Please note that many of the views described are not from official viewpoints with parking areas.
Care should be taken when stopping to look at the mountains from the points described in this book.

Front cover: The view from Herbert Lake, Highway 93 of Mount Temple (left), Fairview Mountain and Haddo Peak, Mount Aberdeen and Mount Lefroy. Photo Dave Birrell.

Back cover: Panorama 21, The Mountains above Canmore. Photo Dave Birrell.

Back cover insets: Right: The author Dave Birrell. Photo Janet Scase.

Top left: Badge of the Royal Dragoon. Courtesy We Stand On Guard.

Bottom left: Black Rock Mountain lookout. Photo Gillean Daffern.

Title page: Tour group at Lake Louise. Mount Victoria in the background. Photo Gillean Daffern.

We acknowledge the financial support of the Government of Canada through the Book Publishing Industry Development Program (BPIDP) for our publishing activities.

Copyright © 2000 Dave Birrell

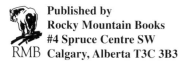

**Published by
Rocky Mountain Books
#4 Spruce Centre SW
Calgary, Alberta T3C 3B3**

ISBN 0-921102-65-8

Canadian Cataloguing in Publication Data

Birrell, Dave, 1944-
    50 roadside panoramas in the Canadian Rockies

Includes index.
ISBN 0-921102-65-8

    1. Rocky Mountains, Canadian (B.C. and Alta.)--Pictorial Works.* 2. Rocky Mountains, Canadian (B.C. and Alta.)--Description and travel.* I. Title. II. Title: Fifty roadside panoramas in the Canadian Rockies.
FC219.B57 2000   971.1'04'0222   C00-910303-1
F1090.B57 2000

ACKNOWLEDGEMENTS

A number of people have been most helpful in providing material and information for this project. I particularly appreciate the assistance of Bill Kerr, Cyril Marshall, Ian Halladay, Wray Hughes, Ken Jones, Janet Mason (British Columbia Geographical Names), Norm Toseland, Trevor Hay, Bruce Fladmark, Chic Scott, Louise Brodersen, Garth and Violet Matkin, Al Bradley, Merrily Aubrey (Alberta Geographical Names program coordinator), Don King, Ruth Oltmann, and the staffs at the Whyte Museum of the Canadian Rockies and Glenbow Archives, Calgary and the Local History Room of the Calgary Public Library.

I am most grateful to Don Beers, Gillean Daffern and Glen Boles who allowed me access to their extensive collections of photographs. Thanks as well to Dan Fox, Tony Daffern, my father Dr. John Birrell, Ray Djuff, Janet Scase, Doug Elias, Greg Redies, Larry Stanier and Murray Anderson of the Castle-Crown Wilderness Association for providing photos. I particularly appreciate the efforts of Gina Brown who solved my dilemma by photographing the Swiftcurrent Creek panorama and Ron Ellis for his drawings of the animals of the Burgess Shale.

The suggestions and guidance provided by Gillean and Tony Daffern, Janice Redlin, Marcelle MacCallum and Ana Tercero at Rocky Mountain Books is appreciated.

Thanks to my wife Leslie for her assistance and encouragement.

Lastly, a special thank you is in order to Tom Hornecker, Jack Soppit, Ron Ellis, Milt Magee, Rocque Goh, Brent Armstrong, Trevor Hay, Garry Sargenia, Maralee Pozzo, Art Barnsley, Andy Lockhart, my wife Leslie and children Gregg, Karen and Janet, my dad and others who have accompanied me on trips to the mountains. They patiently wait while I gaze at the view, take photos and study maps, and then politely listen to all the names and stories.

50 Roadside Panoramas

in the Canadian Rockies

Dave Birrell

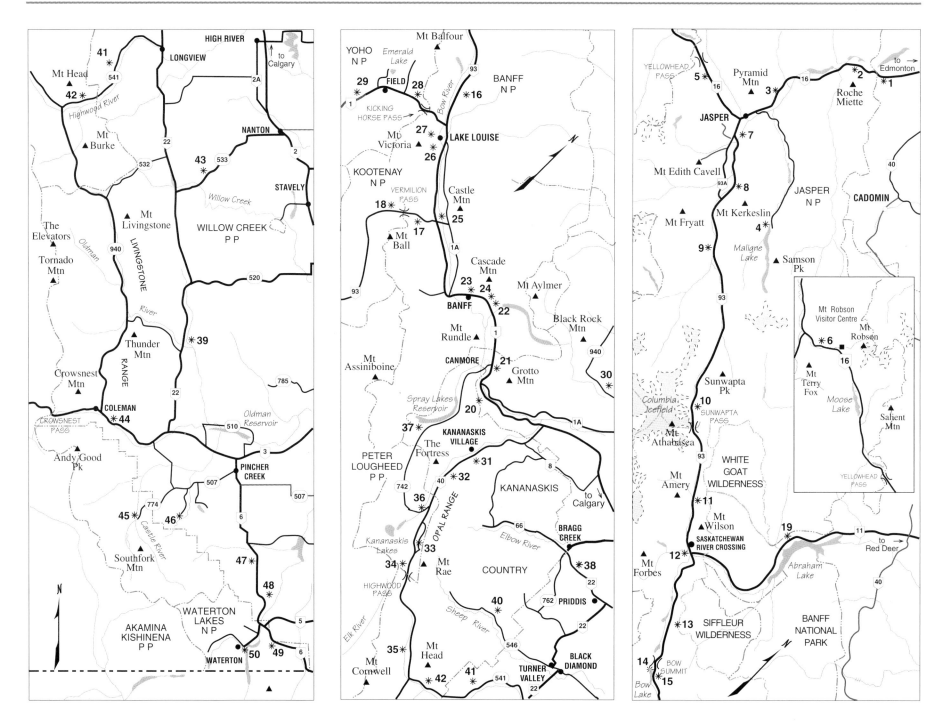

THE FIFTY VIEWPOINTS

INTRODUCTION

A Note to the Reader

"There is a wonderful fascination about mountains. Their massive grandeur, majesty of lofty height, splendour of striking outline—crag to pinnacle and precipice—seem to appeal to both the intellect and to the innermost soul of man, and to compel a mingled reverence and love."[1]

Written by James Outram, who explored and climbed in the Canadian Rockies during the late 1800s and early 1900s, these words sum up the feelings of many of those who enjoy a mountain panorama. To be able to recognize the various peaks and to understand how they relate to one another and to geography as a whole is a source of great pleasure.

However, there is another component to a complete understanding of the mountain panoramas that was not mentioned by the surveyor, perhaps because of his professional focus but more likely because of the fact that he was an explorer and a pioneer. Knowing the history that is associated with these peaks and learning about those who named them adds immensely to one's enjoyment. The names that were chosen provide a window into the past, reflecting what was important to these early visitors as well as to Canadian society itself at that point in time.

The views described are naturally framed panoramas from points of view that are easily accessible to everyone.

There is no question there are innumerable fine viewpoints that may be reached by hiking the trails or climbing the mountains. But we all drive the highways, and even those who do so to reach the trailheads enjoy the views along the way.

All Canadians and our visitors are attracted to the Canadian Rockies by their rugged beauty, their sense of permanence and the quiet pleasures they bring. I hope you will take this book along with you on your travels and that you will take time to stop at the viewpoints to read about these splendid mountains of ours and the people and history associated with them.

Dave Birrell

"Pleasant too, is the recognition of 'Old Friends' among the near or distant summits…. They are friends indeed, and happy is the man who has many such."[2]

Choosing the Names—An Enviable Task

As much of the history related to our Alberta Rockies is associated with the process of naming the mountains, some background is required on the groups and individuals who were involved in a few definable stages in this process.

The vast majority of mountains were named either by the native Indians, members of the Palliser Expedition, George Dawson, various individuals involved in the building and management of the Canadian Pacific Railway, the early climbers and the Interprovincial Boundary surveyors.

The Native Peoples

Although many of the prominent peaks must have been assigned names by the aboriginals, few of these remain. The ones that do are generally descriptive such as Nihahi (rocky) Ridge. Other mountains were assigned Indian names by non-natives. Hungabee (chieftain) and the original names for the mountains in the Valley of the Ten Peaks fall into this category.

The Palliser Expedition

From 1857 to 1860 Captain John Palliser led a group of scientists into what was then virtually unknown territory lying west of what is now Manitoba. Known as the British North American Exploring Expedition, it was charged by the government of the day with the task of exploring, studying and mapping the southern passes through the Rockies and the plains between the North Saskatchewan River and the American border.

John Palliser's background was hunting and wilderness travel in the western United States. He was delegated to organize and lead the expedition but the real work was to be done by respected British scientists in the area of geology, botany, zoology, climatology and geography.

It is difficult to imagine the expedition approaching the front ranges of the Rockies without any sort of map and with virtually all the features unnamed. The vastness of this unknown land and their task must have at times seemed overwhelming and it is not surprising that Palliser chose to split his group into three smaller parties upon reaching the mountains. Lieutenant Thomas Blakiston, the expedition's "magnetic observer," travelled south to the vicinity of Waterton Lakes, then crossed the Kootenay and South Kootenay passes. Palliser himself travelled to the headwaters of the Kananaskis River and down the Palliser River to the Kootenay. Dr. James Hector, the expedition's surgeon and geologist, rode up the Bow Valley and over Vermilion and Kicking Horse passes, and explored the North Saskatchewan Valley, Howse Pass and the Athabasca River.

The Palliser Expedition produced some of the first maps of Alberta's mountainous areas and named many of the prominent features. Generally, the names chosen were those of respected fellow scientists such as one member's anatomy professor at the University of Edinburgh, government officials who supported the expedition such as the governor general of the day, and fellow explorers of the era such as David Livingstone. At times, however, the chosen names related to the appearance of a mountain, such as Molar Mountain, or were named after a bird or animal seen nearby.

George Dawson

Said to be one of the most outstanding scientists Canada has ever produced, George Dawson conducted the first government of Canada survey of the mountains of southern Alberta. Following the Palliser Expedition, any surveying work in the Rockies had been sponsored by the CPR and focused on finding a route through the mountain barrier for the railway. Dr. Dawson's task was more general in nature: to determine the courses of the major rivers and the locations of the main peaks and passes.

George Dawson had a reputation for excellence, his maps containing information phenomenally complete and accurate. The quality of his work was the result of tremendous physical effort in the field despite his short stature complicated by a chronic chest weakness and a back humped by a childhood accident. His biographer, Joyce Barkhouse, wrote that he was, "Possessed of boundless enthusiasm, he seemed never to hunger or tire. He could work all day on a tin of beans and a handful of berries—and expected others to do the same."[3]

During 1884 and 1885 George Dawson travelled extensively through the Rockies. His first summer's work in the mountains began in early July and by the end of the season he had travelled through the country south of Crowsnest Pass to the headwaters of the Oldman River, up the Kootenay and Columbia valleys to the present site of Golden, then through the Kicking Horse Pass and down the Bow River valley. His second summer's studies began in early June and took him from the Bow Valley to the headwaters of the Kananaskis River and south again to the Crowsnest Pass, returning to the Bow Valley in late July. The month of August was spent covering the area from south of Mount Assiniboine to Kicking Horse Pass. During September his party studied the area north of Castle Junction to the Red Deer Valley and west to the headwaters of the Bow River.

Approximately 1000 km were travelled during the two seasons, a remarkable effort considering the general lack of trails. As well, Dr. Dawson would have constantly been stopping and taking side trips for his scientific work.

Appointed director of the Geologic Survey of Canada shortly after his summers in the Rockies, Dr. Dawson's work took him to many other parts of the country. His name is to be found on maps and in numerous reports ranging west from the Alberta Rockies through British Columbia to the Queen Charlotte Islands, and north to the Yukon.

The Canadian Pacific Railway

As the surveying, construction and development along the main line of the CPR proceeded during the last two decades of the nineteenth century, most of the significant features along the route were named. Some honoured prominent visitors of the day such as Sir John A. Macdonald's wife who enjoyed the views from the cowcatcher of a locomotive as she travelled over Kicking Horse Pass. Others were named after important railway officials such as the CPR's first president.

The Early Climbers

Following the completion of the Canadian Pacific Railway in 1885, the word spread that innumerable unnamed and unclimbed mountains rose for hundreds of kilometres on both sides of the tracks. Before long, mountaineers began exploring and climbing both in the regions near to the railway and in the unexplored areas to the north and south. Generally focusing on the high peaks of the Continental Divide, they too had an opportunity to name mountains. This was still the Victorian age and these mountaineers were generally well-read individuals, often university professors, whose interests went far beyond climbing mountains. They often named peaks after fellow mountaineers who had gained fame in the Alps and Himalayas, after the packers, hunters and guides who accompanied their expeditions and sometimes after each other.

Arthur Wheeler and the Boundary Surveyors

Those involved in the survey that established the 1000 km-long Continental Divide were responsible for the naming of more peaks than any other group. The survey was begun in 1913 and continued every summer until 1924. It was a major effort that involved much detailed mapping in the areas adjacent to the border as well as the actual delineation of the boundary itself.

R. W. Cautley was the Alberta representative on the survey and was responsible for the detailed work required in and near the passes. The British Columbia representative was Arthur Wheeler who had previously completed some detailed surveys in the Selkirks and was assigned the mapping in the high mountains between the passes.

Arthur Wheeler became the man most associated with this project. As well as having a professional interest in travelling through the mountains, Wheeler was a co-founder of the Alpine Club of Canada. Through his involvement with the Boundary Survey and the Alpine Club over four decades, he probably saw more of the Canadian Rockies than any other person.

As much of the survey's work was done during and immediately following the First World War when patriotism was at its height, many of the chosen names relate to this conflict. Mountains were named after warships, war heroes, songs of the era, generals and admirals and little known soldiers who had left the survey and lost their lives overseas.

Roche Miette · Mt. Greenock · Gargoyle Mtn. · Roche de Smet · Mt. Thornton · Mt. Cumnock · Roche Ronde · Bedson Ridge

1 Roche Miette and the Entrance to the Mountains

From Roche à Perdrix
Highway 16, 2.6 km east of Jasper National Park entry gate; 2.8 km west of Folding Mountain Campground.

Roche a Perdrix from the viewpoint.

"Suddenly it (the trail) opened out on a lakelet, and right in front a semi-circle of five glorious mountains appeared..... Three of them were so near and towered up so bold that their full forms, even to the long shadows on them, were reflected clearly in the lakelet, next to the rushes and spruce of its own shores. Here is scene for a grand picture.... The mighty column of Roche a Perdrix towered a mile above our heads, scuds of clouds kissing its snowy summit.... We were entering the magnificent Jasper portals of the Rocky Mountains by a quiet path winding between groves of trees and rich lawns like an English gentleman's park."[4] These words were written by Reverend George Grant as he passed this way in 1872. He was accompanying Sir Sandford Fleming, the engineer in charge of the construction of the Canadian Pacific Railway, during an inspection of a possible route through the Rockies.

This view of "the magnificent Jasper portals" is from part way down a long hill at the bottom of which are the entrance gates to Jasper National Park. **Roche à Perdrix** (2134 m) stands to the south of the highway as it enters the mountains, this viewpoint being directly below it. The mountain was named by Reverend Grant because he felt the folding layers of rock resembled the tail of a partridge. Translated from the French, "roche" means rock and "perdrix" means partridge.

During the early decades of the nineteenth century, the valley of the Athabasca River was used regularly by French speaking, fur-

Roche Miette dominates the entrance to Jasper National Park. Photo Don Beers.

trading voyageurs and the names of three of the five peaks in this panorama were obviously named by these hardy travellers. In 1810, the North West Company dominated the Athabasca Valley below these mountains. Eleven years later the Hudson's Bay Company purchased the rights. The efforts of both companies were spearheaded by men of Scottish extraction but the voyageurs who did the work were Metís, Iroquois Indians and French Canadians.

Rising beyond the lower slopes of Roche a Perdrix, **Roche Miette** (2316 m) dominates the entrance to the Rockies and Jasper

National Park. It is also a dominant feature when seen from the opposite direction, the near vertical cliff in marked contrast to the gentler slopes of nearby mountains. As James Hector approached the Rockies from the east in 1859, he wrote that "Miette's Rock is a bold object, bounding the valley of the Athabasca to the south, and resembling the 'Devil's Head,'"[5] which lies to the north of the Bow River. The first ascent is credited to Bonhomme Miette, a legendary figure in French Canadian folklore, who was a hunter, a gifted fiddler and storyteller. When he reached the top, it is said he sat and dangled his feet over the precipice, smoked his pipe and enjoyed a pleasant visit with St. Peter.

Many early travellers wrote of Roche Miette with admiration, but their enthusiasm was tempered by the barrier it presented. Although not visible from this viewpoint, Roche Miette slopes steeply into the Athabasca River and posed a serious obstacle to those travelling along the south bank. Steep, downward sloping slabs of slippery rock often sent horses sliding down into the river at what became known as "Disaster Point." Early travellers attempted to negotiate a dangerous trail that climbed some 395 m above the river. It was said to be a narrow, dangerous path on bare and loose rock, with a steep, slippery slope that dropped over a cliff into the Athabasca River. The dangerous "nose" of Roche Miette remained an obstacle until it was blasted away in the early 1900s by the builders of the Grand Trunk Pacific Railway.

The de Smet Range is a 25 km-long ridge that lies north of the Athabasca Valley and to the west of the valley of the Snake Indian River. **Roche de Smet** (2539 m) is the highest and most massive part of the range. A Jesuit priest, Father Pierre-Jean de Smet travelled widely in the mountains during the mid-nineteenth century as a missionary. The natives at Jasper House, which was located just downstream from the foot of the ridge, had great respect for the missionary and, according to de Smet, decided to honour him. "Each one discharged his musket in the direction of the highest mountain, a large rock jutting out in the form of a sugar-loaf, and, with three loud hurrahs, gave it my name."[6]

Mount Greenock (2065 m) is the small, rounded rise on the southern end of Roche de Smet. In Gaelic, "greenoch" means sunny knoll so perhaps Morris Bridgland, who named it in 1916, climbed to this spot on a sunny afternoon.

Although it is difficult to distinguish at times, the gently sloped, rounded summit of **Gargoyle Mountain** (2693 m) rises behind Roche de Smet to the left of its highest point. Lying beyond Vine Creek valley, it was named by Morris Bridgland because of the rock formations around a stream that flows from its base.

Roche de Smet from Disaster Point.

Sometimes incorporated into the decorative architecture of buildings, gargoyles are waterspouts in the form of a grotesque human or animal figure.

Sir Henry Thornton was the president of the Canadian National Railway from 1922 until 1932. **Mount Thornton** (2752 m) is the highest peak in this panorama and lies 11 km beyond Roche de Smet.

Mount Thornton is visible through a valley that cuts through the de Smet Range, and to its north the pointed summit of **Mount Cumnock** (2460 m) may be seen. Cumnock is a village in Scotland, its name meaning "meeting of the waters." Two creeks that cut through the de Smet Range join the Snake Indian River immediately to the northeast of the mountain, so this may explain why the name was chosen.

"Ronde" means round in French. Lying across the river from Roche Miette, **Roche Ronde** (2138 m) does not appear to be round from this vantage point but the reason for its name becomes apparent when the mountain is seen from the Disaster Point viewpoint. The legendary Snake Indian River flows from the northwest, just beyond Roche Ronde to join the Athabasca River.

In pre-photography days, visitors were, at times, prone to writing "a thousand words." Reverend Grant wrote of the view of Ronde Roche, "Roche Ronde was to our right, its stratification as distinct as the leaves of a half opened book. The mass of the rock was limestone, and what at a distance had been only peculiarly

Crossing Disaster Point, 1863. Courtesy Glenbow Archives, NA-1240-8.

Roche à Boche, Coronach Mountain and Roche Ronde from Disaster Point. Photo Don Beers.

bold and rugged outlines, were now seen to be the different angles and contortions of the strata. And such contortions! One high mass twisting up the sides in serpentine folds; another bent in great waving lines, like petrified billows. The colouring, too, was all that artist could desire. Not only the dark green of the spruce in the corries, which turned into black when far up, but autumn tints of red and gold as high as vegetation had climbed on the hill sides; and above that, streaks and patches of yellow, green, rusty red and black, relieving the gray mass of limestone; while up the valley, every shade of blue came out according as the hills were near or far away, and summits hoary with snow bounded the horizon."[7]

Bedson Ridge (2240 m) frames the northern side of this historic view of the Athabasca Valley's entrance to the Rockies. The Bedson railway siding was formerly located below this ridge and the ridge took its name from the siding. This may be the only feature in the Rockies named after the warden of a penitentiary. Bedson was warden of the Stoney Mountain Penitentiary in Manitoba.

Pierre-Jean de Smet

Father de Smet. Courtesy Glenbow Archives, NA-1391-1.

Father de Smet was a Catholic missionary who travelled through much of the Canadian Rockies in 1845 and 1846. He regularly wrote long and interesting letters to his "Superior," which are delightful descriptions of the landscape and the natives he was working with. His writings, entitled *Oregon Missions and Travels over the Rocky Mountains*, were published in book form in 1847.

Much of the book is concerned with his work as a priest but it also contains some interesting references to the mountains. The accompanying map covers a vast area from 44 degrees to 54 degrees latitude and from the Pacific Ocean to well east of the front ranges of the mountains. Although it is primarily concerned with rivers, it does note the locations of several mountains that must have been considered to be particularly noteworthy at that time. One of these is the legendary Mount Brown with its elevation of 16,000 ft. Another is "Devil's Nose," which probably was the peak we now know as Devil's Head. Also noted on the map is "The Pyramid," which was almost certainly the peak now known as Mount Assiniboine.

The book also contains many amusing anecdotes, many of which describe incidents involving his size and his somewhat limited skills in horsemanship and wilderness travel.

He was said to have been a popular, jovial man but consid–erably overweight, and negotiating between trees on horse-back was difficult for him at times. He wrote, "I have a little word of advice to give all who wish to visit these latitudes. At the entrance of each thick forest, one should render himself as slender, as short, and as contracted as possible.... Not withstanding these precautions, it is rare to escape without paying tribute in some manner to the ungracious forest. I one day found myself in a singular and critical position: in at-tempting to pass under a tree that inclined across the path, I perceived a small branch in form of a hook, which threatened me. The first impulse was to extend myself upon the neck of my horse. Unavailing precaution! It caught me by the collar of my surtout, the horse still continuing his pace. Behold me suspended in the air, struggling like a fish at the end of a hook. Several respectable pieces of my coat floated, in all probability, a long time in the forest, as an undeniable proof of my having paid toll in passing through it. A crushed and torn hat, an eye black and blue, two deep scratches on the cheek, would, in a civilized country, have given me the ap-pearance rather of a bully issuing from the Black Forest, than a missionary."[8]

Cinquefoil Mtn.
Pyramid Mtn.
Morro Peak
The Palisade Mt. Kinross
Mt. Zengel
Buttress Mtn.

2 Pyramid Mountain and the View toward Jasper Townsite

If you're driving up the Athabasca River valley on the Yellowhead Highway (16), pause for a few minutes just after turning south at Disaster Point. There is interesting history associated with this spot, and as well, the traveller is treated to a view of the mountains to the northwest of the town of Jasper, a panorama dominated by Pyramid Mountain.

This view is framed on the left by the sloping ridge of **Cinquefoil Mountain** (2259 m), the northernmost point of the Jacques Range. Cinquefoil is a small yellow flower that takes its name from the fact that its flower has five (cinq) parts. Many different varieties are found throughout Alberta including the mountains.

The low rounded mountain behind the Jacques Range is **Morro Peak**, at 1678 m one of the lowest named mountains in Alberta. It was named by Morris Bridgland after the Spanish word for "round hill." The Athabasca River makes a 90 degree turn just beyond the mountain.

The Palisade (2130 m) is a seven km-long ridge with steep cliffs of Devonian Palliser Formation limestone facing the Athabasca Valley. Early travellers noticed its resemblance to a defensive military position.

Behind and above the wall of The Palisade, **Pyramid Mountain** rises to 2766 m—the highest peak in the vicinity of Jasper townsite. From this viewpoint the mountain appears perfectly symmetric, with long evenly sloped ridges to the

northwest and southeast. Snow tends to accumulate on the east face seen from Disaster Point and because it generally lingers into mid-summer, the mountain makes a striking contrast to the other nearby snowless peaks. The mountain is also part of the view from the Icefields Parkway to the south of Jasper, but is not nearly as outstanding in form. The mountain was first climbed by Reverend George Kinney and Conrad Kain in 1911. A telecommunications tower is now located on the summit.

Pyramid Mountain was named by James Hector of the Palliser Expedition. Sir James passed this way in late January of 1859. His

From Disaster Point
Highway 16, 12.8 km west of Jasper National Park entrance gates; 0.7 km east of Rocky River bridge.

The ridge of The Palisade. Photo Don Beers.

party had spent 18 days travelling from Fort Edmonton when they arrived at Disaster Point en route to Jasper House. Hector wrote, "It was quite dark when we reached the base of Miette's Rock, where a spur of the mountain from the south compelled us again to seek the river.... After searching about for a crossing place… we then got off the ice ourselves, and found, the water took us above the waist, and getting the sleds, loads and all on our shoulders, (we) waded through the rapid, which was about one hundred yards wide, and so reached the left bank. The wind, which had changed at sunset to N.E. was bitterly cold, so that the plunge into the water felt warm at first, but on re-emerging, we at once stiffened into a mass of ice, for as I found half an hour afterwards, the thermometer stood at -15 degrees (Fahrenheit)."[9]

The peaks to the right of Pyramid Mountain are, like Pyramid Mountain itself, part of the Victoria Cross Range. Most were named in 1951 to honour Canadian soldiers who were awarded the Commonwealth's highest award for bravery during the First World War.

The twin peaks of **Mount Kinross** (2560 m) honour Private Cecil John Kinross, who was awarded the Victoria Cross medal while serving with the 49th Battalion in the Alberta Regiment. To its right is **Mount Zengel** (2630 m). In a similar act of bravery, Sergeant Raphael Louis Zengel demonstrated a "most conspicuous bravery and devotion to duty"[10] while serving with the 45th Battalion in the Saskatchewan Regiment.

Surprisingly, the high peak to the right and beyond Mount Zengel is unnamed. It is quite a striking mountain from this location and is in fact the second highest point on the panorama.

Buttress Mountain (2685 m) is the high point on the northwestern end of the ridge to the right of Mount Zengel. Views to the northwest of Buttress are blocked by the slopes of **Esplanade Mountain** (2301 m).

Pyramids of the Canadian Rockies

There are at least seven mountains in the Canadian Rockies that have been known as Pyramid. Only two retain the name and another carried the name for only a time before having it changed in order to avoid confusion with the other Pyramids. The other four, ironically the ones that most resemble the shape, were never formally named Pyramid.

Peter Fidler was the first European to enter the Canadian Rockies and the first to name a peak. His journal entry on December 7, 1792, said he saw a "remarkable high cliff… very much resembling a pyramid—from which very near resemblance I shall call it bythat name."[11] The bearings noted in his journal indicate he was referring to what we now know as Mount Glasgow in the headwaters of the Elbow River.

The best known of the Pyramids is located nine km north of Jasper. Its near-perfect triangular-shaped profile when viewed from the east must have impressed James Hector of the Palliser Expedition, who named the mountain on his approach to Athabasca Pass in 1859. Although the mountain's slopes from this angle are similar to those of Egypt's pyramids, the peak lacks the three dimensional aspect that a true pyramid requires.

Mount Chephren, visible from the Bow Pass viewpoint, was named Pyramid Mountain by J. Norman Collie in 1897. At the same time he named its neighbour, which was covered in snow, White Pyramid. Pyramid Mountain, in contrast, had very little snow.

In 1918 the Interprovincial Boundary Commission decided the mountain's name must be changed in order to avoid confusion with the Pyramid Mountain near Jasper. J. M. Thorington, a prominent mountaineer and author of the era, liked the association of the peak with the pyramids of Egypt and recommended the name Chephren. Chephren, or Khafre, was the fourth pharaoh of the Fourth Dynasty of Egypt and built the second of the three Great Pyramids. The name White Pyramid was thought to be sufficiently different from Pyramid Mountain and was retained.

While travelling in the Bow River headwaters near White Man Pass in 1845, Catholic priest/explorer Pierre-Jean de Smet wrote, "The valley is bounded on either side by a succession of picturesque rocks, whose lofty summits, rising in the form of pyramids, lose themselves in the clouds."[12] On his map he noted only one of these, naming it "The Pyramid." This must have been the peak now known as Mount Assiniboine.

In 1892, Arthur Coleman named the fourth highest peak in the Rockies Pyramid. It was subsequently renamed Mount Clemenceau by the Interprovincial Boundary Commission in 1919 after Georges Clemenceau, the President of France during the final year of the First World War.

Mount McPhail in the upper Highwood Valley was known locally as The Pyramid until 1918 when it was officially named by the Boundary Commission.

Pyramid Mountain from Jasper Lake. Etching from Ocean to Ocean.

Excelsior Mtn. Centre Mtn. Mt. Tekarra Signal Mtn. Mt. Fryatt Whirlpool Mtn. Mt. Edith Cavell

3 Giant Peaks in the Distance

For travellers approaching Jasper townsite from the east, this viewpoint offers the lure of distant, high peaks. The mountains along the Yellowhead Highway are not of a particularly high elevation, few exceeding 2700 m. But two of the three mountains in the distance are over 3350 m in elevation. Both were named to honour British heroes who, despite the fact that they were civilians, were executed by the enemy during the First World War. Morning light on these giants named in their honour tends to draw one farther toward the rugged and beautiful peaks of the upper Athabasca River valley.

The mountains on the left side of this panorama are part of the Maligne Range and lie beyond the Maligne River that joins the Athabasca just eight km south of the Snaring River bridge viewpoint. **Excelsior Mountain** has an elevation of 2744 m. It was named by W. P. Hinton in 1916, probably because it is the highest in the range.

Centre Mountain (2700 m) is one of a group of three peaks that lie perpendicular to the general trend of the Maligne Range. Its position is midway between Excelsior Mountain and Amber Mountain, which from this viewpoint is hidden behind **Mount Tekarra** (2694 m). James Hector named Mount Tekarra after one of the guides who accompanied him on his 1859 winter journey to Athabasca Pass.

During the time that the main fur trade route through the Rockies followed the Athabasca River valley and traversed Athabasca Pass, a hunting lodge named Old Fort was maintained by the North West Company at a prominent point just across the river from the present town of Jasper. At various times signal fires were built on the ridge behind the lodge and for this reason the low peak behind it became known as **Signal Mountain** (2255 m). In 1941 the mountain became the site of the mountain national parks' first fire lookout and for the next four decades a Parks employee kept watch over the forests of the Athabasca River valley.

Lying directly south from the Snaring River Flats viewpoint, the triangular-shaped **Mount Fryatt** (3361 m) is the most distant peak in the panorama, lying almost directly south and over 50 km away. To the right of Mount Fryatt, **Whirlpool Mountain** (2900 m) rises just beyond the point where the Whirlpool River flows into the Athabasca.

Alone and aloof on the right side of this panorama is **Mount Edith Cavell** (3363 m) some 37 km in the distance. It is characterized by a distinctive profile and snow-highlighted beds dipping to the west. When Reverend George Grant saw the mountain from this location in 1872 he referred to it as, "a great mountain, so white with snow that it looked like a sheet suspended from the heavens."[13] It is the peak's precipitous north face that is seen from this angle.

Awe-inspiring north face of Mount Edith Cavell.
Photo Don Beers.

From Snaring River Flats
Highway 16, 1.3 km west of Snaring River bridge; 11.4 km east of the junction with the Maligne Lake road.

Edith Louise Cavell

The Edith Cavell Memorial near Trafalgar Square, London.

Edith Louise Cavell was born in 1865 in Norfolk, England. At the age of 20 she entered the nursing profession and in 1907 was appointed the matron of the Berkendael Institute in Brussels.

After the German occupation of Belgium she cared for wounded German troops, but also became involved with an underground group that assisted some 200 British, French and Belgian soldiers who were trapped behind enemy lines to escape to neutral Holland and rejoin their armies. Sheltered at the institute, which had become a Red Cross hospital, they were provided with money and guides by Philippe Baucq, a Belgian. This was regarded as treason under German martial law and was punishable by death. In August 1915, Edith Cavell was betrayed by a spy and she and several others were arrested, tried by a court-martial, and sentenced to be executed. Her defence was that as a nurse she was duty-bound to save lives and she was doing just that by concealing and helping hunted men to return to their homes.

Although neutral governments, including representatives of the United States and Spain, tried to have their death sentences reprieved, both she and Philippe Baucq were shot on October 12. Her last words were, "I see now that patriotism is not enough. I must have no hatred or bitterness towards anyone."[14]

Technically, the enemy did have a case, but it was one that was not accepted by world opinion because espionage was not involved. She was widely regarded as a martyr. After lying in state in Westminster Abbey, Edith Cavell was buried in Norwich Cathedral.

Edith Cavell's execution was said to have played an important role in ending America's neutrality. One historian wrote, "By two deeds that she did in the earlier days of the war, more than by any that she did before after, Germany hurt herself with America. These were the sinking of a ship, May 7, 1915 (the Lusitania) and the shooting of a woman, October 12, 1915."[15]

The premier of British Columbia was the first to suggest that a mountain be named in her honour, suggesting the highest peak in the Canadian Rockies, Mount Robson. Prime Minister Sir Robert Borden agreed with having a mountain named but instructed the Geographic Board of Canada to make the decision as to which one.

Originally named La Montagne de la Grande Traverse, and later known as Fitzhugh and then Geikie, the mountain was officially named Mount Edith Cavell in March of 1916, just five months after the execution. A memorial service for Edith Cavell is held each year in the Anglican Church in Jasper.

Charles Algernon Fryatt

Captain Fryatt of the Brussels. Courtesy The Great War, Vol. 7.

During the early months of the First World War, the German navy sent their submarines into action around the British Isles for the first time. British anti-submarine measures were largely ineffective as the small patrol ships, often in appalling weather, were spread too thin given the large area to protect. So the British began to arm their merchant ships and ordered their captains to turn toward a hostile submarine, if possible, and force it to dive to avoid being rammed.

On March 28, 1915, Captain Fryatt of the railway ferry *Brussels* made use of this technique, ramming enemy submarine U-33 and then escaping. In doing so, Fryatt made himself a marked man in German eyes. Over a year later, during the night of June 22, 1916, the *Brussels* was intercepted by German destroyers and taken into Zeebrugge. Captain

Fryatt was tried before a military court-martial as a "franc-tireur," an individual outside of the regular armed services who had tried to injure German military forces. He was found guilty and promptly shot.

The British regarded this as judicial murder aimed at terrorizing merchant seamen, but, as in the case of Edith Cavell, German harshness backfired on the diplomatic front. Their action was widely condemned in the world's press, particularly in the then neutral United States where the *New York Times* termed it "a deliberate murder."

Mount Fryatt was named in 1921 to honour the captain of the *Brussels*. A year later, the name Brussels Peak was bestowed on a nearby peak.

Leah Peak

Samson Peak

Mt. Paul
Monkhead Mtn.
Mt. Warren
Valad Peak
Mt. Henry MacLeod
Mt. Charlton
Mt. Unwin

4 The Backdrop to the Lake

As one drives up the valley of the Maligne River, the view of the mountains is limited. Upon reaching the lake, however, the panorama of the peaks beside and beyond the longest lake in the Canadian Rockies is outstanding and well worth the drive. L. S. Amery, a British statesman, climber and author who visited the area, was so impressed that he wrote, "Lake Maligne is the most fantastically varied and beautiful thing the whole range of the Rockies has to show."[16]

Henry MacLeod, a surveyor under the direction of Sandford Fleming of the CPR, was the first non-native to travel up the Maligne River from the Athabasca River valley. After struggling up the long, narrow valley in 1875, he named the lake at its source Sorefoot Lake. The river's name was based on the French word for wicked, which is how the early fur traders felt about the valley and the stream. The lake subsequently took its name from the river.

In 1908 Mary Schaffer, together with her companion Mollie Adams, a botanist friend, a cook and two guides reached the shores of Maligne Lake after a long pack trip from Lake Louise. Her party was following a map drawn for them the previous year by a Stoney Indian, which guided them to the lake from the southwest over what is now known as Maligne Pass. Upon reaching the lake, it became obvious to the group that the best way to continue their exploration was on the lake itself. A raft, which they christened *HMS Chaba* after the Indian name for the lake, Chaba Imne, was assembled. The guides determined that, "we were to go in style regardless of our plea that we were willing to

rough it for a few days; air-beds, tents, and food for three days were to be taken on that raft."[17] The group spent three idyllic days sailing their craft to the end of the lake and back. During the almost two weeks the group spent on and near the lake, they found no sign of man, "just masses of flowers, the lap-lap of the waters on the shore, the occasional reverberating roar of an avalanche and our own voices stilled by a nameless Presence."[18]

From Maligne Lake
The south end of the Maligne Lake road, 43.1 km from Highway 16.

Evening light at Maligne Lake (l-r: Mount Paul, Monkhead Mountain, Mount Warren, Valad Peak, Mount Henry MacLeod, Mount Charlton, Mount Unwin). Photo Don Beers.

Spirit Island with Mount Paul, Monkhead Mountain and Mount Warren looming in the background. Photo by Don Beers.

Oliver Wheeler with Paul Sharples on Maligne Lake, 1911. Courtesy Whyte Museum, V139 PS70.

The boat house in the foreground was built by Curly Phillips, a well-known guide in the Jasper area during the early 1900s. It is recognized as a Registered Historic Resource.

The upper slopes of two peaks, **Leah Peak** (2801 m) and **Samson Peak** (3081 m), form the left side of the panorama and are similar in profile. They were named by Mary Schaffer for a married couple: Samson and Leah Beaver. Samson was the Stoney Indian who provided Mrs. Schaffer with the map she used to find the lake. He had visited the lake with his father when he was 14 years of age, and 16 years later was able to draw the map from memory when he met Mrs. Schaffer at Elliott Barnes' cabin on the Kootenay Plains.

Mount Paul (2805 m) is most impressive from Samson Narrows, probably one of the most recognized viewpoints in Jasper National Park. It lies eight km from the north end of the lake, just over half way to the end. When Mary Schaffer's party reached this point they thought that they had reached the end of the lake until, after navigating the narrows, "There burst upon us that which, all in our little company agreed, was the finest view any of us had ever beheld in the Rockies."[19] It is from here, with the small, treed Spirit Island in the foreground, that Mount Paul rises, towerlike, 1134 m above the lake. The group originally referred to this mountain as The Thumb.

In 1911, during her second visit to the lake, Mary Schaffer was accompanied by her nine year-old nephew, Paul Sharples. The previous winter Paul had suffered from whooping cough and was taken along because Mary felt he needed a summer of fresh air and sunshine. As they passed below the narrows they "looked up to the great buttresses of The Thumb, and sighed a long sigh at the wonderfulness of it all. Even the small boy was silenced by the splendour of the scene for the time being, and then the little voice uttered... 'I suppose I am too little a boy to have a mountain named for me.'"[20] Mary responded, "No, I think if you stayed a very good boy for the rest of the trip and not..." (mentioning a few lapses of good behaviour chronic to small boys), "we might call that mountain Mount Paul.... But remember this, that if you fail to keep your part of the bargain, off comes the name.... He promised, but the name had to be removed twice; however, it was on there when we left. So I hope it may remain for years to come, to mark the visit of the first white child who navigated those waters."[21]

To the right of Mount Paul rises the two heads of **Mount Warren** (3140 m). Schaffer describes how after passing The Thumb, "next rose a magnificent double-headed pile of rock, whose perpendicular cliffs reached almost to the shore.... It was its massiveness, its simple dignity which appealed to us so strongly, and we named it Mount Warren, in honour of 'Chief,' through whose grit and determination we were able to behold this splendour."[22] Billy Warren was Mary Schaffer's packer and chief guide and later became her second husband. Regarding his skills as a guide she wrote, "There are older ones (guides), there are better hunters, perhaps, with wider experience in forest lore, more knowledge of the country, but for kindness, good nature (such a necessary adjunct), good judgment under unexpected stress, he had no superior."[23]

In 1950 the lower, easterly peak of Mount Warren was assigned the name **Monkhead** (3211 m) because of the resemblance to a monk's cloak with a hood.

Glacier-clad **Mount Henry MacLeod** (3288 m), the highest peak in this panorama, was named after the CPR surveyor who first saw Maligne Lake in 1875. Although Arthur Coleman named the mountain in 1902, 44 years passed before the lower rock-covered mountain just to its left was named **Valad Peak** (3250 m) after MacLeod's Metís guide, Valad. Valad made some efforts to retain the original names given to features by the natives and the Metís in the Athabasca River valley area. While guiding Sir Sandford Fleming, the great Canadian scientist and railway executive, he had discussions with Sir Sandford regarding, "the old local titles of the mountains..., but every passer-by thinks that he has a right to give his own and his friends' names to them over again."[24]

The beautiful twin peaks of **Mount Charlton** (3217 m) and **Mount Unwin** (3268 m) lie to the right of Samson Narrows and to the left of the valley from which the Maligne River flows into the lake from its headwaters 14 km to the southeast. Mount Charlton may be the only mountain ever named after an advertising agent. Henry Ready Charlton held this position with the Grand Trunk Railway. He realized that Maligne Lake could become one of the park's major attractions and assisted in arranging for Mary Schaffer to return in 1911 to do a more detailed topographic survey of the area.

Sidney Unwin was Mary Schaffer's second guide during her 1908 visit. She wrote, "Opposite our camp rose a fine snow-capped mountain down whose sides swept a splendid glacier. As we paddled slowly in sight of it, (Unwin) suddenly looked up and said, 'That is the mountain from which I first saw the lake.' So we promptly named it Mount Unwin."[25]

When surveyor Arthur Wheeler visited the area he felt somewhat slighted that a mere amateur had already named all the mountains and suggested alternatives. But Mary Schaffer's choices prevailed and all but three of the peaks in the view from the north end of Maligne Lake were named by her.

Mary Schaffer

Jasper National Park was created in 1907 and it has been suggested that Mary Schaffer was the park's first tourist. But Mary Schaffer was no ordinary tourist; she was the first non-native woman to travel through much of Banff and Jasper national parks.

A native of Pennsylvania, Mary Schaffer's first trip to the Canadian Rockies was in 1889 when she accompanied a group of members of the Philadelphia Academy of Natural Sciences. She was joined by a fellow art student, Mary Vaux, who was visiting Glacier House, the Canadian Pacific Railway's hotel in the Selkirks. Obviously an adventurous pair, they travelled part of the way on top of a boxcar. The following year she returned to the Selkirks, now as the wife of Dr. Charles Schaffer, a physician with a driving interest in botany whom she had met at Glacier House the previous year. Dr. Schaffer had a particular interest in the wildflowers of the mountains and he and Mary visited the Canadian Rockies every year until his untimely death in 1903.

Mary Schaffer returned to the mountains on her own the following year with her friend Mollie Adams. Guided by Tom Wilson and his associate Billy Warren, they explored the Yoho Valley and the Moraine Lake area. Returning again in 1905 and 1906, the ladies became more adventurous, travelling as far north as the Columbia Icefields. Then they began to plan a major expedition for the 1907 season.

It was definitely not the norm for two ladies of the Victorian age in their mid-forties to venture off into the mountain wilderness on a four-month pack trip, but these were not two traditional ladies. Over the years they had become kindred spirits, reinforcing the other's interests and determination. Their answer to those who said they should not go was, "Can the free air sully, can the birds teach us words we should not hear, can it be possible to see, in such a summer's outing, one sight as painful as the daily ones of poverty, degradation, and depravity of a great city?"[26]

Their plan was to visit the headwaters of the Saskatchewan and Athabasca rivers, but they also hoped to reach a lake they had heard of that was called Chaba Imne (Beaver Lake) by the Stoney Indians. Later she revealed that, "our real objective was to delve into the heart of an untouched land, to turn the unthumbed pages of an unread book, and to learn daily those secrets which dear Mother Nature is so willing to tell to those who seek."[27]

They reached the Athabasca River and travelled upstream to Mount Columbia, but an attempt to find the lake failed when they encountered heavy snow as the end of the season approached. During their return to the railway, Mary Schaffer met a band of Stoneys and had dinner with them at the home of Elliott Barnes on the Kootenai Plains in the Saskatchewan River valley. One of the Indians was Samson Beaver who as a boy of 14 had visited the legendary lake with his father nearly 20 years previously. From memory, he sketched a map showing the route.

The winter was spent dreaming of the elusive lake with the, "determination to find our way to it if another summer dawned for us… all four of us had the same goal in mind the moment there came a chance of pushing towards it."[28] With Samson's precious map in hand and Billy Warren and Sid Unwin as guides, the determined ladies set out from Lake Louise on June 8, 1908. Almost a month later they finally reached their lake, probably the first to see it since Henry MacLeod's visit in 1875. Following several days of exploration in the area, the party spent five days attempting to push a trail through the thick, downed timber of the Maligne River valley to the Athabasca River. Finally they gave up and retraced their steps to the upper Athabasca. Then they journeyed northwest as far as Tete Jaune Cache before returning to Lake Louise on September 20.

Clearly, this was a remarkable trip and the two ladies were given much recognition for their efforts, although they in turn gave much of the credit to their guides. Mary Schaffer's book, *Old Indian Trails of the Canadian Rockies*, was published in 1911 and is regarded as a classic.

Mary Schaffer returned to the Rockies each summer until 1912 when she purchased a cottage in Banff and made her home among the mountains. Three years later she and her long-time guide and companion Billy Warren were married. Billy Warren became a successful businessman in Banff.

No other location in the Canadian Rockies is so closely identified with a single individual as Maligne Lake and its panorama. Mount Schaffer, however, is located between Lake O'Hara and Lake McArthur in Yoho National Park.

Mary Schaffer and Billy Warren. Courtesy Whyte Museum, V439 PS-6.

Sidney Unwin

Sidney Unwin. Courtesy Whyte Museum, NA-66-496.

"Unsurpassed in woodcraft and resourcefulness, unequalled in thoughtful kindness to his party, and with the charm of courteous manner that adds the final touch of perfection to the little self-centred microcosm that a party in the wilderness constitutes."[29] This was the tribute paid to Sid Unwin by B. W. Mitchell following several trips in the Rockies with this legendary outfitter.

Regarded as one of the most capable of the trail guides during the years of exploration in the Canadian Rockies, Sid Unwin lived an adventurous but short life. Born in London, England, he was for some reason drawn to the mountains of Canada where he set up a guide and outfitting business and spent the winters trapping in the Mistaya Valley near Waterfowl Lakes. While crossing Bow Lake one winter afternoon, the ice broke beneath him and, with a heavy pack and snowshoes he "felt for a minute that it was all over. Then it came to me that I just couldn't die yet. I'm young and life is good."[30] An incredible effort must have been required to save himself. After regaining the ice surface, he struggled to the shore, his clothes frozen stiff, and with matches from a waterproof metal box he carried just for such emergencies he lit a whole tree on fire to get warm. Then he built a bonfire, disrobed and dried his clothes.

In 1908 Sid was one of the guides for Mary Schaffer and Mollie Adams as they set out to search for the lake now known as Maligne. After struggling for days through burnt-out forests, they began to descend the Maligne River from Maligne Pass. The party was becoming dispirited and beginning to doubt the accuracy of the map they were following. After stopping for lunch Sid abruptly announced, "I'm going off to climb something that's high enough to see if that lake's within twenty miles of here and I'm not coming back till I know!"[31] On his return to camp at 10:30 that night, all were excited to hear that he had climbed a mountain to the east of their camp (Mount Unwin) and was able to look down upon the elusive lake they were seeking. Later they all enjoyed the explorations of the longest lake in the Rockies. Together with Mary Schaffer, Sid returned to the lake in 1911 to complete a more detailed survey of the area at the request of the Parks Department.

Sid Unwin's adventures in the tranquillity of the Canadian Rockies were preceded and followed by other adventures amongst the horrors of war. Prior to coming to Canada he had fought with distinction in the South African War. Then, when the First World War broke out in 1914 he asked his sister Ethel to take over his pack and saddle-horse business and enlisted in the Canadian Army, which assigned him to the 20th Artillery Battery at Lethbridge. In January 1916, the battery saw its first action in France and a year-and-a-half later during the Battle of Vimy Ridge, Sid was severely wounded after single-handedly manning an artillery battery. The position was being shelled and Sid ordered all his men to leave the battery and go back to their dugout. Sid did all the loading and firing single-handedly even when one of his ammunition pits was set on fire by a direct hit. Lieutenant E. K. Carmichael, Sid's commanding officer, wrote, "I was so much pleased with, and admired his conduct, that I committed the circumstances to paper at once in case of accidents, so that if anything did happen to me, the paper would bear witness."[32] Sid later died of his injuries in a military hospital.

A last letter, written in a left-handed scrawl from a military hospital, proved that his spirit had not been broken: "Aside from having my right arm blown off, being almost stone deafened by shell fire, and having my head full of shrapnel fragments, I'm fine and dandy."[33] Despite his desire to serve his country and his indomitable spirit while in the horrid trenches of France, he must have longed to return to the days he spent sailing *HMS Chaba* on Maligne Lake.

Right: Mount Unwin.

Lucerne Peak   Tête Roche   Mt. O'Beirne   Caledonia Mtn.   Mt. Bridgland

5 Mountains of the Yellowhead Pass

The approach to Yellowhead Pass is a gentle one. From this viewpoint at the top of a small hill just east of the bridge over Clairvaux Creek, an attractive group of peaks on the Continental Divide comes into view. The border is still nine km to the west, but is only about 25 m higher in elevation.

This view of the mountains near the Pass features **Caledonia Mountain** (2856 m) as the highest and most distant peak. Simon Fraser named the area between the Rocky Mountains and the Coast Range (north of 51°30') New Caledonia because the country reminded him of his mother's descriptions of her native Scotland. The name was retained when fur traders of the Hudson's Bay Company began to regularly traverse the Yellowhead Pass while travelling to and from this portion of the HBC's empire. During mid-summer the mountain features a number of distinctive, long, thin lines of snow rising steeply from left to right on its upper cliffs. In contrast, the lower mountain directly in front of Caledonia has an almost vertical, long, thin line of snow descending from its highest point to the valley below.

Lucerne Peak (2412 m) on the far left side of the panorama is one of four named high points on Yellowhead Mountain that lies north of Yellowhead Lake and west of the pass. Seven Sisters was the name originally given to Yellowhead Mountain. Interestingly, there remains a Seven Sisters near the Continental Divide just north of Crowsnest Pass. Lucerne Peak takes its name from a railway town that briefly flourished in the valley below.

The Canadian Northern Pacific Railway reached Yellowhead Lake in 1913 and named their station there after Lucerne, Switzerland, which is also situated on a lake. This provided the nucleus of a town that for a time had a population approaching 300 and rivalled Jasper. The station was not demolished until after the Second World War.

Tête Roche (2418 m) is the high point at the northeastern end of Yellowhead Mountain. It is believed the name was suggested by Pierre Bostonais who was also known as "Tête Jaune" (Yellow Head), an Iroquois fur trapper with some strands of blonde hair.

From Clairvaux Creek
Highway 16, 4.1 km west of Meadow Creek bridge; 9.8 km east of the B.C. border.

The Caledonian Valley. Etching from Ocean to Ocean.

Mount O'Beirne (2637 m) rises beyond Tête Roche, the valley of Rink Brook lying between the two. Eugene Francis O'Beirne travelled across western Canada with Reverend John McDougall and later, in 1863, joined the party led by Viscount Milton, an English nobleman, and Walter Cheadle, a physician. They were on a "pleasure trip across Canada" that included traversing the uncharted Yellowhead Pass.

The two made the mistake of inviting Mr. O'Beirne to join them while they were in Fort Edmonton. It is not clear why Viscount Milton and Doctor Cheadle agreed to take him. He had acquired such a reputation as a sponger and general pest that the residents of Fort Edmonton were so pleased to be rid of him that they provided O'Beirne with a saddle and a horse. He certainly did provide for some entertaining anecdotes in Cheadle's journal, which was later published in book form.

Although a jovial and entertaining character at times, Mr. O'Beirne appears to have been a less than desirable hitchhiker. He was described as very lazy, accident prone and a chronic complainer during the difficult trip. For example, while building a raft to cross the Athabasca River, Milton noticed that O'Beirne not only consistently chose the small end of any logs that had to be carried, but, "After the first few steps O'Beirne began to utter the most awful groans, and cried out, continually, 'Oh, Dear! Oh, Dear! this is most painful—it's cutting my shoulder in two—not so fast, my lord. Gently, gently. Steady, my lord, steady; I must

Cheadle and Milton's party fording a river. (O'Beirne is holding onto the horse's tail.) Courtesy Glenbow Archives, NA-1240-13.

stop. I'm carrying all the weight myself….' And then with a loud 'Oh!' and no further warning, he let his end of the tree down with a run, jarring his unhappy partner most dreadfully." All this was despite the fact that O'Beirne was a bigger man than Cheadle. Cheadle later commented, "I never saw such an old woman in my life or such a nuisance."[34]

It is no surprise that Mount O'Beirne was not named by either Viscount Milton or Walter Cheadle who, when assessing the assets of their party following the desertion of their guide, wrote that "Mr. O'Beirne represented a minus quantity."[35] Rather it was Arthur Wheeler of the Boundary Survey who named this fine peak in his honour. Why Wheeler immortalized O'Beirne in this way is not known, but perhaps it was because Eugene O'Beirne was clearly one of the more interesting characters that passed through the Yellowhead Pass in the nineteenth century.

The Miette River flows from the northwest between the mountains of the Continental Divide and **Mount Bridgland** (2930 m). Arthur Wheeler originally chose a rather unusual name for the mountain. While surveying in the vicinity of Yellowhead Pass in 1911, the usually staid surveyor decided the peak looked similar to a child's toy locomotive and should, therefore, be called Mount Toot Toot. He referred to it as such on the map he made at the end of the season's work. Later, however, he must have had second thoughts and in the final maps and reports, the peak was named in honour of Morris P. Bridgland, one of his ablest assistants.

Morris Bridgland

Guides at the Alpine Club of Canada camp in Yoho Valley. (l-r: Edouard Feuz, H. G. Wheeler, Morris Bridgland, Gottfried Feuz.) Courtesy Whyte Museum, Cdn. Alpine Journal Vol. 1, 1907.

Morrison P. Bridgland was educated at the University of Toronto and became qualified as a Dominion Land Surveyor. In 1902, he came west as an assistant to Arthur Wheeler. Athletic and very powerful, "Bridge" became respected as a tireless worker as he produced detailed and accurate maps over extensive areas of the Rockies, particularly in Jasper National Park.

Through his work he became a highly proficient climber. His climbing while undertaking topographical surveys was accomplished while carrying instruments and equipment weighing about 35 pounds. Like Arthur Wheeler, he was a founding member of the Alpine Club of Canada within which he was highly regarded both as a mountaineer and as a teacher. Arthur Wheeler's son wrote that, "He led party after party up the same climb, to him an easy and uninteresting climb, always safely, always with patience and good temper, and always with the utmost consideration for his party."[36]

Morris Bridgland's obituary in the *Journal of the Alpine Club of Canada* suggested that he was deserving of a higher, more prominent mountain than the peak that was named in his honour in 1918. Its author, C. B. Sissons wrote that, "The mountain which none too worthily bears the name of a great alpinist, who, I suppose, has climbed more peaks and pioneered more trails than any other Canadian, is near the Yellowhead Pass."[37]

Cinnamon Peak ↓

Mt. Robson ↓

The Dome ↓

Resplendent Mtn. ↓

Campion Mtn. ↓

The Rainbow Range

Panorama photos Georgina Brown.

6 Mount Robson, the Monarch of the Canadian Rockies

"Mount Robson is not only the highest mountain in the Canadian Rocky Mountains but one of the great mountains of the world, and deserving of inclusion in any select list on account of many striking characteristics and a form, beauty, and grandeur transcending any other of the greater peaks of the Rockies.... The mountain is unique, and its massive precipices, seamed with different-coloured rock strata, enhance it in both beauty and stature."[38] These words were written by Frank Smythe, an English mountaineer who wrote dozens of books about the mountains of the world during the mid twentieth century and was widely regarded as an authority on the subject.

The first people to write about this view were Viscount Milton and Dr. Walter Cheadle who reached this location in 1863. Although much less knowledgeable about the mountains of the world than Frank Smythe, they were obviously very impressed, writing, "On every side the snowy heads of mighty hills crowded round, whilst, immediately behind us, a giant among giants, and immeasurably supreme, rose Robson's peak. This magnificent mountain is of conical form, glacier-clothed, and rugged. When we first caught sight of it, a shroud of mist partially enveloped the summit, but this presently rolled away, and we saw its upper portion dimmed by a necklace of light feathery clouds, beyond which its pointed apex of ice, glittering in the morning sun, shot up into the blue

heaven above, to a height of probably 10,000 or 15,000 feet. It was a glorious sight, and one which the Shuswaps of the Cache assured us had rarely been seen by human eyes, the summit being generally hidden by clouds."[39]

No convincing is required to have us believe that **Mount Robson** is the highest peak in the Canadian Rockies as it towers above the Fraser Valley and the neighbouring peaks. Clearly the most impressive thing about this view of Mount Robson is the height of the peak above the Fraser River valley. The mountain has an elevation of 3954 m, 200 m higher than Mount Columbia, the second highest. Because the viewpoint is at the relatively low elevation of only 825 m, one is looking up 3129 vertical metres to the summit. No other view in the Rockies even approaches this base to peak statistic.

As a result of this, the prevailing westerly winds must achieve a tremendous vertical rise to pass over this massive mountain and, therefore, regardless of weather in the valley below, the summit is often obscured in clouds. For this reason the peak was referred to by some early visitors as Cloud Cap Mountain.

The height to which the winds must rise to pass over the summit accounts for two remarkable features on the mountain. Below its southwestern cliffs, particularly heavy levels of precipitation result in a unique rainforest. As well, the moisture-laden air tends to deposit a series of teethlike icy pinnacles across the summit crest that may be seen from the highway under good viewing conditions.

From Swiftcurrent Creek bridge
Highway 16, 4 km west of Mount Robson Visitor Information Centre; 12.6 km east of the junction with Highway 5.

21

From the Swiftcurrent River bridge Mount Robson is a massive, somewhat symmetric peak with two broad shoulders. A glacier flows between the summit and the south shoulder, which has been named **The Dome** (3078 m). Beginning just below the summit, a long, steep and often snow-filled couloir descends to the valley of the Robson River.

The distinctive horizontal rock strata is highlighted by partially melted snow in mid and late summer. The Shuswaps are said to have referred to Mount Robson as The Mountain of the Spiral Road because the strata angles upwards to the east, giving it the appearance of spiral tracks running around the mountain.

On the hidden side of the mountain lies one of the most impressive glacier systems in the Rockies and it is from this point that most mountaineers attempting the peak begin their climbs. But there is no easy route up this mountain and this, in combination with the usual bad weather on the mountain, results in few successful ascents.

Resplendent Mountain from Snowbird Meadows.

Conrad Kain, who is honoured by a peak to the southwest of Resplendent Mountain, wrote of the mountain, "In all my mountaineering in various countries, I have climbed only a few mountains that were hemmed in with more difficulties. Mount Robson is one of the most dangerous expeditions I have made. The dangers consist in snow and ice, stone avalanches, and treacherous weather."[40]

In the early years of the nineteenth century, the North West Company outfitted parties to hunt and trap in the mountains near the Athabasca River. One party was led by a man whose name was carelessly pronounced "Robson" and had a camp near the mountain. This was likely Colin Robertson who worked for both the North West Company and the Hudson's Bay Company around 1815. The spot became a gathering place for the various parties of hunters and the peak was named after him. The first written reference to the name is by George McDougall, a fur trader, in his diary of 1827.

The low ridge to the left of Mount Robson and the Robson River is **Cinnamon Peak** (2667 m). In 1911 Arthur Wheeler climbed the mountain to study the route taken by Kinney and Phillips when they climbed to Robson's summit ridge two years previously. Wheeler referred to the mountain as Little Grizzly, "on account of its resemblance, on a smaller scale, to Mount Grizzly in the Selkirks."[41] Later the name was changed to Cinnamon, a colour variation of the bear.

To the right of Mount Robson is another low ridge known as **Campion Mountain** (2484 m). While surveying in the area, Arthur Wheeler noted that moss campion, a moss-like plant with hundreds of pink blooms, grew abundantly on the slopes of the mountain.

Beyond Campion Mountain rises **Resplendent Mountain** (3245 m), a mountain that, sadly, is often overshadowed by its more renowned neighbour. Following his 1911 expedition to the area, Arthur Wheeler wrote about the view of Resplendent Mountain from the north and described the mountain as "...clad from top to base in pure white snow. On a fine sunny day this mountain presents such an ethereal brilliance that there is little wonder that the name given it by Coleman, which fits so aptly, should have 'hit' him."[42] From the Swiftcurrent Creek bridge one can see the edge of this beautiful glacier as it forms the northeast ridge of the mountain.

To the right of Resplendent and beyond Campion Mountain lie unnamed peaks of the **Rainbow Range**.

The First Ascent of Mount Robson

"Oh what a glorious sight he was that day we first saw him. There, buttressed across the whole valley and more, with his high flung crest manteled with a thousand ages of snow, Mount Robson shouldered his way into the eternal solitudes thousands of feet higher than the surrounding mountains."[43] This was George Kinney's reaction in 1907 to his first view of the mountain that entranced him and was the focus of his life for the next four years.

Kinney was born in New Brunswick, had investigated the fossil beds on Mount Stephen and completed a solo ascent of that high mountain in October of 1904. A founding member of the Alpine Club of Canada, Kinney joined Arthur and Quincy Coleman on what was the first expedition to attempt to climb the highest mountain in the Canadian Rockies.

Arthur Coleman had spent several years searching for the legendary Mount Brown and Mount Hooker, which had been touted as having elevations of about 5000 m, only to find that a "mistake" had been made. Understandably, he was concerned that the height of this peak, which it was claimed rose over 3000 m above its base, might be grossly exaggerated as well. The trio left Lake Louise and after struggling through burnt timber and wilderness for 41 days, reached the base of the mountain. Unfortunately, the weather was bad and as they were too late in the season, they were only able to explore the base of the peak.

Kinney and the Colemans returned again in 1908 and after two attempts again retreated in bad weather. Kinney set out on a solo attempt on September 9, this time reaching an elevation of 3200 m before avalanches drove him off the mountain. The following day the trio reached a high point of 3500 m.

The Colemans and Kinney made arrangements to continue their efforts the following year. However, following reports that a "foreign" party (Arnold Mumm, Geoffrey Hastings, Leopold Amery and Moritz Inderbinen) had their eyes on the peak, Kinney set out alone earlier in the season than planned, "...hoping to pick up someone on the trail to share fortune with me."[44]

The Athabasca River had reached very high levels and both Curly Phillips and George Kinney had been marooned on islands for a few days before their chance meeting at John Moberly's cabin above Jasper Lake on July 11. Curly Phillips had also entered the mountains by himself, hoping to start an outfitting business. Even though Phillips had never climbed a mountain, Kinney thought the, "blue-eyed, curly headed clean-lived Canadian" was "perfectly fit for the undertaking I had in hand."[45] Fourteen days later they reached the base of Mount Robson. Despite 20 days of bad weather, they made three attempts on the northwest face.

Finally, with their provisions nearly depleted, a clear day dawned. This would be George Kinney's twelfth attempt. After overnighting on the mountain, they reached the summit ridge, now known as Emperor Ridge, on August 13 in dense clouds and high winds. The final climb to the summit was a tremendous effort in bitter cold over steep ice and snow. Curly Phillips had no prior mountaineering experience and did not even have an ice axe, using instead a stout pole from the forest below.

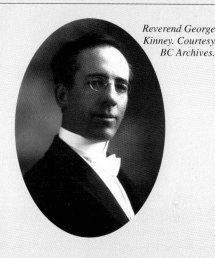

Reverend George Kinney. Courtesy BC Archives.

Mount Robson and Berg Glacier from the north. Photo Dr. John D. Birrell.

Conrad Kain. Photo Byron Harmon. Courtesy Whyte Museum, NA-66-408.

In 1913 a team of experienced climbers organized by the Alpine Club of Canada journeyed to the peak under very different circumstances than those endured by George Kinney during his attempts. The group was able to travel to the base of the peak by railway, then to their base camp at Berg Lake beneath the mountain's northern cliffs by pack train under the guidance of Curly Phillips himself. Conrad Kain, an Austrian guide who had a well-established reputation with the Alpine Club, was to lead two experienced mountaineers, Albert MacCarthy and William Foster, to the summit. The route Kain had chosen was quite different to that climbed by Kinney and Phillips, in that most of it was on ice. According to the club's official records, thirteen hours of strenuous fighting up rock cliffs and dangerous slopes of snow and ice was involved and 1600 steps had to be cut before they reached the summit at 5 o'clock in the evening. Kain later wrote that "Mount Robson is one of the most beautiful mountains in the Rockies and certainly the most difficult one."[46]

Although no one questions the fact that George Kinney and Curly Phillips reached the summit crest of Mount Robson in 1909, controversy continues to this day as to whether or not they reached the highest point on the ridge. Kinney is quoted as stating, "We finally floundered through these treacherous masses and stood, at last, on the very summit of Mount Robson."[47] Curly Phillips is reported to have confided to William Foster that he and Kinney were unable to climb a 60 foot-high dome of ice on the top of the ridge. Some suggest that Arthur Wheeler and the Alpine Club of Canada pressured Curly to say that they had not reached the actual summit in order that the 1913 expedition could claim credit for the first complete ascent.

In his book, *Pushing the Limits, the Story of Canadian Mountaineering*, mountaineer and historian Chic Scott thoroughly reviews all aspects of what is one of the few genuine controversies in the history of Canadian climbing. Chic leaves it for his readers to draw their own conclusion but his research indicates that George Kinney has been "much abused" by historians.

What is clear is that the perseverance and courage demonstrated during the climb by George Kinney and Curly Phillips is one of the most outstanding achievements in the mountaineering history of the Canadian Rockies. Conrad Kain maintained, "They deserve more credit than we, even though they did not reach the highest point, for in 1909 they had many more obstacles to overcome than we; for at that time the railway…was no less than two hundred miles from their goal and their way had to be made over rocks and brush, and we must not forget the dangerous river crossings."[48]

The pole that Curly used on his ascent remains one of the most prized possessions of the Whyte Museum of the Canadian Rockies.

Curly Phillips with his stick at 12,000 feet on Mount Robson. Courtesy Whyte Museum, NA-66-508.

Donald "Curly" Phillips

"Everyone held the same high opinion of this man, who in all things was simple and straightforward."[49]

Curly Phillips was born in Ontario in 1884 where he learned the basics of wilderness travel and canoeing. After travelling west in 1908 at the age of 24, Curly headed to the mountains where he heard there were jobs available working on the construction of the Spiral Tunnels east of Field. A brief visit to the site convinced him that blasting out rocks with dynamite was not for him. After spending the winter in the Edmonton area, he headed to the Yellowhead Pass with a few horses in the hope of outfitting hunters and other visitors.

About 10 km above Jasper Lake he met Reverend George Kinney who was also on his own and began the adventure that ended with the first ascent to the summit ridge of Mount Robson. Curly's accomplishments on the mountain established his reputation amongst climbers and others in the area. Evidence of this was the fact that the following year Norman Collie, a highly respected veteran mountaineer, named the 3250 m mountain immediately across the Robson River from Mount Robson in his honour. This was done even though Curly was only 26 years old and had spent but a single season in the Rockies. Soon Curly Phillips was well established in the guiding and outfitting business.

In 1911 he led a joint party of the Alpine Club of Canada and the Smithsonian Institute on a journey of exploration in the Mount Robson area. Arthur Wheeler and club photographer Byron Harmon were in the group as well as a number of scientists from the American organization. Two years later, Curly was back in the Robson area again as guide and outfitter for the Alpine Club of Canada's camp during which Conrad Kain guided a party to the summit of the peak.

Later that year Curly settled in Jasper. In 1915 he guided two legendary lady explorers, Caroline Hinman and Mary Jobe, on a two month trip into the country northwest of Mount Robson where they attempted to climb Mount Sir Alexander.

He served briefly during the First World War but did not see action overseas. Over the following two decades he continued his outfitting business, guiding J. Monroe Thorington to the Sunwapta Pass area for his first ascents of Mount Saskatchewan and the Twins and the second ascent of Mount Columbia.

A well-read individual who kept a diary from 1905 until 1923, Curly developed other interests that included building canoes, establishing boat trips for visitors on Medicine and Maligne lakes, managing the Maligne Lake Chalet, guiding power boat trips on the Athabasca and Peace rivers, and operating an irrigated market gardening business. He also operated a "dude trap line" to take "city people" by dog team into the northern wilderness and in 1937 pioneered the concept of flying groups of hunters into remote areas.

In 1936, at the age of 52, Curly took up skiing. Two years later, while investigating the idea of building a cabin for the use of skiers, he was tragically killed in an avalanche near Elysium Pass in the Victoria Cross Range northwest of Jasper.

Following Curly's untimely death, an article written by J. Monroe Thorington was published in the *American Alpine Journal*. It included the following tribute, "Curly is remembered as a man of quiet reserve always ready to laugh, as one who moved like a shadow in the woods, and carved his own brand of woodsmanship out of old Indian ways and his own integrity—as a person who relied on himself. These are the qualities for which the man and his times should be remembered for these are the strengths modern people need most."[50]

Donald Phillips. Courtesy Whyte Museum, V14 AC027-18 (15).

Mount Phillips from Campion Mountain. Photo Greg Redies.

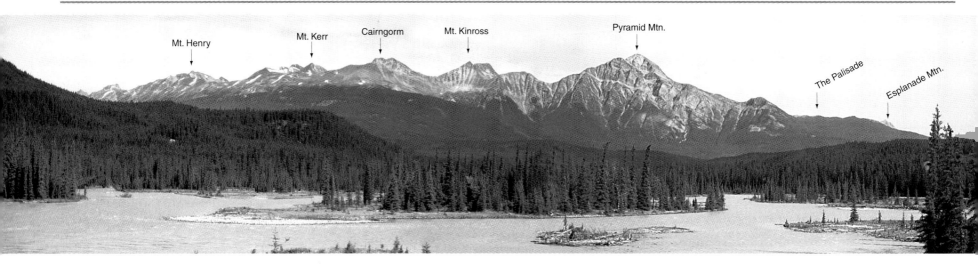

Mt. Henry   Mt. Kerr   Cairngorm   Mt. Kinross   Pyramid Mtn.   The Palisade   Esplanade Mtn.

7 The Backdrop to Jasper Townsite

From Athabasca River bridge

Highway 93, 7.5 km south of the junction with Highway 16; 23 km north of Athabasca Falls junction.

The bridge over the Athabasca River provides an excellent opportunity to enjoy the panorama to the north without trees obstructing the view. From a mountain viewing perspective this is an area of transition, the form and colour of the mountains to the north, which form the backdrop to the town of Jasper, being markedly different from the mountains to the south.

The peaks behind Jasper townsite appear gently contoured, relatively low and have a reddish-orange hue to them. This comes from the oxidization of iron minerals that are found in the rock that forms much of the Victoria Cross Range. The mountains in most other areas of the Rockies are steeper, sculptured with cliffs and are generally the blue-gray colour that inspired the Wilf Carter song *In the Blue Canadian Rockies*.

Most of the peaks you see from this viewpoint are made of Cambrian and Precambrian gritstone (sandstone, with the addition of grains of feldspar and mica) and slate, which tends to erode easily, leaving the mountains with a rounded and worn profile. The mountains are similar in age and in composition to the mountains in the very southern part of the province from the Castle River to Waterton National Park.

Although **Mount Henry** (2629 m) is part of the Victoria Cross Range, William Henry was an early North West Company fur trader who, in 1811, built a trading post on the Athabasca River near the mouth of the Miette River. This was the point where travellers heading west into the mountains switched from travel by canoe to horseback.

Mount Kerr (2560 m) was named to honour Private John Chipman Kerr VC, a native of Edmonton who was awarded the Victoria Cross while serving with the 49th Battalion. In 1916, near the town of Courcelette during the Battle of the Somme, Private Kerr "ran along the parados under heavy fire until he was in close contact with the enemy when he opened fire at point-blank range, inflicting heavy losses. The enemy, thinking that they were surrounded, surrendered—62 prisoners were taken and 250 yards of enemy trench captured. Earlier, Private Kerr's fingers had been blown off, but he did not have his wound dressed until he and two other men had escorted the prisoners back under fire and reported for duty."[51]

Cairngorm (2610 m) is not Mount Cairngorm or Cairngorm Peak, just Cairngorm. It was named by surveyor Morris Bridgland after a group of granitic mountains in the Scottish Highlands called the Cairngorms of which Cairn Gorm is one of the higher peaks. Gorm in Gaelic means blue-green and in July and early August, the upper slopes of the mountain do indeed exhibit shades of green. However, the ancient name for the Scottish Cairngorms is Monadh Ruadh, meaning "red mountains," which these peaks of the Victoria Cross Range certainly are. We can only speculate as to what Morris Bridgland's thoughts were when he chose the name.

Mount Kinross (2560 m) was named after Private Cecil John Kinross VC of Calgary, who was awarded the Commonwealth's highest award for bravery while serving with the 49th Battalion. At the Battle of Passchendaele in 1917, Kinross's company came under heavy attack and further advance was held up by very severe fire from an enemy machine-gun. After making a careful survey of the situation, Private Kinross left all his equipment behind except for his rifle and bandolier and advanced alone over open ground in broad daylight. He charged the enemy machine-gun, killed the crew of six, and destroyed the gun. It was reported that, "his superb example and courage enabled a highly important position to be established."[52]

Although **Pyramid Mountain** (2766 m) is the highest peak seen from this viewpoint, this is not its best side. Its pyramidal shape is only visible as one approaches the town of Jasper from the east.

The forested slope to the right of the Pyramid is the back of **The Palisade** (2130 m), which overlooks the Athabasca Valley east of Jasper. Some 13 km beyond the Palisade stands **Esplanade Mountain** (2301 m), named by Morris Bridgland because its summit is an esplanade or flat-topped ridge. Clearly he wasn't looking at it from this angle when he chose the name.

Pyramid Mountain from the south.

The Victoria Cross

Instituted by Queen Victoria in 1856, the Victoria Cross is the highest award that can be given to a Canadian for gallantry in the face of the enemy. Another important factor in the awarding of a Victoria Cross is that, "neither rank, nor long service, nor wounds, nor any other circumstance or condition whatsoever, save the merit of conspicuous bravery"[53] should be considered in determining an award. This placed all service personnel on an equal footing for the decoration.

The medal was first awarded during the Crimean War and among the recipients was a Canadian lieutenant, Alexander Roberts Dunn, who won the VC for heroism during the charge of the Light Brigade at the Battle of Balaklava.

Over the years 93 Canadians have been awarded the Victoria Cross and two of them were further honoured by having mountains in this panorama named after them. A total of six mountains named after Victoria Cross recipients may be seen from viewpoints described in this book.

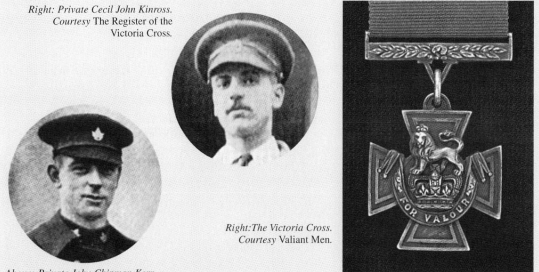

Right: Private Cecil John Kinross.
Courtesy The Register of the Victoria Cross.

Above: Private John Chipman Kerr.
Courtesy The Register of the Victoria Cross.

Right:The Victoria Cross.
Courtesy Valiant Men.

Mt. Christie | Brussels Peak | Mt. Lowell | Mt. Fryatt | Divergence Peak | Whirlpool Mtn. | Mt. Brown | Mt. Edith Cavell

8 Whirlpool Valley and Much More

From Hardisty Hill

Highway 93, 5.3 km north of Athabasca Falls junction; 17.7 km south of Athabasca River bridge.

The magnificent view from the top of the hill below Mount Hardisty is one of the most outstanding in the Canadian Rockies. It features two high peaks named in memory of civilian heroes of the First World War, the "Three Sisters of the Athabasca Valley," a view up the Whirlpool Valley to the vicinity of a legendary pass that was first travelled in the early years of the nineteenth century and a look at what was for a time the most talked about mountain in Canada.

Southwest face of Mount Fryatt. Photo Glen Boles.

There are two established viewpoints on the hill. The northern one has signage related to David Thompson and Athabasca Pass, but unfortunately the view toward the pass is blocked by a nearby ridge. Though the southern viewpoint is better, the ideal spot from which to contemplate the rich history of this valley requires you to walk 200 m south along the highway from the southern viewpoint.

From this point, **Mount Kerkeslin** limits the view to the left and seems to loom over the valley. Although only 2984 m high, this classic mountain often dominates the view from the north as one travels south from Jasper, an excellent viewpoint being the Athabasca River bridge. Its strata is such that snow often highlights its many layers, which form a gentle synclinal fold.

Being such a prominent peak, it is not surprising that it was named by James Hector when he travelled up the Athabasca Valley in 1859. Just who or what Kerkeslin was remains a mystery. This is very unusual as the history of the naming of our mountains has generally been well documented. Mount Kerkeslin is probably the most prominent peak in Alberta that carries a name whose derivation is not known.

Lying just beyond the Fryatt Creek valley, **Mount Christie** (3103 m), **Brussels Peak** (3161 m) and **Mount Lowell** (3150 m) are, from this viewpoint, quite like the Three Sisters of the Bow Valley.

Mount Christie is the highest of the three and was named by James Hector when he passed by on his way to Athabasca Pass. William Joseph Christie was the chief factor at the Hudson's Bay Company's Fort Edmonton when Hector was there during the winter of 1858-59.

Brussels Peak remains the only peak in the Rockies named after a ferry boat. Frank Smythe, a widely travelled mountaineer who wrote numerous books related to mountains during the 1940s, wrote that, "It is a conspicuous object from the road, and strongly resembles one of those minor dolomite peaks which jut out surprisingly from an otherwise normal landscape."[54] He went on to be, for some reason, unkindly critical of the mountain, writing that there is, "no particular grace or dignity about it. In fact it is one of those absurd little mountains that shouldn't be there, stuck on an otherwise impeccable landscape as an afterthought."[55] He was perhaps referring to how different its profile is compared to the "sisters" to its left and right.

His attitude toward the mountain may have been coloured by the fact that he made three attempts to complete the first ascent but was unsuccessful. He later wrote, "Most mountains have their weaknesses, but not so Brussels. Most mountains have cracks or chimneys leading through otherwise impassable cliffs or pitches; but the cracks and chimneys on Brussels peter out into overhangs or are merely incidental, beginning and ending nowhere. Most mountains have ledges whereby difficulties can be circumvented, but there are few ledges in the cliffs of Brussels."[56] The peak was finally climbed in 1948 by R. C. Garner and J. Lewis, but only with the use of a considerable amount of hardware including recently developed expansion bolts.

Mount Lowell features an attractive notched summit. It was named in 1934 by members of the Harvard Mountaineering Club after the university's president. The name remains unofficial and is one of four impressive peaks in this panorama that are officially unnamed.

Dominating the view to the south, the symmetric **Mount Fryatt** (3361 m) stands majestically behind a closer, horizontal ridge. An example of a horn peak, Fryatt has been eroded by glaciers from all sides—a feature best seen from the Mount Christie viewpoint, 16.2 km to the south. Named by the Boundary Commission in 1921, the mountain honours Charles Algernon Fryatt, the captain of the merchant ship *Brussels,* who was executed by the enemy during the First World War.

The valley containing the three Geraldine Lakes lies between two impressive, but unnamed peaks. Beyond the lakes in the distance lies **Divergence Peak** (2827 m), the northernmost of two similarly shaped mountains. It was named by Arthur Wheeler of the Boundary Survey because the Continental Divide abruptly turns from its typical SSE orientation to SSW at its summit. The boundary continues SSW for another 11 km with Alberta to the west and British Columbia to the east, the opposite of what one is used to.

The legendary valley of the Whirlpool River lies directly to the southwest of this viewpoint, to the right of the peak known unofficially as **Whirlpool Mountain** (2900 m). The infamous **Mount Brown** (2799 m) may be seen some 40 km in the distance. During the latter years of the nineteenth century, this mountain was one of the most talked about and pursued peaks in the Rockies. It lies just to the west of Athabasca Pass.

Mount Edith Cavell (3363 m) completes this impressive panorama. Just two m higher than Mount Fryatt, it lies four km beyond a high ridge forming the west side of the Whirlpool River valley. The mountain was referred to as La Montagne de la Grande Traverse by travellers in the fur trade era. It was here that those traversing Athabasca Pass had to ford the Athabasca River and begin ascending the Whirlpool, and so the mountain became a very significant landmark. Later, in 1916, it was officially named after Edith Louise Cavell, an English nurse who was executed during the First World War.

Brussels Peak. Photo Larry Stanier.

Mount Christie. Photo Tony Daffern.

Athabasca Pass

Interprovincial Boundary Survey monument at Athabasca Pass. Photo Glen Boles.

It is somewhat confusing that Athabasca Pass lies at the headwaters of the Whirlpool River and not at the headwaters of the Athabasca River. This is because early travellers considered the Whirlpool to be the main branch of the Athabasca. The pass became so significant historically that the original name remains.

The first white man to cross Athabasca Pass was David Thompson of the North West Company in 1811. Thompson had discovered Howse Pass in 1807 and using it as a trade route had established his company as a trading partner with the Kootenay Indians in British Columbia. In the fall of 1810 he set out to cross Howse pass, but was blocked by a Peigan war party who objected to his dealings with the Kootenais. Instead of retiring to Rocky Mountain House, Thompson set off in the dead of winter to look for another pass over the Continental Divide.

With 13 men on snowshoes and eight dogsleds, Thompson passed below what is now Mount Edith Cavell in early January and began the 48 km ascent to the headwaters of the Whirlpool River. He was well aware of the difficulties he faced and had selected only the hardiest available for the ordeal.

After six days of struggling though metres of fresh, wet snow they reached the treeline. "The view now before us was an ascent of deep snow, in all appearance to the height of land between the Atlantic and the Pacific Oceans; it was to me an exhilarating sight, but to my uneducated men…the scene of desolation before us was dreadful."[57] At the summit of the pass, Thompson's men built a fire on a platform of poles they had cut and dragged along for the purpose, as they were camped on 20 feet of snow. That night "My men were not at their ease, yet when night came they admired the brilliance of the stars, and as one of them said, he thought he could almost touch them with his hand…."[58] Thompson reflected that "a new world was in a manner before me, and my object was to be at the Pacific Ocean before the month of August."[59] Thompson and his party persevered, reaching the Columbia River and on July 15 the Pacific Ocean.

The pass became the main fur trade route across the Rockies for the next half century. An exchange of goods, letters and individuals often took place on the summit, one group having made the journey up the Columbia River by boat to Boat Encampment, and then up the Wood River and finally Pacific Creek to the pass. The party from the east would journey from Edmonton by boat and pack train, following the Athabasca and Whirlpool rivers.

Hudson's Bay Company governor George Simpson traversed the pass himself in 1824. He wrote, "At the very top of the pass or height of Land is a small circular Lake or Basin of water which empties itself in opposite directions and may be said to be the source of the Columbia and Athabasca Rivers as it bestows its favours on both these prodigious Streams. That this basin should send its Waters to each side of the Continent and give birth to two of the principal rivers in North America is no less strange than true both the Dr. [John McLoughlin] and myself having examined the currents flowing from it East and West and the circumstance appearing remarkable I thought it should be honoured by a distinguishing title and it was forthwith named the 'Committee's Punch Bowl.'"[60] Fur-trade travellers paused at this natural campsite to drink a toast to the governing committee of the Hudson's Bay Company in London.

In 1854 the Hudson's Bay Company closed its operations in Oregon and moved its centre of activity to Fort Victoria on Vancouver Island. With no commercial significance, traffic through the pass virtually ceased.

The Committee's Punch Bowl. Photo Glen Boles.

Mount Brown

"Being well rested by one o'clock, I set out with the view of ascending what seemed to be the highest peak on the north,"[61] wrote botanist David Douglas during his crossing of Athabasca Pass in 1827. "Its height does not seem to be less than 16,000 or 17,000 feet [5000 m] above the level of the sea. The view from the summit is of too awful a cast to afford pleasure. Nothing can be seen, in every direction as far as the eye can reach, except mountains towering above each other, rugged beyond description. This peak, the highest yet known in the northern continent of America, I feel a sincere pleasure in naming 'Mount Brown,' in honour of R. Brown, Esq., the illustrious botanist.... A little to the southward is one nearly the same height, rising into a sharper point. This I named Mt. Hooker...."[62] David Douglas, whose name is associated with the Douglas fir tree, was Professor Brown's student and his ascent was the first recorded climb of a mountain in the Canadian Rockies.

When Douglas's book recounting his experiences in Canada's mountains was published, Mount Brown and Mount Hooker became well known. J. Monroe Thorington wrote, "When I was little, when you were a school-child, geography books taught that the highest mountains of North America—Mount Brown and Mount Hooker—lifted their unsurpassed heights on either side of Athabasca Pass."[63] Douglas's determination of their elevations was probably based upon an estimate of the elevation of Athabasca Pass made by an earlier traveller who had lost his barometer and overestimated the altitude by 1800 m. Adding further to the confusion, it is difficult to understand how Douglas, even with his acknowledged eyesight problems, could have failed to notice that the other mountains nearby were much higher than the one he had climbed.

In the late nineteenth century the first mountaineers to visit the Rockies were very anxious to find and climb these "giants." Arthur P. Coleman, a geology professor from Toronto, later wrote, "A high mountain is always a seduction but a mountain with a mystery is doubly so.... I studied the atlas and saw Mounts Brown and Hooker...(and) I longed to visit them."[64] In 1893, during his third summer of explorations, he finally reached the pass but the nearest highest mountain he

Mount Brown. Photo Don Beers.

David Douglas. Courtesy Whyte Museum, M106/7.

could find was only about 2800 m in height. Disappointed, he wondered, "What had gone wrong with these two mighty peaks that they should shrink seven thousand feet in altitude and how could anyone, even a botanist like Douglas, make so monumental a blunder?"[65]

But these mythical pair of giant mountains had been talked about for so long and appeared on so many maps that the legend did not die easily. Even mountaineers experienced in the Rockies such as Walter Wilcox and J. Norman Collie still believed they may have existed and continued the search.

The search for Douglas's huge peaks was finally brought to a close, not in the mountains of Canada, but in a library in England when Collie carefully read Douglas's original journals and noticed that he had claimed to have climbed Mount Brown in a single afternoon. "If David Douglas climbed a 17,000 foot peak alone on a May afternoon," he wrote, "when the snow must have been pretty deep on the ground, all one can say is that he must have been an uncommonly active person.... For nearly seventy years they have been masquerading in every map as the highest peaks in the Canadian Rocky Mountains; they must now retire from that position, and Mts. Forbes, Columbia, Bryce, and Alberta will, in future, reign in their stead."[66]

Mt. Morden Long · Mt. Palmer · Mt. Confederation · Mt. King Edward · Blackfriars Peak · Mt. Quincy · Dragon Peak

9 The Peaks of the Upper Athabasca

From Ranger Hill
Highway 93, 4.2 km north of the road to Sunwapta Falls; 19.3 km south of the road to Athabasca Falls.

This spectacular panorama features one of the most rugged areas of Jasper National Park and a look at the very source of the Athabasca River. Because trees obscure the view from the highway viewpoint, it is necessary to cross the Icefields Parkway about 100 m to the south and climb 30 m up the slope to see the complete panorama.

If you enter the mountains on the Yellowhead Highway (16) and then turn south on the Icefields Parkway (93), you will have followed the Athabasca River for about 100 km when you reach this viewpoint. This is where the Athabasca Valley turns, heading south to its headwaters at the Columbia Icefield while the highway continues southeast, following the Sunwapta River to Sunwapta Pass.

The Athabasca River does not have its source at or near an easily traversed pass like most major rivers in the Canadian Rockies. If you travel up this valley to the headwaters of the Athabasca you meet a wall of steep rock and glaciers only traversable by experienced mountaineers.

Mount Morden Long (3040 m), just visible behind a lower ridge, is located at the northern end of the Sir Winston Churchill Range, which includes the peaks between the Athabasca Valley and the Sunwapta Valley as far south as the Columbia Icefield. It was named for Morden Heaton Long, a professor at the University of Alberta who wrote extensively about the history of western Canada and was the first chairman of the Geographic Board of Alberta.

Mount Confederation features a spectacular twin tower.
Photo Don Beers.

In the distance, **Mount Palmer** (3150 m) rises behind the near ridge and 6.5 km beyond the southeastern cliffs of Mount Confederation. The mountain is actually made up of two summits but the westerly one is hidden. Howard Palmer climbed widely in the Selkirks and Rockies, completing the first ascent of Mount Sir Sandford, the highest mountain in the Selkirk Range in 1912. He was the author of *Mountaineering and Exploration in the Selkirks*, one of the classics of mountaineering in Canada.

Mount Confederation (2969 m) rises in front of and to the right of Mount Palmer. Named in 1927, it commemorates John A. Macdonald and the other Fathers of Confederation who negotiated the formation of Canada in 1867. A striking peak, its rose-brown towers culminate in a pyramid-shaped summit that from this and, indeed, all angles, appears to be a rather difficult climb. In fact, six attempts to reach the summit failed before Mr. and Mrs. John Mendenhall, who had failed their attempt in 1940, returned in 1947 to complete the first ascent. They noted that part of the mountain's "allure" was that it was one of the few unclimbed mountains visible from what was then known as the Banff-Jasper Highway.

Just hidden behind the slopes of Mount Confederation, Mount Columbia towers above the source of the Athabasca River. The next page describes a nearby viewpoint from where you can view Alberta's highest mountain.

Mount King Edward (3490 m) is the distant peak that forms the head of the valley from this viewpoint. Lying some 43 km to the south, this impressive, glacier-draped mountain is the easternmost of the six highest peaks that lie adjacent to the Columbia Icefield. A glimpse of this giant in the early morning light of a summer morning is a special treat.

King Edward VII was the eldest son of Queen Victoria and was 65 years old when he became King in 1901. His mother had allowed him no political influence at all and it is said that he resented this. Affectionately known as Bertie by his family, he lived a self-obsessed life complete with many mistresses and much self-indulgence. However, he did change British foreign policy, gaining the goodwill of France and beginning active rearmament, his concern being Germany under Kaiser Wilhelm.

A large "massif" of extremely steep terrain lies between the Athabasca River to the east and the Chaba River valley to the west. In 1901, at the suggestion of Jean Habel, the high point on the eastern edge was named **Blackfriars Peak** (3210 m). The mountain reminded Dr. Habel of a peak in Europe with a similar name. Unclimbed until 1953, the summit was attained by a party

Mount King Edward (left) and Blackfriars Peak (right). Photo Don Beers.

led by Walter Perren, who in 1950 had become one of the last two Swiss guides brought to Canada by the Canadian Pacific Railway.

Some 60 m lower than Blackfriars Peak, **Mount Quincy** (3150 m) features a beautiful glacier on its broad summit. Arthur P. Coleman, a professor of geology at the University of Toronto who travelled widely in the northern Rockies, named the mountain in 1892. Perhaps the name honours his mother's family name, but more likely it honours his brother, Lucius Quincy Coleman, who ranched in the Morley area of the Bow Valley. In his book *The Canadian Rockies, Old Trails and New*, Professor Coleman praises him highly for his ability in packing, tracking, and cooking and for his pleasant disposition. One of Quincy Coleman's neighbours at Morley referred to him as, "a man of sterling character and a gentleman in every way."[67]

To the mountain's left is a spectacular rock tower. It is situated on the western end of a broad high ridge that lies between Mount Quincy and Blackfriars Peak. The isolated nature of the tower is best seen from north of the viewpoint.

This wonderful view is framed on the right side by **Dragon Peak** (2940 m), named because rock formations at the summit were thought to resemble a dragon by members of the Alberta-British Columbia Boundary Survey.

Arthur Coleman. Courtesy Whyte Museum, V14 ACOOP-82.

Mount Columbia

Mount Columbia from Ranger Creek viewpoint. Photo Don Beers.

In order to get a glimpse of Mount Columbia (3747 m), the highest mountain in Alberta, travel 2.6 km north of the Ranger Hill viewpoint to Ranger Creek. Although it can be seen through the trees from the highway just south of the creek, a fine, unobstructed viewpoint can be attained by walking about 20 m up the south side of the creek, then climbing another 20 m to the top of the scarred area above the highway. An unknown lover of mountains has built a small cairn to mark this very special spot.

"Chisel shaped at the head, covered with glaciers and snow...I at once recognized the great peak I was in search of."[68] Norman Collie thought at the time that he had found the legendary Mount Brown and was undoubtedly disappointed to learn later that he had not. However, he had become one of the first to see the magnificent peak that would be named Mount Columbia, the second highest mountain in the Canadian Rockies.

From this viewpoint one can see the north and east faces of the mountain that rise to the pointed summit almost 2300 m above the Athabasca River.

The opposite side of the peak is quite different: the Columbia Icefield drapes over its relatively gentle southern and eastern slopes almost to the summit. The edge of the ice may be seen above the cliff on the left-hand ridge.

Approaching the mountain from the Columbia Icefield side, James Outram and guide Christian Kaufmann made the first ascent in 1902. Outram described the view from the summit as "simply marvellous."[69] He later wrote, "The vast extent of these mountain-tops is extremely striking, especially in such untrodden regions as the Canadian Rockies freely offer. The charm of the unknown is mingled with the pleasures of recognition."[70]

A much more challenging climb, technically, was completed in 1970 by C. Jones and G. Thompson when they spent two-and-a-half days climbing the north face.

Mount Columbia takes its name from the river that loops through British Columbia before entering the United States.

The spectacular northeast face of Mount Columbia. Photo Glen Boles.

Mount Columbia (as Collie first saw it) from the summit of Mount Athabasca. Photo Glen Boles.

Mt. Athabasca   Mt. Andromeda   Snow Dome   Mt. Kitchener   Athabasca Glacier

10 The View from the Icefields Centre

"The country here was much more open and the going perfectly easy. Our course lay W.N.W.; and, passing through some pretty park like glades, the outfit emerged into a broad, green, and nearly level valley. We had passed the watershed unawares; for the tiny rivulet that now meandered, parallel with us, peacefully through the meadows was the infant Athabasca starting on its long journey to the Great Slave Lake and the Arctic Ocean."[71] Norman Collie and his party had just arrived at Sunwapta Pass and were about to be the first to see and explore the Columbia Icefield that lay hidden above them.

Sunwapta Pass is the boundary between Banff and Jasper national parks, the waters from its summit flowing south to the Saskatchewan River and north to the Athabasca River. From the summit of the pass the highway travels north through Collie's "broad, green, and near level valley"[72] for five km before reaching the Icefields Centre. These meadows are at an elevation of over 2000 m, beautiful on many days in summer, but often windswept and barren during the winter. Whatever the weather, the construction of the Icefields Centre below the western slopes of Mount Wilcox has made for a very comfortable viewpoint from which to enjoy this panorama featuring four of the high peaks bordering the Columbia Icefield.

In 1896, Walter Wilcox, R. L. Barrett and guides Tom Lusk and Fred Stephens discovered Sunwapta Pass and were the first to enjoy this panorama. They were on a 60-day expedition and searching for a pass through which to reach the Athabasca River. Impressed by "the tremendous grandeur of mountain scenery,"[73] the group explored the area, Barrett even attempting to climb, "a beautiful, glacier-hung peak"[74] that must have been Mount Athabasca.

In order to determine if the party could continue over the newly discovered pass, Fred Stephens reconnoitred between the toe of the Athabasca Glacier and the steep slopes of a rocky peak to the east but found that, "the route which first appeared most promising was blocked by a canyon."[75] The party then proceeded over a high grassy pass to the east of the rocky peak, eventually descending into the Sunwapta River valley beyond the Tangle Creek canyon. To honour Walter Wilcox, the pass and the rocky peak were later named **Wilcox Pass** and **Mount Wilcox** (2884 m).

The outstanding, glacier-draped peak on the left side of the panorama is **Mount Athabasca** (3491 m), one of the classic peaks of the Canadian Rockies and an easy climb from this direction. A view of the mountain's east-facing slopes may be seen from a point four km south of Sunwapta Pass. From here the peak is "horn-like" and features a glacier lying in the cirque below.

To the right of Mount Athabasca and closer to the icefield is **Mount Andromeda** (3450 m). This mountain was named for the nearest galaxy to our Milky Way at the suggestion of Major Rex Gibson, a former president of the Alpine Club of Canada.

Below the northern cliffs of Andromeda, the **Athabasca Glacier** descends seven km from the rim of the Columbia Icefield to the valley below. En route it flows over three cliffs, resulting in steep, broken icefalls.

From the Icefields Centre at Sunwapta Pass
Highway 93, 105 km south of Jasper; 53.3 km north of Saskatchewan River Crossing.

Mount Wilcox and Wilcox Pass to its right.

Athabasca Glacier. Photo Gillean Daffern.

The day after climbing Mount Athabasca, Norman Collie and party ascended the right side of the Athabasca Glacier and bivouacked for the night. Setting off at 1:30 the next morning, they reached the Columbia Icefield and headed toward the chisel shaped, glacier-draped mountain they had seen towering above the opposite side of the icefield (Mount Columbia). At noon, when they seemed no closer to their goal, they turned back, more aware now of the size of the icefield they had discovered.

Collie and Stutfield later wrote, "To the eastward of where we stood, and almost on our way home, rose a great white dome, and we determined to ascend it. After a hot and very tiring climb through snow that broke under our feet at every step, we finally reached the summit at 3:15. We have named this peak The Dome."[76]

The smooth summit of what is now called **Snow Dome** (3456 m) is the hydrographic apex of North America. This means that water from this point flows to three oceans; via the Saskatchewan and Nelson rivers to the Atlantic, via the Columbia to the Pacific, and via the Athabasca and eventually the Mackenzie River to the Arctic.

Below Snow Dome, between the Dome and Athabasca glaciers lies an isolated and unique forest. It is a remnant of a much larger forest that existed prior to the Little Ice Age. One of the surviving trees, an Engelmann spruce, has been determined to be 720 years old, proving that this little forest continued to grow during the much harsher conditions of the Little Ice Age.

Although the three km-wide summit of **Mount Kitchener** (3505 m) may be seen from the highway a few kilometres to the north, from the Icefields Centre one is only able to see the northeastern tip of what is the sixth highest mountain in Alberta. Horatio Herbert Kitchener, a British field marshall, was secretary of state for war from 1914 until 1916 and was responsible for organizing the British Army during the early years of the First World War.

Mount Kitchener is just one of the peaks at the northern end of the Sir Winston Churchill Range. Lying between the Sunwapta and Athabasca rivers and covering 500 sq. km of some of the most rugged and picturesque mountain country in the Rockies, the range was named in 1965 to honour the great man who had led Britain and the Commonwealth to victory during the Second World War. As a young man Sir Winston had climbed in the Alps, in 1894 climbing the Wetterhorn with a party that included Christian Kaufmann, a guide who is himself honoured by a peak near Saskatchewan River Crossing.

To the right of Mount Kitchener a long, gentle slope descends into the Tangle Creek canyon that blocked Walter Wilcox's party in 1896.

A question that is often asked by visitors at the Icefields Centre is: If the glaciers flowed down the mountain valleys and onto the prairies during the ice age and then retreated, why are there lateral moraines at the sides of Athabasca? The explanation lies with the "Little Ice Age" that began in the thirteenth century and lasted until the mid-nineteenth century. During this time, increased sunspots cooled the earth's climate and the glaciers advanced into the valleys, piling up moraines at the sides of the valley. The cooling effect was world wide. The Baltic Sea froze and ice forced the Vikings to abandon Greenland. Villages and farms were abandoned throughout northern Europe as growing seasons decreased by three to five weeks.

Though Walter Wilcox's party reached Sunwapta Pass when the Little Ice Age was ending, the Athabasca Glacier in 1896 extended to where the Icefields Parkway is today. The glaciers have retreated dramatically since that time, leaving behind the lateral moraines.

Mount Athabasca and the Columbia Icefield

Mount Athabasca and Mount Andromeda from the Upper Sunwapta Canyon viewpoint. (Five km northwest of the Icefields Centre.)

"Immediately opposite our camp, to the south-west, rose a noble snow-crowned peak, about 12,000 feet in height, with splendid rock precipices and hanging glaciers; and on its right the tongue of a fine glacier descended in serpentine sinuosities to the bottom of the valley. We named them Athabasca Peak and Glacier respectively. The spirits of us three climbers rose high, and our blood was stirred within us at the thought of being once more on the ice and snow…. It was decided, therefore, that we should attack the peak next day."[77]

When they completed the first ascent of Mount Athabasca on August 18, 1898, J. Norman Collie and Hermann Woolley became the first people to grasp the extent and significance of the Columbia Icefield. Collie's description of the view from the summit is classic Canadian Rockies literature and it is a testament to his intelligence that he understood the geographical significance of what he saw. "The view that lay before us in the evening light was one that does not often fall to the lot of modern mountaineers. A new world was spread at our feet; to the westward stretched a vast ice-field probably never before seen by human eye, and surrounded by entirely unknown, un-named, and unclimbed peaks. From its vast expanse of snows, the Saskatchewan Glacier takes its rise, and it also supplies the headwaters of the Athabasca; while far away to the west, bending over in those unknown valleys glowing with evening light, the level snows stretched, to finally melt and flow down more than one channel into the Columbia River, and thence to the Pacific Ocean."[78]

What Collie and Woolley had the pleasure of discovering was the largest icefield in the Canadian Rockies, encircled by a most spectacular collection of nine high peaks—Stutfield Peak, North Twin, South Twin, Mount King Edward, Mount Columbia, Mount Bryce, Mount Athabasca, Snow Dome, Mount Andromeda and Mount Kitchener. Seven of them were named by the party.

Only a small portion of the icefield is visible from the Icefields Parkway. The Athabasca Glacier is the most accessible and most visible of the glaciers that flow from the icefield, but there are numerous others.

Over 300 sq. km in area, the depth of the icefield varies from 100 to 365 m. The average annual snowfall on the upper reaches is seven m.

Norman Collie and Hugh Stutfield. Lantern slide by H. Woolley. Gillean Daffern collection.

The Columbia Icefield from the high point south of the upper Saskatchewan Glacier: (l-r) Castleguard Mountain, Mount Columbia, The Twins, Snow Dome, Mount Andromeda and Mount Athabasca. Fifteen km of icefield lie between this viewpoint and Mount Columbia.

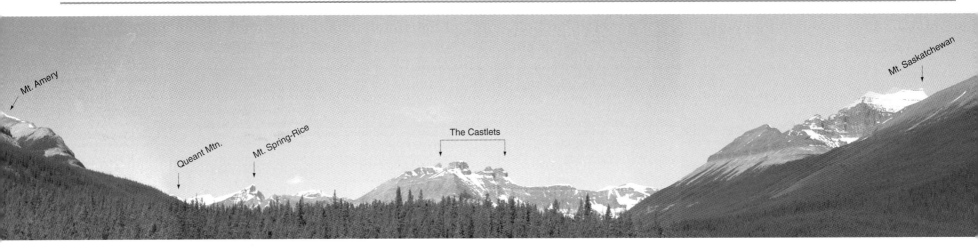

11 Spring-Rice, the Castlets and Mount Saskatchewan

From Alexandra River Flats

Highway 93, 18.3 km north of Saskatchewan River Crossing; 27.1 km south of the Banff-Jasper national parks boundary.

Mount Amery from the northern end of Alexandra River Flats.

"Filling the great angle between Alexandra River and the North Fork, a thing of towers and battlements, rises Mount Saskatchewan. Formidable in appearance, and long sought by climbers, it had never failed to attract the attention of those who came into the region. A symmetrical monolith on the jagged northeast ridge is well known as the 'Lighthouse' and serves as a landmark in the valley of the North Saskatchewan."[79] In The Glittering Mountains of Canada, *J. Monroe Thorington summed up the appearance of Mount Saskatchewan from the valley.*

This panorama can be seen from a pull off on a small hill immediately south of the gravel flats where the Alexandra River joins the Saskatchewan. To see the complete view, cross the highway and climb up above the ditch on the east side. If it is July, you may enjoy fresh strawberries.

Mount Amery (3329 m) looms directly across the river from this location, its northern slopes forming the left side of this panorama. While it is most impressive, the best viewpoint for the mountain is 1.7 km to the north where its smoothly contoured, glacier-covered summit may also be seen.

Mount Spring-Rice (3275 m) and the glacier-clad slopes of **Queant Mountain** (3120 m) lie at the head of the Alexandra River.

Arthur Wheeler named Mount Spring-Rice in 1920 after Sir Cecil Spring-Rice, a British diplomat. From this direction it is an outstanding peak with its glacier-covered southern slopes and perpendicular north face. It was first climbed in 1923 by a professor of philosophy and psychology at McGill University in Montreal, J. W. A. Hickson, led by guide Edward Feuz Jr. The two often climbed together, Feuz estimating they had climbed between 200 and 300 mountains, 25 of them first ascents. Feuz had great respect for his favourite client, saying, "If you ever saw him walk down the street, you'd never think he was a mountaineer. He could hardly walk. Years ago a horse he was riding slipped and rolled over his leg and it never healed well. Physically, he was not strong either. But he had an iron will, and he was the most stubborn man I ever met; after all that's what gets you up mountains."[80]

The First Ascent of Mount Amery

Leopold Amery served in the British parliament for 34 years. In the latter years of his career he played a role in bringing down the Chamberlain government in 1940, thus opening the way for Winston Churchill to become the wartime prime minister.

Amery had visited the Canadian Rockies in 1909 but, "it was not until a disagreement with the electorate in the spring of 1929 released me from the cares of office that I felt that I was justly entitled to a real holiday."[81] He had a special motive for this visit, however, as Mount Amery had been named in his honour. As a parliamentarian, Amery had promoted trade reforms with Canada and had worked toward advancing the constitutional arrangements with former British colonies. The Canadian government of the day must have had great respect for him. "To me the challenge (of making the first ascent at the age of 56) was obvious as well as proving myself, as a mountaineer and not merely as politician, justified of the appellation."[82] Amery was joined by Brian Meredith, a skier and Canadian Pacific Railway public relations officer, and by guide Edward Feuz Jr.

It was difficult to locate a route up the steep cliffs, which were quite "rotten" and broke away easily. Unfortunately, the weather did not cooperate either and deteriorated to the point that Feuz suggested turning back. Amery insisted that they press on, writing later that when they reached the summit, "Here we felt the full force of the blizzard and were more than once hard put to it to keep our feet…. I had made good my claim to Mount Amery in the mountaineering sense. The view I had to forgo."[83] Amery was most pleased with his climb and Edward Feuz must have been too. The guides took great pride in getting someone famous to the top of "their" mountain.

The following evening Amery commented, "Well, you know Edward, when we got onto my mountain, it bothered me a little…this bad weather we had and…I was worried we weren't quite on the top."[84] Feuz replied, "We'll fix that…. Let's climb Mount Saskatchewan. It's right opposite your peak, just across the valley…. I'll show you the stoneman."[85]

Upon reaching the summit of Mount Saskatchewan the following day Feuz said, "Now sit down here. Here is the glass. Look right across."[86] Amery took the glass and smiled saying, "You're right Edward, it's right on the very top."[87]

Edward Feuz Jr. (l) and Leopold Amery (r) on the summit of Mount Amery. Photo Brian Meredith. Courtesy Whyte Museum, NA-66-2117.

Edward Feuz Jr.

Edward Feuz Jr. was the son of Edouard Feuz, one of the first guides brought to Canada from Switzerland by the CPR during the 1890s. William Van Horne, the president of the railway, was attempting to promote a program that would attract tourists to the Rockies and the CPR's hotels. One of his ideas was to supply guides for mountaineering parties.

When Edward Jr. arrived in Canada in 1903, he apprenticed under his father, then began work at Glacier House near Rogers Pass for the CPR, who continued to employ him until his retirement in 1949. When based at Lake Louise, he was instrumental in the building of the Swiss style alpine hut on Abbots Pass (between Mount Lefroy and Mount Victoria) at an elevation approaching 3000 m.

He guided privately until 1953, completing a 50-year career as a mountain guide without a fatal accident.

The *Climber's Guide to the Rocky Mountains of Canada* is a listing of all the first ascents and important routes in the Rockies. The name of Edward Feuz Jr. seems to be on every page. He climbed virtually all the significant peaks in the Rockies and many in the Selkirks as well.

Edward Feuz climbed Mount Victoria, the backdrop to Lake Louise, on numerous occasions, the last time being when he was 85 years old—11 years before his death in 1981.

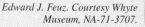

Edward J. Feuz. Courtesy Whyte Museum, NA-71-3707.

Mount Saskatchewan with Lighthouse Tower on the ridge to the right. Photo Don Beers.

Ladd, Thorington made the first ascent of this challenging peak and was, "satisfied beyond expression that we had been the first to ascend a mountain whose impressive and imposing architecture had for years excited our admiration."[89] Because of his close association with Conrad Kain, Thorington completed and edited Kain's autobiography after the guide's early death. *Where the Clouds Can Go i*s a classic of mountain literature. Thorington, together with Howard Palmer, also compiled the first *Climber's Guide to the Canadian Rockies* in 1921.

The spectacular pinnacle known as Lighthouse Tower, or as it is sometimes called, "Cleopatra's Needle," rises over 75 m from a ridge that extends eastwards from the highest part of Mount Saskatchewan. It cannot be seen from this viewpoint. One must drive 4.9 km south of the Alexandra River Flats viewpoint to a pull-off. Another view of the Tower is through a gap in the ridges 5.2 km north of the Alexandra Flats viewpoint. Although the spire is much closer, it is not nearly as needle-like as it appears from farther south. Lighthouse Tower was first climbed in 1964.

Lighthouse Tower. Photo Glen Boles.

Queant Mountain was named after a village in France that was captured by Canadian troops at the end of the First World War. It is surrounded by the North, South and East Rice glaciers whose names are derived from Mount Spring-Rice, with the word "Spring" omitted.

The Castlets (2865 m) are an attractive and suitably named group of towers that lie beyond Terrace Creek, which flows into the Alexandra from the northwest. They were thought to resemble small castles when they were named in 1920.

The low, smoothly contoured peak to the left of the lower slopes of Mount Saskatchewan is an outlier of **Terrace Mountain** (2917 m), the top of which cannot be seen from this viewpoint.

Mount Saskatchewan (3342 m) was named from its position near the headwaters of the Saskatchewan River. The upper cliffs of its southern face, which one can see from Alexandra River Flats, are almost always covered with snow. Its unseen northern slopes feature a large glacier.

J. Monroe Thorington was a prominent mountaineer in the 1920s and 1930s who completed 52 first ascents in the Rockies and Selkirks. He definitely had his eye on this peak when he rode up the valley in 1923. "We knew the mountain well by this time. From the east, on the slopes of Mount Coleman, we had gazed upon its unclimbed heights, wondering at its sheer forbidding face of snow-powdered cliff."[88] With guide Conrad Kain and W. S.

Peak Mt. Chephren White Pyramid Mt. Epaulette Kaufmann Peaks Mt. Sarbach Howse Pass Mt. David Mt. Outram Mt. Forbes Messines Mtn. Mons Peak Survey Peak

12 Mount Forbes and the Peaks of the Lower Mistaya

"...we had a grand view of the mountains, more elevated and craggy than any we had before seen. The upper parts of some of them are curiously formed, some closely resemble citadels, round towers, and pinnacles rising to a great height, with perpendicular summits, so steep that no human being could ascend them."[90] One of the first to be impressed with this panorama was Alexander Henry who wrote this description in his journal on February 8, 1811.

Almost 90 years later, when Norman Collie and Hugh Stutfield came to Canada specifically to climb these very peaks that Alexander Henry had said could not be ascended, they wrote of the view, "In every direction is a landscape to delight an artist's eye. Great mountain masses, bare and rugged to the north, their flanks more gently sloping and richly wooded towards the west and south, and remarkably diversified in form, tower around the spectator on all sides, but at a distance sufficient to enable him to gauge their true dimensions and grandeur."[91] They went on to suggest that, "the place seems an ideal one for a tourist centre; and we may fairly anticipate that at the mouth of Bear Creek (Mistaya River) will be the Chamonix or Grindelwald of the Canadian Alps."[92]

Saskatchewan River Crossing has always been an important junction for those travelling through the Alberta Rockies. This is the point where the North Saskatchewan River, after flowing south from its source at the Saskatchewan Glacier, turns east to flow through the front ranges and foothills and onto the plains. As well, this is the confluence of the North Saskatchewan with the Mistaya and Howse rivers.

Since the early nineteenth century this has been a place to pause, meet friends and camp. As well, it was often necessary to spend some time here waiting for the river levels to subside following heavy rains or very warm weather. With these major valleys all meeting at Saskatchewan River Crossing, it is not surprising that visitors, who may have stopped for other reasons, are able to enjoy one of the most spectacular panoramas of peaks in the Rockies. The exact location of this viewpoint is 100 m east of the actual highway junction, on the south side of Highway 11.

The towering cliffs of Mount Murchison frame the view on the left. The eastern summit of **Aries Peak** (2996 m) is the first mountain seen, lying beyond Cirque Lake. To its right are two of the dominant peaks of the Mistaya Valley, **Mount Chephren** (3266 m) and **White Pyramid** (3275 m) with its lovely glacier rising to the summit along three ridges. Until Mount Chephren was renamed in 1918, travellers would have referred to it as Pyramid.

Mount Epaulette (3095 m) was not officially named until 1961. The glacier that seems to hang on a narrow shelf above steep cliffs dropping into the valley was thought to resemble the shoulder ornament of some military uniforms worn by fairly high-ranking individuals.

The **Kaufmann Peaks** (3109 m) are a striking pair of very similar mountains that share a lovely glacier below them. Their summits are almost identical in outline, within 15 m of being the same height, and both appear to be split near the top, creating twin summits. On the right-hand summit, this effect is caused by a patch of snow near the top. Quite appropriately they are named for two brothers, Christian and Hans Kaufmann, who were members

From Saskatchewan River Crossing
Highway 93 at the junction with Highway 11.

Peter Sarbach, George Baker and Norman Collie, 1897. Courtesy Whyte Museum, V701-LC9.

of a well-established Swiss guiding family and worked as guides for the CPR. Both were highly respected and in constant demand because of their mountaineering skills and to some extent because they spoke excellent English.

Dominating the panorama is **Mount Sarbach** (3155 m). Norman Collie had great respect for the early guides and named the peak in honour of Peter Sarbach, the first of the Swiss guides. Collie's first ascents of Mount Lefroy and Mount Victoria in 1897 were led by Sarbach who, later that summer, guided Collie's party to the summit of this mountain. The view of high, unclimbed peaks to the north inspired Collie to return the following year and continue his explorations.

Beyond the long northern slope of Mount Sarbach, **Mount David** (2780 m) is seen in the distance. The Howse River flows northward between Mount Sarbach and Mount David from its headwaters at Howse Pass and the Freshfield Icefield.

As one of the world's great geographers, David Thompson was the first to map the main travel routes in western Canada and the northwestern United States. During his explorations in the late eighteenth and early nineteenth centuries, it is estimated he travelled some 8000 km by canoe, horse and on foot.

In the spring of 1807, as an employee of the North West Company, he paddled up the North Saskatchewan from Rocky Mountain House, seeking a passage to the Columbia River and the Pacific. After passing what has become Saskatchewan River Crossing, and travelling six or seven km up the Howse River, it became impossible for the canoes to proceed any farther. According to Thompson's journal, "Here among the stupendous and solitary Wilds covered with eternal Snow, and Mountain connected to Mountain by immense Glaciers… I staid fourteen days more, impatiently waiting the melting of Snows on the Height of Land…."[93] During these 14 days the party made the necessary preparations to proceed over Howse Pass with horses and on June 22 he wrote that he had reached a "rill whose current descends to the Pacific Ocean—may God in his mercy give me to see where its waters flow into the ocean, and return in safety."[94]

In 1920, the mountain above David Thompson's 1807 campsite on the Howse River was, most appropriately, officially named Mount David. It is unusual that a mountain should be given the first name of an individual rather than the last. Arthur Wheeler named the peak and was aware that a peak adjacent to the Wapta Icefield to the south had already been given David's surname in 1898 in honour of Charles Thompson.

Mount Chephren and White Pyramid. Photo Don Beers.

Named after James Outram who made the first ascents of some 28 peaks in the Rockies, **Mount Outram** (3240 m) features near vertical cliffs on its northeastern face, below which lies a large, square patch of snow that persists into the fall. To the left of Mount Outram lies the valley of the Howse River and to its right, the valley that contains the largest lake in Banff National Park, Glacier Lake.

The mountain looming over the north shoulder of Mount Outram is one of the outstanding in the Rockies and is, in some ways, quite similar to Mount Assiniboine. At 3612 m, **Mount Forbes** is only six m lower, and like Assiniboine, towers some 350 m higher than neighbouring peaks. Its pyramidal summit is often hidden in the clouds while lesser, but still very respectable, nearby mountains are visible. It is not surprising that a peak as prominent as Forbes was named by James Hector of the Palliser Expedition. Edward Forbes was Hector's professor of natural history at the University of Edinburgh.

James Outram and Norman Collie's parties combined forces in 1902 to attempt Mount Forbes. Collie had a high regard for the mountain. Admiring it from a nearby peak he wrote, "…by far the most commanding feature on view was the stately pyramid of Forbes; and we scanned for the first time, and with critical eyes, the western side of the arête by which we hoped to climb it."[95]

There had been some competition and even animosity between the two when Outram made the first ascent of Mount Columbia following Collie's preparatory exploration of the area. The fine Victorian manners of both gentlemen were demonstrated on this challenging first ascent. At one point Collie, rather than increase the risk to his companions of being the fourth on the rope, abandoned the ascent. After Outram successfully climbed the second cliff, he sent the two guides, Christian and Hans Kaufmann, back down to accompany Collie up the difficult section, feeling that Collie, "more than all the rest, deserved the gratification and honour of being the first to conquer Mount Forbes."[96]

To the right of Mount Forbes, pinnacles at the summit of **Messines Mountain** (3100 m) may just be seen beyond a glacier-covered ridge. This peak lies on the Continental Divide at the southern end of the Mons Icefield, five km beyond Mount Forbes. The capture of Messines Ridge by the British Army was a much publicized "highlight" during the First World War. In preparation for the attack a massive tunnel project placed large concentrations of high explosive immediately under the enemy trenches. Nineteen enormous explosions reduced the enemy's front lines to a series of craters and the positions were quickly taken. However, a very heavy bombardment of the recently taken ridge resulted in

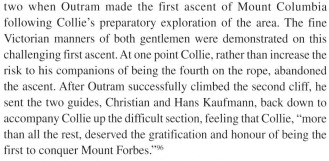

Christian Kaufmann far left, Hans Kaufmann far right. Courtesy Whyte Museum, NA-66-186.

The Kaufmann Peaks. Photo Don Beers.

James Outram

James Outram. Courtesy Whyte Museum, V14 ACOOP-80.

James Outram was probably the most ambitious of the early climbers to visit the Canadian Rockies. He was a British clergyman with experience of climbing in the European Alps. Outram's focus on first ascents was made clear when he wrote that the mountaineer's soul, "will crave—and rightly so—the chief joy of the climber's ambition, a 'first ascent.'"[97] This unabashed competitive urge brought him into conflict with some of the other early mountaineers. J. Norman Collie referred to him as an "interloper"[98] and wrote that the climbers who had done the early exploration of an area should, "get some of the scalps."[99]

Outram's 28 first ascents were concentrated into the years 1901 and 1902. One of the most notable was Mount Assiniboine, climbed in September of 1901.

Many of the high mountains he climbed were in the headwaters of the North Saskatchewan River where Outram was able to take advantage of Norman Collie's preliminary explorations of 1898. During the summer of 1902, he and guide Christian Kaufmann completed the first ascents of 10 peaks exceeding 10,000 feet during the 54-day outing.

An incident during this trip resulted in outfitter Jimmy Simpson recalling later that "Outram wanted all the glory himself,"[100] and that he treated Kaufmann as "just help."[101] Simpson had accompanied Outram and Kaufmann on a long, late day hike to reconnoitre Mount Columbia, which with an elevation of 3747 m is the highest peak in Alberta. When a promising route was discovered, Jimmy Simpson became quite excited about the climb that was planned for the next day and asked if he could accompany Outram to the summit, but his request was refused.

Outram and Kaufmann left camp at 1:00 a.m. the following morning and 11 hours later, "planted the Union Jack upon the broad white platform which crowns the summit of the highest point so far occupied in Canada."[102]

Outram spent his remaining years in Canada, having found "in the lonely woods or on the solitary mountain tops of Canada, the long-sought sanctuary of the storm-tossed soul. There, burdens that seemed too heavy to be borne are rolled away."[103]

Mount Outram and Mount Forbes. Photo Don Beers.

16,000 British casualties. Later analysis suggested the Germans knew the attack was coming and had withdrawn their frontline troops and guns.

Mons Peak (3083 m) and the Mons Icefield lie to the south of the head of the valley containing Glacier Lake and above it the Glacier River. The Royal Highlanders of Canada and the Royal Canadian Regiment captured the city of Mons, Belgium, the evening prior to the armistice that ended the First World War.

The largest lake in Banff National Park, Glacier Lake was first visited in 1807 by David Thompson from his camp on the Howse River. Thompson marvelled at the fact that all the mountains at the end of the lake were covered with ice. The lake was visited 51 years later by James Hector who travelled beyond the end of the lake and climbed high onto the glaciers where "we had a splendid view over the 'Mer de Glace' to the south and west, the mountain valleys being quite obliterated, and the peaks and ridges standing out like islands through the icy mantle."[104]

This spectacular panorama is bordered to the north by the appropriately named **Survey Peak** (2334 m). In 1898 Norman Collie and Hugh Stutfield climbed the mountain and used the summit as a site from which to base a plane table survey of the area. The slopes that we can be seen from Saskatchewan River Crossing show signs of a fairly recent forest fire. The darker shade of green is older forest while the lighter green is younger, post-fire growth.

Howse Pass

Lying at the head of the Howse River, just five km beyond Mount David, Howse Pass was first crossed by David Thompson in 1807. His employers, the Hudson's Bay Company, were anxious to find a practical route to the Pacific and China, having determined that Alexander Mackenzie's 1793 route was impractical for trade.

The newly discovered pass was named for Joseph Howse, a Hudson's Bay Company trader who crossed it a few years later. Howse was in charge of Carlton House near present-day Prince Albert, Saskatchewan, from 1799 to 1809.

Thompson was on his way to the pass again in 1810 and this time it was his intention to follow the waters on the western slope to the mouth of the Columbia River. But when he reached Rocky Mountain House he found that Chief Big Bear of the Peigans was camped upstream. Having been defeated in battle by a group of Indians who had been using arms provided them by the white traders, the chief was angry. Thompson felt his life was in danger so retreated to seek another route through the Rockies. The discovery of Athabasca Pass resulted from these efforts and was heavily used by the fur traders for the next 50 years despite the fact that Howse Pass would have been a much easier route to the Columbia River. Howse Pass remained unused for another 50 years.

James Hector reached the Saskatchewan River Crossing area in the fall of 1858 and briefly attempted to locate Howse Pass. Travelling up the Howse River valley, he was slowed by dense forests and ended up at Glacier Lake, which he named for the huge snowfield at the head of the valley. The season was coming to a close, but Hector spent one more day travelling up the Howse River, reaching the point below Mount David where Thompson had camped while waiting for the snow to melt in 1807.

After reaching Athabasca Pass during the following winter, Hector was back searching for Howse Pass again the following fall. Soon after being abandoned by their guide Nimrod, Hector and his party arrived at what is now Saskatchewan River Crossing and headed up the Howse River. After two false starts up the Freshfield and Forbes Brook valleys, they proceeded along the main valley, which seemed to stretch on and on, and was densely forested. After travelling another five km he noticed a small creek that flowed in the same direction he was travelling in and was surprised to find he was now across the Divide, having not reached any particularly noticeable height of land. Hector descended the Blaeberry River, which he named because of the blueberries he enjoyed there, and reached the Columbia Valley.

In 1871, Walter Moberly, who was in charge of finding the best route through the Rockies for the Canadian Pacific Railway, surveyed the route over the pass from the Columbia River valley. Again in 1881, the pass was visited by surveyors of the CPR but only weeks later the decision was made that the railway would be built through Kicking Horse Pass.

Howse Pass's history is one of widely spaced, intermittent visits, with no regular traffic through to the Columbia. It is interesting to speculate what the Howse River valley and the pass beyond Sas-katchewan River Crossing would look like today had the CPR made a different choice. A highway heading west from here would certainly have been built parallel to the railway and it is likely that a major hotel complex would have been built by the railway, not at Lake Louise, but at Hector's Glacier Lake.

Howse Pass. Photo Gillean Daffern.

Mt. Patterson · Barbette Glacier · Breaker Mtn. · Aries Peak · Midway Peak · Aiguille Peak · Mt. Synge · Howse Pe

13 Tightly Packed Peaks along the Continental Divide

From Silverhorn Creek bridge

Highway 93, 11 km north of Bow Pass; 25.3 km south of Saskatchewan River Crossing.

Aiguille Peak from the northern end of Lower Waterfowl Lake.

The forest downstream from the bridge over Silverhorn Creek was cleared to facilitate the construction of the Icefields Parkway and a campground. This artificial clearing allows travellers to enjoy an excellent view to the west, which features five peaks along a four km long-section of the Continental Divide.

Mount Patterson (3197 m) is a massive peak that towers 1500 m above the Icefields Parkway. The mountain rises in three tiers, with glaciers hanging picturesquely between each. John Duncan Patterson was a founding member of the Alpine Club of Canada and became its third president in 1914.

Between the main portion of the peak and a high outlier to its right, a smoothly contoured line of moraine—left following the last advance of the Snowbird Glacier—adorns a very large cirque on the northeast side of the mountain. One of the most attractive glaciers in the Rockies, the Snowbird drapes over the cliff bands with wings spread in a manner similar to those of the Angel Glacier on Mount Edith Cavell. This is one glacier whose appearance has probably changed very little over the past century. The extent of the wings are limited by the width of the ledges upon which they rest, so any additional build up of ice simply falls over the cliffs to the snowbird's tail below.

Only the left wing of the Snowbird Glacier can be seen from Silverhorn Creek bridge viewpoint. The best view lies 3.1 km south of the bridge. On calm days in the summer, the roar of the waterfalls and meltwater streams in the cirque is constant.

To the west of Mount Patterson, Barbette Glacier occupies a large circular-shaped basin below a band of cliffs. A higher glacier rests on the cliff bands and the almost completely ice covered summit of **Barbette Mountain** (3072 m) looms above. The peak is just hidden behind the slopes of Mount Patterson, but may be seen by walking just 100 m or so north of the bridge.

A barbette is a platform on a ship or fort from which guns may be fired over a parapet. The name was probably chosen with the view from this point in mind as the cliffs below the peak form a broad platform for the summit.

The meltwater from the Barbette Glacier flows into Mistaya Lake, which fills the valley for some five km in front of the remaining peaks of the panorama.

Breaker Mountain (3058 m) is a broad, smoothly-contoured peak that features a glacier spilling over its lower cliffs like a breaking wave approaching a beach.

A flat-topped, dark-coloured mountain, **Aries Peak** (2996 m) can just be seen beyond the highest point of a nearer ridge featuring numerous avalanche slopes. The name was chosen by Arthur Wheeler of the Boundary Survey after the Latin word for sheep. The mountain actually has two summits, one lying on the Continental Divide and the other lying entirely in Alberta, the two separated by a glacier-filled col.

Aries Peak is the first of the five mountains above the viewpoint. To the right of the near ridge, the symmetric **Midway Peak** (2871 m) may be seen. With so many mountains so close together, Arthur Wheeler and his surveyors must have been running out of ideas because the name of this mountain was chosen only because it was midway between Stairway Peak, which is hidden behind the ridge, and **Mount Synge** (2972 m).

Captain Millington Henry Synge was a soldier and author. After visiting the Rockies, he drew a map that showed the route through the mountains to be followed by the Canadian Pacific Railway some years later.

Small but distinctive mountains have a particular appeal and **Aiguille Peak** (2999 m) is one of those that can become a favourite as one travels this section of the Icefields Parkway. In order to accommodate the peak, the Divide makes a very abrupt jog to the southwest of Mount Synge, then back again. So even though Aiguille appears to the left of Mount Synge, it is actually a few hundred metres farther along the border. The upper portion of the slopes can be seen rising sharply between Midway Peak and Mount Synge.

If you're travelling north it is interesting to watch Aiguille disappear behind Mount Synge and then, as you reach the northern end of Lower Waterfowl Lake, reappear dramatically but now between Mount Synge and Howse Peak. The mountain is most impressive from this viewpoint, with its vertical cliffs and needle-like spires.

"Aiguille" is the French word for needle, and is the term used in a general sense for any sharp, alpine peak. Numerous peaks in the Alps use the word in their names.

Mr. and Mrs. J. D. Mendenhall made the first ascents of Midway Peak, Mount Synge and Aiguille Peak in 1952.

With an elevation of 3290 m, **Howse Peak** is the highest in the panorama from Silverhorn Creek bridge and the highest in the Waputik Range that parallels the Icefields Parkway from the Saskatchewan River to the Bow River. Geographically, it is significant because at its summit the Continental Divide makes a 90 degree turn and trends northeast-southwest for 20 km, one of the largest shifts from the usual northwest-southeast direction. Howse Pass lies beyond the mountain and the huge basin occupied by the Freshfield Icefield lies even farther to the west.

A dome-shaped mountain, its base is composed of dark, almost black limestone that forms a steep cliff with little indication of layering. In contrast, the upper portion of the mountain is primarily reddish-tinged layers of dolomite that allow for attractive patterns of snow highlighting in early summer.

The mountain takes its name from the pass that was traversed by James Howse in 1810, three years after its discovery by David Thompson. Norman Collie and party completed the first ascent of Howse Peak in 1902.

Bottom left: Mount Patterson and Snowbird Glacier.
Bottom right: Howse Peak.
Photo Gillean Daffern.

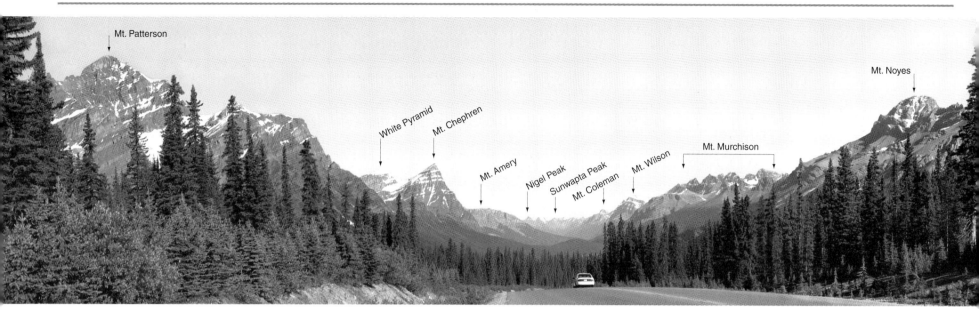

Mt. Patterson

White Pyramid · Mt. Chephren

Mt. Noyes

Mt. Amery · Nigel Peak · Sunwapta Peak · Mt. Wilson · Mt. Murchison

Mt. Coleman

14 Mistaya Valley Peaks and Beyond

From Bow Pass

Highway 93 at Bow Pass, 41.4 km north of the Trans-Canada Highway; 36.1 km south of Saskatchewan River Crossing.

*Mount Coleman from Sunset Pass.
Photo Gillean Daffern.*

The approach to Bow Pass from the south is by a long, gently-sloped alpine meadow with low-lying bushes and clumps of trees that remind the traveller of the elevation that has been reached. The view from the pass features some spectacular mountains in the Mistaya Valley and, if it's not too hazy, high, distant peaks beyond the Saskatchewan headwaters in the vicinity of the Columbia Icefield.

Upon reaching this important divide on the Icefields Parkway by car, it is still well worth the time to pull over and enjoy the distant peaks beyond the Saskatchewan as well as some splendid, nearer mountains that may be seen from this high viewpoint. The Mistaya River valley follows a very straight line, paralleling the general northwest-southeast trend of the ranges, and this enables one to see mountains beyond the next pass to the north, Sunwapta at the Columbia Icefield.

The closest peak, just six km away, is **Mount Patterson** (3197 m), which from this viewpoint lies beyond Peyto Lake.

White Pyramid (3275 m) is one of the few mountains that does not have the word "mount" before the name or "mountain" or "peak" after it. Because the mountain was covered in snow when Norman Collie first saw it, he named it in contrast to its darker neighbour, Pyramid. Pyramid or **Mount Chephren** (3266 m) as it is now called, is a spectacular peak when viewed from Waterfowl Lakes, its tower of dark, purplish rock rising some 1600 m above the valley floor.

Only the very top of the broad summit of **Mount Amery** (3329 m) may be seen 25 km beyond the shoulder of Mount Sarbach. Amery is an outstanding peak when viewed from the Saskatchewan River valley a few kilometres north of

Saskatchewan River Crossing near Viewpoint 11. Leopold Amery was a British parliamentarian, alpinist, author and skier.

Beyond Mount Amery and 75 km from the viewpoint lies **Nigel Peak** (3211 m). This mountain is actually north of the Athabasca Glacier that flows east from the Columbia Icefield. Nigel Vavasour was a packer who accompanied Norman Collie and Hugh Stutfield to the Columbia Icefield area in 1898. It was named by the mountaineers during a sheep hunt in which Vavasour was involved. Collie later wrote, "We gave them another hour and then followed them up an open valley, towards a lake that lay at the foot of a high snow-clad peak of which Nigel is now the eponymous hero."[105]

The most distant peak seen from Bow Pass is an amazing 88 km away, some 15 km inside Jasper National Park. In late July, generally only one of the peaks has snow cover and this is how **Sunwapta Peak** (3315 m) can be identified between Nigel Peak and Mount Coleman. A lovely and much closer view of this outstanding peak may be enjoyed from the Sunwapta River valley south of Jonas Creek. The mountain takes its name from the river that was given the Stoney term for "turbulent river."

The helmet-shaped **Mount Coleman** (3135 m) was named in 1902 after Arthur P. Coleman, a professor of geology from Toronto who was one of the first climbers and explorers in this area of the Rockies. After an initial visit in 1884 he returned several times, spending most of his time attempting to locate the legendary Mounts Brown and Hooker, which were reputed to be 5000 m high. He later wrote of his travels in *Canadian Rockies, Old and New Trails.*

Mount Wilson (3260 m), the mountain named in honour of outfitter Tom Wilson by Norman Collie in 1898, lies just to the north of the point where the North Saskatchewan River turns east toward the prairies. It covers a large area, its high cliffs stretching for 11 km above both the Icefields Parkway to the north and Highway 11 to the east. Billy Warren, one of the early outfitters to pass this way, once said, "I don't like Mount Wilson. I once travelled around its base for two days and it seemed as though I should never get away from it."[106] The northeastern slopes of Mount Wilson feature a large snowfield that forms the summit of the mountain from this angle. The entire glacier may be seen from the David Thompson Highway, 10 km to the east of the junction with the Icefields Parkway. North of Saskatchewan River Crossing, numerous slender waterfalls tumble down Mount Wilson's western cliffs during snow melt in the early summer.

The first ascent of Mount Wilson was the last climb in James Outram's very successful summer of 1902, during which he recorded eight first ascents of major peaks including Mount

Columbia. Of the view from Mount Wilson he wrote that, "The view was one of the most delightful of the year. Besides the new country now displayed to the north and east, the panorama furnished a complete resume of our entire trip, and no other mountain could have offered so perfect an ideal for a consummation of the summer's mountaineering…. The vast sea of mountains, in all their majesty of might, the attendant valleys, filled with treasures of most perfect beauty, glacier and forest depth, sparkling stream and flower-decked glade, have graven with imperishable strokes upon my memory a record that will be a never-ceasing joy throughout life."[107]

Mount Murchison (3333 m) lies across the North Saskatchewan River from Mount Wilson. It was named by James Hector in 1858 after Sir Roderick Murchison, who at the time was the director of the Geological Survey of Great Britain and had recommended that Hector be chosen as a member of the Palliser Expedition. In a letter written in 1859, Sir Murchison thanked Hector for honouring him with a high mountain in such a prominent location.

Mount Murchison is the highest peak in the panorama and one of the most massive with a base covering an area measuring five km by seven km. The main northwest peak and many of the seven "towers" of approximately the same elevation are visible from this viewpoint.

Mount Noyes (3084 m) is the peak on the right side of this panorama. It was named after Reverend Charles L. Noyes who travelled with Norman Collie's party and was the first to explore Peyto Glacier.

Mount Murchison. Photo Don Beers.

Tom Wilson

During the summer of 1882, a former member of the North West Mounted Police and his Stoney Indian companion known as "Gold Seeker" journeyed westward up the Bow Valley. Tom Wilson was employed by the Canadian Pacific Railway and was working for Major A. B. Rogers, chief engineer of its Mountain Division, who was conducting surveys in the valley. While camped, they heard the sound of distant avalanches, which were explained by Gold Seeker as coming from a mountain above the "Lake of Little Fishes." The following day the two climbed out of the valley and Tom Wilson became the first non-native to visit what we now know as Lake Louise. Tom named the lake Emerald Lake, a name that eventually became attached to another lake that Tom discovered.

Following his work with the railway, Tom Wilson became one of the most renown early outfitters in the Rockies. He led many pioneering explorations into remote areas such as Mount Assiniboine, the Yoho Valley and the Saskatchewan River headwaters. Many of his assistants, such as Bill Peyto and Jimmy Simpson, went on to become legendary guides in their own right.

Tom Wilson at his Kootenay Plains cabin.
Courtesy Whyte Museum, NA-66-764.

In 1904 he sold his outfitting business. Retaining ownership of many of his horses, he continued to live in Banff, but spent most of his time raising horses in the Kootenay Plains, a unique area of prairie-like grassland in the valley of the North Saskatchewan River downstream from Mount Wilson.

The following story demonstrates Wilson's remarkable stamina. One winter Tom was at his horse ranch and as Christmas Day approached he decided to join his family in Banff for dinner. Despite the fact that conditions were not favourable, he set off up the Siffleur River. Arthur Wheeler described the trip as involving, "a snowshoe tramp alone of seventy miles through lonely tree-clad valleys, through rock-bound gorges and over wind-swept passes, where all nature lay stark and stiff in the icy grip of winter."[108] At one point he fell through a snowbridge during a fierce windstorm and had great difficulty drying his wet socks and moccasins. "It was drifting and snowing so hard that the snow covered my sox and moccasins as fast as I could wring them dry, and, owing to the fierce wind, the flames leaped in every direction, making it impossible to get near the fire, so at half past nine I gave it up, put on my wet footgear and snowshoes and started down the valley. I could not see and felt the way with a stick…. It kept the circulation going."[109] When daylight came he was in heavy timber and was able to dry his footgear. The last three days of his journey were made without food. Tom wrote, "…the last day I could only make about fifty yards without resting, and my back tracks did not leave a very straight line. The chief trouble I had was to keep from going to sleep; it would have been so much easier to quit than to go on."[110]

Tom Wilson was active in the mountains until 1920 when he moved to Vancouver. However, the old lure proved too strong and he returned to spend the years from 1927 to 1933 providing "local colour" for the CPR by entertaining guests at the Banff Springs Hotel with stories of the old days in the Rockies.

Mount Wilson.

Bow Peak · Crowfoot Pass · Crowfoot Glacier · Crowfoot Mtn. · Mt. Olive · St. Nicholas Peak · Wapta Icefield · Portal Peak · Mt. Thompson · Lower slopes of Mt. Jimmy Simpson

15 Jimmy Simpson's View

"The scenery at the head of the Bow Valley, surrounding the upper Bow Lake, is grand, and will not disappoint anyone who should make the journey there."[111] These words were written by Hugh Stutfield and Norman Collie in 1903 and remain true almost a century later.

On a clear summer's day, the striking contrast of the dark blue sky above the pure white of the snow of the Crowfoot Glacier dominates the view as one begins the descent from the summit of Bow Pass. As the waters of Bow Lake come into view it is a good time to pull off to the side of the road and enjoy this outstanding view of the mountains at the headwaters of the Bow River.

Goat Mountain was the name that James Hector gave to what is now known as **Bow Peak** (2868 m). Its smoothly-contoured slopes descend into **Crowfoot Pass**, which features beautiful snow patches until well into the summer.

The view is dominated by the three summits of **Crowfoot Mountain** (3050 m), whose highest point rises above the **Crowfoot Glacier**. The mountain, glacier and high pass to the right of Bow Peak were not named to honour the great native leader who, trusting in the North West Mounted Police, signed Treaty #7. Rather, the name's origin derives from the lower part of the glacier that formerly had the shape of a crow's foot. A viewpoint beyond the southern end of Bow Lake provides an opportunity to see what remains of the crow's foot. Since the beginning of the twentieth century, this and all the glaciers in the Rockies have receded considerably.

To the right of Crowfoot Mountain one can see a small portion of the **Wapta Icefield**. Below the heavily crevassed **Bow Glacier** the fledgling Bow River may be seen tumbling over a steep cliff as Bow Glacier Falls.

Both **Mount Olive** (3130 m) and **St. Nicholas Peak** (2970 m) lie on the Continental Divide with a portion of the icefield to the east of them but with most of it lying to the west. Olive Dixon was the wife of Harold Baily Dixon, a British alpinist and chemist who named the mountain in 1899. Arthur Wheeler, while surveying the Alberta-British Columbia boundary through the icefield, thought that rock formations on St. Nicholas resembled Santa Claus when viewed from a certain angle.

To Charles Thompson, one of the earliest alpinists to visit the area, the mountain to the right of the Bow Glacier seemed to be one side of a gateway leading from the lake to the alpine area to the west and so chose the name **Portal Peak** (2911 m) for the feature. **Mount Thompson** (3084 m) to the north of Portal Peak was named after Thompson.

Framing this wonderful vista on the right side are the lower slopes of **Mount Jimmy Simpson** (2789 m). Named shortly after Jimmy's death, it forms the backdrop to Bow Lake when it is approached from the south, and during mid-summer features an attractive band of snow just below the summit ridge.

St. Nicholas Peak from the upper Bow Glacier. Photo Gillean Daffern.

From above Bow Lake
Highway 93, 4.4 km south of Bow Pass; 0.6 km north of Num-te-jah Lodge.

The Wapta Icefield

From this viewpoint one is able to see only a very small part of the Wapta Icefield, but it is an interesting glimpse into what is a very different type of mountain landscape. This is the southernmost icefield of several that lie along the Continental Divide. All are remnants of the last major glacial ice age that covered most of Canada from about one million years ago until just 20,000 years ago.

The upper part of an icefield, generally above 2500 m in the Canadian Rockies, is known as the accumulation area. In this area each winter's snowfall exceeds the amount that melts and is compacted and recrystallised into ice. In the lower part, the ablation area, each winter's snowfall melts in summer and exposes older layers of ice. Here the ice often takes the form of slowly downward moving glaciers. Above Bow Lake the distant snowfield is always white, whereas the blue ice of the Bow Glacier can be seen extending from the accumulation area.

Wapta is the Stoney Indian word for "running water." The name, originally given to the Kicking Horse River, was later applied to this icefield, which is its source.

The Wapta is connected to the Waputik Icefield, which lies to the south, the two combining to cover an area of between 500 and 600 sq. km. It is a vast area, desolate but beautiful, where nothing but rock, ice and snow can be seen.

The most popular access route to the icefield is to travel beyond Bow Lake and behind the northern slopes of Crowfoot Mountain. From here, skiers and mountaineers ascend to the high ridge above the lower cliffs upon which is located the Bow Hut, operated by the Alpine Club of Canada.

*Bow Glacier and the Wapta Icefield beyond.
Portal Peak at right. Photo Don Beers.*

Charles Thompson's Close Call on the Wapta Icefield

On August 10, 1897, Charles Thompson, Hugh Stutfield and Norman Collie camped on the shore of Bow Lake and undoubtedly enjoyed this magnificent view. The following day they climbed the glacier, which at that time descended farther down into the valley, and crossed the Wapta Icefield to reach the summit of Mount Gordon above the Yoho Valley. From this viewpoint they were surrounded by unnamed mountains and took the liberty of naming one of the nearby peaks Mount Thompson. A short time later, Charles Thompson very nearly became the Canadian Rockies' second climbing fatality. The story of his brush with death is one of the most exciting incidents in the early years of mountaineering in the Rockies.

Collie described the accident: "Not far from this second summit a huge crevasse partially covered with snow had to be crossed. All the party had passed over but Thompson who unfortunately broke through and at once disappeared headlong into the great crack that ran perpendicularly down into the depths of the glacier…. Although Thompson was too far down to be seen, yet he could be heard calling for help and saying that although he was not hurt, he would be extremely grateful to us if we could make haste and extricate him from the awkward position he was in, for he could not move and was almost upside down, jammed between the two opposing sides of the crevasse."[112]

Collie, being the lightest of the party as well as unmarried, was "lowered into the gaping hole. On one side the ice fell sheer, and the other it was undercut, but again bulged outwards about eighteen feet below the surface, making the crevasse at that point not much more than two feet wide. Then it widened again, and went down into dim twilight. It was not till I had descended sixty feet, almost the whole available length of an eighty foot rope, that at last I became tightly wedged between the two walls of the crevasse, and was absolutely incapable of moving my body. My feet were close to Thompson's but his head was further away, and about three feet lower than his heel. Face downwards, and covered with fallen snow, he could not see me. But, after he explained that it was entirely his own fault that he was there, I told him we would have him out in no time. At that moment I must say I hardly expected to be able to accomplish anything. For, jammed between two slippery walls

Approaching Mount Gordon on the Wapta Icefield. Photo Gillean Daffern.

of ice, and only able to move my arms, cudgel my brains as I would, I could not think what was to be done. I shouted for another rope. When it came down I managed to throw one end to Thompson's left hand, which waved about until he caught it. But when pulled it merely dragged out of his hand. Then with some difficulty I managed to tie a noose on the rope by putting both my hands above my head. With this I lassoed that poor pathetic arm which was the only part of Thompson that could be seen. Then came the tug-of-war. If he refused to move, I could do nothing more to help him; more-over I was afraid that at any moment he might faint. If that occurred I do not believe he could have been got out at all, for the force of the fall had jammed him further down than it was possible to follow. Slowly the rope tightened, as it was cautiously pulled by those above. I could hear my heart thumping in the ghastly stillness of the place, but at last Thompson began to shift, and after some short time he was pulled into an upright position by my side."[113] From this point Thompson and then Collie were pulled to the surface of the icefield.

Jimmy Simpson

Jimmy Simpson on his 90th birthday.
Photo Dr. John D. Birrell.

Jimmy Simpson first saw this view in 1898. Tom Wilson, one of the early outfitters in the Lake Louise area, had a contract with the CPR to construct a trail up the Bow Valley and Jimmy was put in charge of the work. As Jimmy rode around Bow Peak on that spring day, he passed Crowfoot Glacier, looked across Bow Lake to the Wapta Icefield with Bow Glacier tumbling out of it and thought it was, "the most beautiful thing I'd seen in Canada."[114] The party camped at the north end of the lake where Jimmy fell in love with the spot and vowed, "I'll build a shack here sometime."[115]

Jimmy had emigrated from England, arriving in Winnipeg in 1896. His uncle had arranged for him to buy a farm, but Jimmy was unimpressed and returned to Winnipeg. Having parted with all of his money in the taverns, he then pawned his gold watch and chain and bought a train ticket to Calgary. Hearing of work with the railway in Golden, he stowed away on a westbound passenger train, but was discovered by the conductor and summarily tossed off the train at Castle Mountain from where he walked to Laggan below Lake Louise. It was probably during this walk that Jimmy became rooted to the Canadian Rockies.

The next year Jimmy worked as a cook for Tom Wilson and began learning the guiding and outfitting business from Tom and from the legendary Bill Peyto and Tom Lusk. In 1902, while working for Peyto, he was given the responsibility of leading James Outram's very successful climbing expedition into the headwaters of the North Saskatchewan and the Columbia Icefield. It was on this trip that his client refused Jimmy's request to accompany the party on the first ascent of Mount Columbia, the highest peak in Alberta. Jimmy was not pleased with this rebuff and a few days later when asked to join in the first ascent of Mount Lyell, and help carry a heavy camera to the summit, it was Jimmy's turn to say no.

Before long, Jimmy left to go into the business on his own, combining a guiding business in the summer with trapping in the winter. Snowshoes were a requirement for trapping and he soon learned to travel on them with such speed that the Stoney Indians gave him the name Nashan-esen, which meant "wolverine-go-quickly."

In 1920 Jimmy made an application to the Parks branch to lease five acres of land, which included the spot at which he had camped on his first trip up the Bow Valley in 1898. A small log building was completed on the site in 1922, and the plan was to use it in conjunction with his outfitting business. Because of the stunted trees in the vicinity, Jimmy designed an octagonal-shaped building with sides each 10 feet long. He named the building Num-te-jah, the Indian word for pine marten. During the 1930s Jimmy's business operations shifted from Banff to Bow Lake. The building of the Banff-Jasper Highway during the Depression years brought automobile traffic to the area and Jimmy found it necessary to begin a major expansion in 1937. This is the red-roofed structure one can see today from the highway. The original building became Jimmy's personal residence and he spent his later years living in what became known as "the Ram's Pasture."

Jimmy continued actively guiding parties until the end of the Second World War when his son took over the business. He remained quite active at Num-te-jah, enjoying his well-earned status as "Grand Old Man of the Mountains" until his death in 1972 at the age of 95. Two years later the mountain to the northwest of the lodge was named Mount Jimmy Simpson in his honour.

From the Bow Lake viewpoint one can reflect on Jimmy Simpson's words, "There is something up in the mountains, something that is far ahead of human beings and will always be far ahead of human beings."[116]

Mount Jimmy Simpson.

16 Peaks in the Heart of the Canadian Rockies

In his book The Glittering Mountains of Canada, *J. Monroe Thorington wrote of this view that was welcomed by parties returning on horseback from explorations and adventures to the north of Lake Louise as follows: "Down the valley one sees the peacock-blue waters of Hector Lake... and finally, through a rift in the clouds, the groups above Lake Louise burst into view, Mount Temple and the Victoria Ridge rising above all the rest."*[117]

This is clearly one of the most magnificent roadside views in the Rockies. Although an excellent location for a properly constructed viewpoint, one can only pull onto the shoulder of the Icefields Parkway at the moment.

From this viewpoint the mountains around Lake Louise—which is often thought of as the heart of the Canadian Rockies—seem to form a fairly compact group. Ten peaks with elevations in excess of 3000 m rise from the south side of the Kicking Horse Pass route through the Continental Divide. Because the peaks are viewed from the north, one can see more glaciers and snow-covered features. This also means that for most of the day the peaks are in shadow, which gives them a somewhat forbidding appearance. Early morning or late evening in early summer is the best viewing time.

Because this viewpoint is about 200 m higher than the river valley below, this enables one to see some distance down the Bow Valley toward Banff. **Storm Mountain** (3100 m) is the beautiful peak that towers above Castle Junction just south of the point where Highway 93 passes over Vermilion Pass into Kootenay National Park. During the summer a large, triangular-shaped snowpatch near the top of the gentle western shoulder helps to identify it.

The mountain was named by George Dawson in 1884 after storm clouds were seen on its summit. The government department that regulates place names attempts to avoid having the same name for two different features, particularly when they are fairly close to each other. In the case of the name "Storm Mountain," there are two of them only 100 km apart and both were named by George Dawson in the same year and for the same reason. An additional coincidence is that the mountains are within five m of each other in elevation. The other Storm Mountain lies in the Misty Range at the headwaters of the Highwood River. As a "postcard" mountain it cannot compete with the Vermilion Pass Storm Mountain, which is somewhat isolated and looks very picturesque.

Storm Mountain and the unnamed high point beyond and to its right are peaks of the Ball Range. John Ball, as an undersecretary of state for the colonies, assisted in the organization and funding of the Palliser Expedition. He was also a proficient mountaineer, the first president of the Alpine Club, and the author of the first guidebook to the Swiss Alps. The range was named in his honour by James Hector.

From the Upper Bow Valley
Highway 93, 14.7 km north of the junction with Highway 1; 21.7 km south of Bow Lake.

Storm Mountain. Photo Glen Boles.

Panorama Ridge (2824 m) is an aptly named, low mountain that lies to the south of the valley containing Consolation Lakes. The panoramic view from its summit features a number of high mountains in the Moraine lake area.

One of the special features about this viewpoint is the peek one gets of the spectacular high mountains at the head of Consolation Lakes valley. **Mount Bident** (3084 m) and **Mount Quadra** (3173 m), together with the high icefield in front of them, are just visible behind and to the left of the highest mountain in this panorama.

Mount Temple (3543 m) dominates the Lake Louise area. This view from the north is ideal for admiring the beautiful glacier below its summit and the steep cliffs that rise from Paradise Valley. An unusual and distinctive feature of the mountain is the narrow line of snow that accumulates in a very steep debris channel that extends for a long distance down the left side of the peak. Sloping at an angle of about 85 degrees, it is perpendicular to other lines of snow on the mountain that are parallel to the sedimentary layer.

The smoothly-rounded summit of **Fairview Mountain** (2744 m) can be seen below and directly in line with Mount Temple.

Mount St. Piran (2649 m), like Fairview Mountain, does not form part of the skyline from this viewpoint.

Haddo Peak (3070 m) and **Mount Aberdeen** (3152 m) rise beyond St. Piran and above the valley that contains Lake Louise.

Mounts Niblock, Lefroy, Pope's Peak and Mount Victoria.

This is an excellent viewpoint for Aberdeen: one can clearly see the glacier hanging off the east ridge of the mountain. Lord John Campbell Gordon was the marquis of Aberdeen as well as the governor-general of Canada from 1893 until 1898. To commemorate his visit to Lake Louise during his first term of office, the mountain was named in his honour by J. J. McArthur in 1897. Prior to 1897 it was referred to as Hazel Peak, but there is no record of who Hazel was.

Mount Niblock (2976 m) rises directly from the valley containing the CPR and the Trans-Canada Highway. It is the nearest peak in this group so it appears somewhat higher than it really is. It dominates the view for much of the way through the Kicking Horse Pass from Lake Louise to Wapta Lake.

Entirely ice covered from this angle, **Mount Lefroy** (3423 m) looms majestically behind two lower, unnamed high points. The mountain is one of three peaks over 3400 m that dominate the Continental Divide in the Lake Louise area.

At 3492 m, **Mount Hungabee** is the highest of the three. Only the top of its narrow summit can be seen rising beyond the western slopes of Mount Lefroy. It lies at the heads of three valleys: Paradise Valley, whose river flows into the Bow River, Opabin Valley in the Lake O'Hara area of Yoho National Park and Prospector's Valley in Kootenay National Park. Samuel Allen recognized the peak's geographic significance in 1894 when he named it using the Stoney Indian word for "chieftain."

Pope's Peak (3163 m), its glacier-covered summit rising smoothly above steep, north-facing cliffs, lies near the head of a glacier-filled valley in British Columbia. It was formerly known as Boundary Peak because the Continental Divide descends from this mountain into Kicking Horse Pass. John Henry Pope was minister of railways and canals when the mountain was named in 1887.

Always snow covered, **Mount Victoria** (3464 m) rises spectacularly behind Pope's Peak. Most visitors to the Canadian Rockies know Victoria as the backdrop to Lake Louise in the view from the chateau where the full width of the mountain is visible. From this point, however, one is looking somewhat along its long summit ridge and, therefore, the mountain appears narrower. As one travels down toward the main valley below this viewpoint, Victoria disappears behind much closer peaks.

This wonderful panorama is framed on the right by the southern end of the **Waputik Range**.

James Hector and Kicking Horse Pass

James Hector was a doctor, geologist, naturalist and member of the Palliser Expedition. In August of 1858 the expedition reached the Rockies and at this point Palliser divided his party, telling Hector to explore whatever areas appeared to be geologically the most interesting. Hector was delighted to be in an area with cliffs and gorges where the rocks could be studied, and spent the remainder of the summer travelling up the Bow River, through Vermilion Pass (now traversed by Highway 93), down the Columbia River to the present-day site of Golden, and back eastward over Kicking Horse Pass. The party then turned north just before reaching what would become Mount Hector, and travelled past a lake that George Dawson would later name Hector Lake to the headwaters of the Bow River at Bow Pass. After descending the Mistaya River, they reached the Saskatchewan River, which took them out to the prairies and eventually to Fort Edmonton. The mountain portion of this amazing journey, at a time when there were few trails and when finding food was a significant problem, was completed in only 38 days.

Kicking Horse Pass got its name after a horse kicked Hector. As the party was struggling eastward toward the pass, one of the pack horses, in an attempt to escape the fallen timber, plunged into the river. Hector described what followed: "…the banks were so steep that we had great difficulty in getting him out. In attempting to recatch my own horse, which had strayed off while we were engaged with the one in the water, he kicked me in the chest, but I had luckily got close to him before he struck out, so that I did not get the full force of the blow."[118]

Peter Erasmus was Hector's guide during this part of his exploration and he later wrote, "We all leapt from our horses and rushed up to him, but all our attempts to help him recover his senses were of no avail…. Dr. Hector must have been unconscious for at least two hours when Sutherland yelled for us to come up; he was now conscious but in great pain. He asked for his kit and directed me to prepare some medicine that would ease the pain."[119] Hector's men thought it appropriate to name the river in honour of the "Kicking Horse."

This happened at a time when the party was having great difficulty finding food and was near starvation. They struggled toward the pass, eating blueberries along the way until they reached Wapta Lake where they camped and were able to kill a grouse. They "were happy to boil it up with some ends of candles and odd pieces of grease, to make something like a supper for the five of us after a very hard day's work."[120] The next day a moose was shot and the men began to regain their strength.

When George Dawson, himself a scientist renown for detailed and accurate work, studied the geology of western Canada 25 years later, he was most impressed with Hector's description and explanation of the geological structure west of the Great Lakes. Following his work in western Canada with the Palliser Expedition, Hector continued to make significant contributions to geology, particularly in New Zealand. He was knighted in 1887.

In his book *Buffalo Days and Nights*, Peter Erasmus describes how Hector was admired by his fellow travellers. "Dr. Hector alone of all the men of my experience asked no quarter from any man among us, drivers or guides. He could walk, ride, or tramp snowshoes with the best of our men, and never fell back on his position to soften his share of the hardships, but in fact gloried in his physical ability after a hard day's run to share in the work of preparing camp for the night, building shelters from the wind, cutting spruce boughs, or even helping get up wood for an all-night fire."[121]

John Palliser and James Hector. Courtesy Glenbow Archives, NA-588-1.

Mount Hector from the south. Photo Gillean Daffern.

Castle Mtn.

Eisenhower Peak

Helena Ridge

Sawback Range

17 Castle Mountain and the Sawback Range

From Storm Mountain Hill

Highway 93, 5.2 km west of Castle Junction; 5 km east of the Alberta/British Columbia border.

As he travelled up the Bow Valley in 1858, James Hector of the Palliser Expedition thought the peak he named Castle Mountain was "a most remarkable mountain."[122] *Entering the higher elevations approaching Vermilion Pass, he undoubtedly continued to be impressed by the entire panorama that becomes visible from this viewpoint. After admiring this vista, he continued westward into the Columbia Valley, becoming the first white man to cross Vermilion Pass.*

This viewpoint was also highly thought of by officials of the Canadian Pacific Railway who in 1923 built Castle Mountain Bungalow Camp, later known as Storm Mountain Lodge. This was the same year Highway 93 from the Bow Valley to Radium was completed.

The broad summit of **Castle Mountain** (2862 m) frames the left side of this panorama, with **Eisenhower Peak** (2752 m) to its right. The separation of this peak from the main portion of the mountain is not seen at its best from this location; it is much more impressive from the Trans-Canada Highway at Castle Junction. Formerly referred to as the "South-east Tower," it is a challenging rock climb first climbed by Lawrence Grassi and P. Cerutti in 1926.

Helena Ridge (2862 m) can be seen gradually descending from behind Castle Mountain to the valley containing Johnston Creek. Charles D. Walcott spent many summers studying the geology of the Canadian Rockies and chose to name this feature after his first wife, Helena Stevens. A high point hidden behind Castle Mountain was named for his son Stuart.

A summary of Dr. Walcott's work in this area was published by the Smithsonian Institute in 1928. The 368-page book is filled with detailed geological information, but there is a single reference to his wife in the introduction to the "Wild Flower Canyon Section," where he notes that, "Mrs. Walcott identified 82 species in blossom in July within a short distance of the pond."[123]

Rising in the distance, midway along Helena Ridge, is an unnamed high point of the Sawback Range. Farther to the right one gets an unobstructed view of a 15 km-long section of this distinctive range.

Mount Ishbel (2908 m) is the range's highest point, rising beyond Johnston Canyon. Ishbel MacDonald was the daughter of Prime Minister Ramsay MacDonald of Great Britain.

The next high point, **Mount Cockscomb** (2776 m), lies beyond Ranger Creek and was named because it was thought the outline of its summit resembled a rooster's comb.

Located on an unnamed high point of the Sawback Range beyond Mount Cockscomb, **The Finger** (2545 m) was brought into prominence through a poem written by Earle Birney. A distinctive spire outlined against the sky when seen from the south near the Muleshoe picnic site on the Bow Valley Parkway, the feature seems to disappear into the jagged Sawback Range when viewed from the west and cannot be picked out from this viewpoint.

The poem *David* was written in 1940 and though fictional is based on Birney's climbing experiences when he worked in Banff during a few summers. It tells of two young men becoming knowledgeable in the ways of the mountains.

> *By the fading shreds of the shattered stormcloud. Lingering*
> *There it was David who spied to the south, remote,*
> *And unmapped, a sunlit spire on Sawback, an overhang*
> *Crooked like a talon. David named it the Finger.*[124]

In the poem the author slips on the summit, and in the process of regaining the author's balance, David's foothold breaks and he falls to a ledge below. His back broken, he begs the author to push him over the cliff to avoid spending his life in a wheelchair. If you read the poem you will never drive past The Finger without remembering *David*.

The Bow Valley lies between the Sawback Range and the forested ridges that rise gently toward the smooth summit of **Copper Mountain** (2795 m) on the right side of the panorama.

Copper Mountain was named in 1885 by George Dawson four years after prospectors John Healy and J. S. Dennis discovered copper high on its slopes. From the mine site Dr. Dawson first saw and named Mount Assiniboine.

The Finger from near Muleshoe picnic site on the Bow Valley Parkway.

Castle Mountain

James Hector's 1858 sketch of Castle Mountain. Courtesy Palliser, Capt. John et al. The Journals....

James Hector was still 19 km down the Bow Valley from what is now known as Castle Junction when he decided what the name of this mountain should be. He noted, "a very remarkable mountain...which looks exactly like a gigantic castle."[125]

One of the most imposing peaks in the Bow Valley, the bold, castellated southwest front of the mountain dominates the view for much of the journey from Banff to Lake Louise. Its bulk, prominent position and reddish colour combine to make this a favourite of most who pass this way.

Two tiers of steep cliffs form the "castle" part of Castle Mountain. The ledge between is the Stephen Formation that correlates to the rocks that contain the Burgess Shale fossils in Yoho National Park.

Despite the appropriateness of Dr. Hector's name and the fact that it had been used for almost 100 years, the mountain was renamed Mount Eisenhower in 1946 in honour of American General Dwight D. Eisenhower, the Supreme Commander of the Allied Forces in Europe during the final year of World War II.

The decision to rename Castle Mountain was made by Prime Minister Mackenzie King on the day before the president was to pay a visit to Ottawa. As much as Eisenhower was respected, this arbitrary decision so enraged the Alberta government it immediately formed its own geographical names board. It took 33 years and an Albertan as prime minister before Castle Mountain regained its original name in 1979. As a compromise, the prominent tower on the southern end of the mountain was given the name Eisenhower Peak.

Bottom left: Castle Mountain with Eisenhower Peak at right. Photo Gillean Daffern.

Bottom right: Eisenhower Peak. Photo Gillean Daffern.

Main Ranges and the Sawback Range

Having had considerable geological training, Dr. James Hector would undoubtedly have noticed the abrupt change in geology between Castle Mountain and the more distant Sawback Range as he looked into the Bow Valley from this viewpoint.

Geologists separate the Rocky Mountains of western Canada into four different zones, which relate to the style and degree of their structural deformation. In the Foothills area the rock layers have been folded and faulted but not uplifted to a great extent. Farther west the front ranges appear, their eastern edge forming a very distinct boundary where older limestones have been exposed. These ranges are composed of a series of thrust faults that underlie panels of rock that overlap like the shingles on a roof. They are almost always tilted down to the west in varying amounts. To the west of the front ranges lie the main ranges of the Rockies, in which the sedimentary layers remain relatively undisturbed although they have been uplifted significantly and moved eastward. Farther west, the layers of the western ranges are severely broken, faulted and folded. The western boundary of the Rockies is the "Rocky Mountain Trench," a wide valley filled with thick deposits of sands and gravels and containing major rivers such as the Columbia.

Castle Mountain is noteworthy because it is the easternmost mountain of the main ranges in the Bow Valley. The rock is Precambrian and Cambrian in age and the rock layers are relatively horizontal. The Castle Mountain Fault has thrust the older (400-600 million years) limestone that forms the cliffs and underlying older rocks over younger (200 million years) rock that has eroded and is responsible for the tree-covered, gently-sloped base of the peak. This fault defines the boundary between the main ranges and the front ranges and can be traced throughout Banff Park and into Jasper National Park where it passes between the Palisade and Pyramid Mountain just east of Jasper townsite.

Castle Mountain is, appropriately, a "castellate" type of mountain in which the flat-lying layers feature near vertical cliffs alternating with flat or gently sloped terraces that have been sculptured by various forms of erosion. The layers of rock involved vary in their resistance to erosion, the harder rock such as limestone being more resistant than the softer shales.

Mount Ishbel.

While Castle Mountain is the easternmost of the main ranges, the Sawback Range, which was appropriately named by James Hector, is the westernmost of the front ranges. In this range the strata has been tilted to near vertical. "Sawtooth" type mountains have been formed as the steeply dipping, thin layers of sedimentary strata are eroded by cross gullies to form a series of inverted Vs that resemble the teeth of a saw.

Cross section of the Rocky Mountains by David M. Baird. Courtesy Geological Survey of Canada.

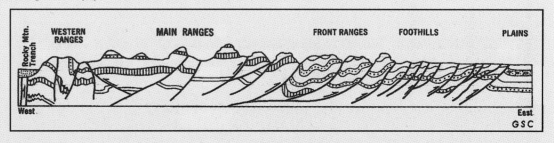

Stanley Peak

Mt. Whymper

Vermilion Peak

Mt. 10,060

Mt. 10,240

Slopes of
Storm Mtn.

18 A View into British Columbia

From Vermilion Pass

*Highway 93, 8.4 km west of Castle
Junction; 1.8 km east of the
Alberta/British Columbia border.*

*Friday, August 20, 1858, was a very important day for
James Hector and his party, for they finally reached "the
first water we had seen flowing to the Pacific."[126] It must
have been exciting for the party to begin the descent while
enjoying this magnificent panorama of peaks on the western
side of the Continental Divide.*

The treed slopes of **Storm Mountain** (3100 m), which form the
left edge of this view, show signs of the 1968 forest fire that
burned for four days and consumed 2500 ha of forest. Lodgepole
pine seeds wait for the heat of a fire to be dispersed, so this species
dominates the forest as nature renews the area. Highway 93 was,
of course, closed as were parts of the Trans-Canada Highway that
were used as a landing strip for water bombers.

Clearly, the highest summit from this viewpoint is the glacier-
draped **Stanley Peak** (3155 m), which rises 1600 m above the
valley bottom. Despite the fact it is a major peak in the Ball Range
that forms the Continental Divide, Stanley Peak lies entirely in
British Columbia. It was named by Edward Whymper after
Frederick Arthur Stanley, who was Canada's sixth governor-
general but is probably best known as the person responsible for
the Stanley Cup.

The ideal viewpoint for Stanley Peak is from a point three km
southwest of Vermilion Pass. From here one can look into the
beautiful hanging valley of Stanley Creek and enjoy the
impressive northeast face of the mountain. The Stanley Glacier
descends to a fairly low level, its retreat slowed by the steep cliffs
of the mountain's north face.

Four hours after crossing the pass, Hector's party reached the
Vermilion Plain where Ochre Creek joins the main valley. He
wrote in his journal that, "Its surface is completely covered with
yellow ochre, washed down from the ferruginous shales in the
mountains. The Kootanie Indians come to this place sometimes,
and we found the remains of a camp and of a large fire which they
had used to convert the ochre into the red oxide which they take
away to trade to the Indians of the low country, and also to the
Blackfeet as a pigment, calling it vermilion."[127] The attractive peak
to the east of the ochre beds takes its name from the colour of the
pigment that the Indians obtained in the flats below.

The smooth, southern slopes of **Vermilion Peak** (2636 m) are
covered in meadow, unusual for a peak in this area. Highway 93
passes to the north of the peak before turning to the south below
the impressive eastern slopes of the Vermilion Range. From this
viewpoint, most of these steep cliffs are hidden behind a high

ridge. Known as the Rockwall, they stretch for 25 km and the central portion provides the focus for a classic 30 km hike along what is known as the Rockwall Trail.

Separated by a U-shaped gap, the two peaks one can see remain unnamed despite their substantial elevation and prominence from Highway 93. In the past they have been referred to as **Mount 10,060** (3097 m) and **Mount 10,240** (3121 m), the numbers being their elevations in feet. It was the first ascent of Mount 10,240 that helped launch Ken Jones on a remarkable guiding career that has continued for over 65 years.

Katie Gardiner and guide Walter Feuz are best known for their numerous first ascents in the Kananaskis Valley. During the summer of 1933 they visited Kootenay National Park to attempt some unclimbed peaks in the Vermilion Range and invited along a young 23 year-old friend from Walter's home town of Golden, Ken Jones.

The threesome completed the first ascent of Foster Peak in July, then returned the following month. After reaching their campsite at treeline below the Rockwall by noon, Ken and Walter left to do some preliminary reconnaissance, got carried away, and made the first ascent of a second mountain. The following day Katie, Walter and Ken made the first ascent of Mount 10,240.

Ken remembers that Katie was primarily interested in first ascents that summer and there seemed to be real competition between her and another outstanding lady climber of the era, Georgia Engelhard. The two placed fourth and fifth in the list of first ascents by "non-guides," Katie edging out Georgia 33 to 32.

Mount Whymper (2845 m) is the striking peak that forms the right-hand edge of this panorama. During the summer of 1901, British mountaineer Edward Whymper became the first climber to visit the upper Vermilion Valley. With four guides who had travelled with him from Europe, he made the first ascents of both Stanley Peak and his own mountain. Compared to some of his experiences in the Alps 30 years earlier, Whymper's climb of Mount Whymper must have seemed quite simple and monotonous as a mountaineering challenge. Today the ascent is regarded only as a moderate "scramble," not requiring ropes and certainly not requiring four alpine guides.

Stanley Peak.

The twin peaks of Mount 10,240.

Edward Whymper

Edward Whymper. Courtesy Whyte Museum, V14 ACOOP-251.

"Every night, do you understand, I see my comrades of the Matterhorn slipping on their backs, their arms outstretched, one after the other, in perfect order at equal distances—Croz the guide, first, then Hadow, then Hudson, and lastly Douglas. Yes, I shall always see them...."[128]

Edward Whymper became the most renowned climber in the world after completing the first ascent of the Matterhorn in 1865. This most significant accomplishment came after a number of other impressive ascents in the Alps, but the tragedy during the descent that took the lives of four members of his party haunted him for the rest of his life and was likely responsible for his extensive use of alcohol.

During the winter of 1900-01, Whymper suggested to the CPR that they invite him to spend a summer in the Rockies at their expense and in return he would promote the Canadian Rockies and the railway in his written reports and speaking engagements in England and Europe. The railway officials thought this was a good idea and even arranged to have an unclimbed peak named in his honour prior to the trip.

Much was expected of the legendary Whymper and the newspapers were full of stories about him. Other climbers such as Norman Collie and James Outram were openly hostile and concerned that despite the fact that he was over 60 years old he would claim many of the remaining unclimbed peaks including the "Canadian Matterhorn," Mount Assiniboine. But it soon became apparent that Whymper, largely because of his alcoholism, was somewhat limited in what he could accomplish.

He journeyed to the Rockies every summer from 1901 until 1905 and returned for a final visit in 1909. But he climbed few peaks and the ones he chose were not as challenging as expected. Sadly, his personality was such that he antagonized those he worked with, particularly his guides and outfitters. Practical jokes were played including placing a chipmunk in a tin can under his bed and setting up staged photographs of his empty liquor bottles.

One of those who apparently had a personality conflict with Edward Whymper was the legendary guide Bill Peyto. After arriving in Canada from England in 1886, Peyto worked for the CPR, homesteaded and prospected before entering the outfitting business with Tom Wilson. By the time he was chosen to lead Whymper to Vermilion Pass he had acquired a solid reputation for his work with Walter Wilcox, Norman Collie and others.

Peyto and Whymper seemed to get along reasonably well during their initial trip together and although Whymper found numerous faults with his Swiss guides, he felt that Peyto had properly executed his commission. Later in the summer, however, after a severe tongue-lashing from Whymper for coming back to camp too early from trail-clearing work in the Yoho Valley, Bill walked out on him with the excuse that he had to take two sick horses back to Field.

It was expected by the CPR and others that Whymper would eventually write a book about his experiences in the Canadian Rockies and that it would promote them in climbing circles across Europe, but presumably he lacked the energy and enthusiasm to complete the project.

Mount Whymper.

Ken Jones

"Ken Jones is a real guide, he takes people out, has them do more than they ever thought possible, and brings them home laughing and talking about an early start for tomorrow."[129]

Lizzie Rummel, a mountain legend in her own right, used to say these words about the man who made three first ascents in the Vermilion Range during the summer of 1933.

Born in Golden in 1910, Ken was raised on a homestead in the Columbia Valley. His early experiences with Walter Feuz and Katie Gardiner in 1933 marked the beginning of a remarkable career as a mountain guide. The first alpine guides in the Rockies had been "imported" from Europe in the late nineteenth century and even 35 years later all the practicing guides were European. Ken was able through hard work and a winning personality to become the first Canadian born mountain guide.

As well as being an alpine guide, he is a civil engineer, has worked in the Yukon in the mining industry, became a pilot during World War II, trained the legendary Lovat Scouts in mountain warfare, trained to become a commando himself, became accomplished in the construction of log buildings and studied polar bears in Churchill, Manitoba. In addition, from 1967 until 1974 he was the first warden of Mount Assiniboine Provincial Park.

Mummery Icefield, Jones Peak (right). Courtesy Ken Jones collection.

After literally making his own first pair of skis, Ken was a pioneer in the development of skiing in the Rockies and Columbia Mountains. He was a leader during the early years of skiing at Mount Assiniboine Lodge and Skoki. He entered competitions whenever he could, including the Dominion Championships where he competed in cross country, jumping, slalom and downhill events.

In the foreword to *Ken Jones, Mountain Man* by Lorne and Kim Tetarenko, his colleague and longtime admirer Chic Scott wrote, "His life has been a wonderful adventure, shared with the most interesting and unique individuals in our mountain heritage."[130]

Jones Peak, a glaciated mountain in the Mummery Icefield area, is a fitting tribute. Ken was climbing in the area and suggested ascending the mountain. Illness kept Ken in camp but the others in his party climbed the mountain and one of them, Andy Kauffman, saw to it that the mountain was named after his friend.

Ken currently resides in Nanton, Alberta, with his family, but is a regular visitor to the Assiniboine and Skoki areas where he continues to lead visitors into the mountains he loves and knows so well.

Ken Jones, Mount Assiniboine Provincial Park warden. Photo Hans Gsellmann. Courtesy Ken Jones collection.

Ken's warden cabin at Mount Assiniboine Provincial Park. Courtesy Ken Jones collection.

19 The Peaks above Kootenay Plains

From Abraham Lake

Highway 11, 21.1 km west of Big Horn River bridge; 6.9 km east of the Cline River bridge.

Badge of the 1st Canadian Parachute Battalion. Courtesy We Stand on Guard.

This view to the south along the valley of the North Saskatchewan River changed forever with the construction of the Big Horn Dam. Now, instead of the Kootenay Plains providing the foreground for this panorama, there is a reservoir known as Abraham Lake. In the distance lie the headwaters of the Siffleur River and some distant peaks near the head of the Clearwater River.

Behind the forested ridge on the left side of the panorama rises a complex mountain with five peaks. It was referred to as Kadoona Mountain by Mary Schaffer, but the name was not formally adopted and it wasn't until 1994 that the feature was officially named. **Ex Coelis** (2545 m) is Latin for "Out of the Clouds" and is

Ex Coelis Mountain across the Kootenay Plains.

the motto of the First Canadian Parachute Battalion, one of eight battalions that made up the Sixth British Airborne Division during World War II. When the mountain was named, the battalion association's president referred to the peaks as "A bold memory of jumpers buried on foreign soil."[131]

When the invasion of France began on D day, members of the battalion were among the first Allied force on the ground, taking off from their base at 23:30 and landing in France shortly after 01:00 on June 6, 1944. The unit had orders to demolish a bridge over the Dives River, thus hampering any German advance to the invasion beaches, then to cover British paratroopers attacking a coastal artillery battery.

Though they accomplished these tasks, 19 men were killed, 10 wounded and 84 taken prisoner. The large proportion taken prisoner occurred because many of the paratroopers became isolated when they landed far beyond the intended drop zone.

In 1997, names were assigned to the five peaks of Ex Coelis Mountain. Normandy Peak, Ardennes Peak and Rhine Peak were named after battles in which the battalion participated. Elbe Peak was named after a river in Germany near the point where the battalion met the Russian Army that had been advancing from the east. The fifth peak, Stan Waters Peak, was named after a battalion member who had an outstanding career both as a soldier and a civilian.

Stan Waters joined the Calgary Regiment (Tank) in 1940 and, while serving in the First Special Service Forces, was awarded the U.S. Silver Star for gallantry in action in Italy. He commanded the first battalion to liberate Rome in June, 1944, and in 1945 saw action as a company commander with the First Canadian Parachute Battalion. After retiring from the military in 1975 with the rank of lieutenant general, he had a successful business career and was involved with a wide variety of community service organizations in Calgary before being appointed to the Canadian Senate.

Forty-five km away at the head of the Escarpment River, a distant icefield is visible with **Icefall Mountain** (3221 m) rising to its right. The icefield is the highest point of the Ram River Glacier, which is the headwaters of the Ram River. Icefall Mountain features a hanging glacier separate from the Ram River Glacier.

A number of high, unnamed peaks lie between Escarpment River and Siffleur Creek, some reaching elevations in excess of 3300 m.

It is not surprising that the most prominent mountain in this panorama—**Siffleur Mountain** (3129 m)—was named by James Hector as he journeyed east on his way to Fort Edmonton in 1858. Siffleur is the French word for the hoary marmot.

In 1940 Ernest Ross became the first person to drive from Rocky Mountain House to Saskatchewan River Crossing. In 1969, the year after the David Thompson Highway was constructed, the mountain to the right of Siffleur Peak was named **Mount Ernest Ross** (2454 m) in honour of Ross' efforts over a 40-year period to have the highway completed.

Framing this view on the right side is **Elliott Peak** (2872 m), an attractive little mountain some 1200 m lower than Siffleur Mountain. It was originally named Sentinel Mountain by Arthur Coleman as he descended Whiterabbit Creek in 1892. He described it as "jutting boldly into the belt of prairie"[132] and noted that it was prominent from a number of different directions.

Elliott Barnes Sr. had a horse ranch on the Kootenay Plains that he named Kadonna Tinda (Stoney for Windy Plains). In 1906, when he was only eight years old, his son, Elliott Barnes Jr., climbed the mountain above the ranch that was named in his honour the following year.

An accomplished photographer, Elliott Barnes Sr. spent only the summers ranching on this now partly submerged part of the Kootenay Plains. Silas Abraham, after whose family the lake is named, looked after the operation during the times that Elliott was away. But winter conditions in the mountains, it turned out, did not suit the purebred Clydesdale horses he was raising, and after three years Barnes moved his operation to a ranch near Calgary. It was in his cabin below Elliott Peak, one fall evening in 1907, that Samson Beaver drew the map that Mary Schaffer followed to Maligne Lake the following summer.

Elliott Barnes Jr. on the summit of Elliott Peak, 1906. Courtesy Whyte Museum (Barnes collection), NA-65-90.

Elliott Peak.

20 The Mountains above Wind Valley

From Dead Man's Flats
Highway 1 at Dead Man's Flats, 7.3 km west of Lac des Arcs overpass; 6 km east of the Bow River.

This mountain panorama is a classic, particularly in the way it unfolds to the south as one drives through Dead Man's Flats. These peaks at the headwaters of Wind Creek are the first high mountains encountered on the drive west of Calgary on the Trans-Canada Highway, rising some 675 m above those that lie to the east. Their height, coupled with the fact that one is looking at their north faces, means that they are often highlighted by snow well into the summer.

The mountains on the left side of this panorama are quite different from those on the right side. Composed of shale and sandstone of the Mesozoic age, they are easily eroded and form gentle slopes that are generally grass covered.

Both of the grassy ridges are part of **Mount Allan** (2789 m), although the lower one to the left is referred to, unofficially, as **Mount Collembola** (2758 m). One of the more unusual names in the area, collembola are 16-eyed snow fleas that appear in the thousands after a thaw. The long ridge on the right leads to the summit of Mount Allan, which may also be seen from the Kananaskis Highway (40).

The peaks on the right side of the panorama are the northern part of the Kananaskis Range. The triangular-shaped **Wind Mountain** (3153 m) is one of the four summits of **Mount Lougheed** (3105 m). The least attractive southeast summit is actually the highest point. The northwest summit is the spectacular one and the one generally referred to as Mount Lougheed. It honours Sir James Lougheed who had been

appointed Queen's Council for the North West Territories in 1885 and became a prominent lawyer, businessman, senator and federal cabinet minister.

A beautiful peak, the gently folded strata of Mount Lougheed's northern cliffs are often highlighted by snow that lingers on the narrow ledges. W. S. Drewry and A. St. Cyr claimed the first ascent of Mount Lougheed, but this was disputed in later years by Tom Wilson, the most famous of the early outfitters of Banff National Park and the first non-native to reach the shores of Lake Louise. He claimed to have made the first ascent two days prior to Drewry and St. Cyr. At the time all three were in the employ of J. J. McArthur who was conducting a survey for the CPR.

Windtower (2688 m), on the right side of the panorama, is a unique mountain that features an interesting curved ridge with near vertical sides. The gentle, forested slopes of Wind Ridge limit the view on the right side of this panorama.

Right: The four summits of Mount Lougheed from Mount Collembola. Wind Mountain at far left. Photo Gillean Daffern.

The Lougheed Family and the Mountains of Wind Valley

The Palliser Expedition was travelling up the Bow Valley in 1858 when Eugene Bourgeau, the expedition's botanist, first saw the magnificent mountain that dominates the panorama from Dead Man's Flats. It must have been just as much of a surprise to him as it is to those who now travel up the Bow Valley by car on the Trans-Canada Highway. Clouds were swirling around the summit, so he named it Wind Mountain. He ascended the lower slopes and to his delight was able to collect about 50 varieties of alpine plants. Unlike some other explorers of the era, when Bourgeau got a chance to name a peak he preferred to choose a name based on something natural rather than use the name of a famous person who more often than not would never even see the peak.

But some 70 years later a decision was made that this was too spectacular a peak to have the simple name of "Wind." Sir James Lougheed had recently passed away and it was decided that a mountain west of Calgary should be named in his honour. Lougheed had practised law in the city in partnership with the future prime minister of Canada, R. B. Bennett. Sir James had been appointed to the Senate and later became a privy councillor and cabinet minister in Robert Borden's government.

Originally, a mountain near Healy Creek in Banff National Park had been chosen to carry the name of Sir James Lougheed. However, the Lougheed family did not approve of this particular peak and, perhaps assisted by R. B. Bennett, successfully exerted pressure in the right places to have the much more spectacular Wind Mountain renamed Mount Lougheed in 1928.

Sir James Lougheed's grandson Peter was the premier of Alberta in the 1970s and early 1980s and during his time in office succeeded, with other members of his family, in climbing the mountain with guides.

However, the renaming of the mountain was not the end of the name "Wind." The impressive southernmost peak of Mount Lougheed was named Wind Mountain in 1985. So there still is a Wind Mountain in the panorama but it is not the mountain that Eugene Bourgeau named in 1858. To further complicate matters, the steep-cliffed mountain to the right of Mount Lougheed is known as Windtower and the ridge immediately southwest of Dead Man's Flats is called Wind Ridge.

James Lougheed. Courtesy Glenbow Archives, NA-3918-14.

Wind Ridge from Wind Creek. Photo Gillean Daffern.

21 The Mountains above Canmore

George McDougall. Courtesy Glenbow Archives, NA-659-44.

From below Harvie Heights

Highway 1, 2.2 km east of Banff Park gates, 8.1 km west of the Bow River bridge.

Shortly after leaving Banff National Park eastbound toward Calgary, this magnificent panorama comes into view and serves to remind the traveller that there are many beautiful mountains to be found between the park and the prairies.

It is interesting to note that the eastern side of almost all of the mountains in this panorama are part of the skyline as seen from the city of Calgary.

The gentle slopes of **Grotto Mountain** (2706 m) form the left border of the view. In August, 1858, James Hector and Eugene Bourgeau of the Palliser Expedition followed a small creek up the slopes of the mountain to above timberline. During their explorations they found a large cave strewn with the bones of a goat and thus chose the name Grotto for the mountain.

Between these peaks, the twin summits of **Mount McGillivray** (2454 m) rise in the distance. Although not officially named until 1957, the peak honours one of the first non-natives to visit the Bow Valley.

Duncan McGillivray was inspired by the explorations of Alexander Mackenzie, who, though he had travelled extensively across the continent to the Pacific, had failed to find a navigable river that reached the Pacific Ocean. McGillivray was determined to find the source of the Columbia whose mouth was explored by Captain Vancouver's party in 1792.

In November of 1800, McGillivray and David Thompson, in the employ of the Hudson's Bay Company, rode south from the recently established Rocky Mountain House. They passed the present site of the city of Calgary and travelled south to the Highwood River. Thompson's journal suggests they had difficulty determining where they could enter into the mountains. However, they eventually rode west up the Bow Valley as far as what is now Mount McGillivray. But it was late in the season and not practical to travel farther up the valley to search for a pass into the headwaters of the Columbia. After further explorations west of Rocky Mountain House, McGillivray returned to Rocky Mountain House for the remainder of the winter. In the spring, he was too ill with rheumatism to carry on his explorations and on crutches returned to the East.

Duncan McGillivray was highly regarded by many people including David Thompson. As evidence, on the map of western Canada that Thompson made following his travels, he referred to all of the Rocky Mountains south of the Saskatchewan River as "Duncan's Mountains."

Pigeon Mountain (2394 m) was for a few years the site of a downhill ski resort. However, a combination of little snow, warm chinook winds and a southern exposure forced it to close. The old ski runs can still be seen as you drive closer to the mountain. It was named "Pic de Pigeons" by Eugene Bourgeau, after he saw flocks of wild pigeons in the area.

Skogan Pass lies between Pigeon Mountain and **Mount Collembola** (2758 m), a shoulder of **Mount Allan** (2789 m). This gap has a long history and was noted as an old Indian trail on George Dawson's 1886 map. The name "Skogan" was applied by Don Gardner in 1972. This Norwegian word means a magic forest with elves and trolls.

The distant mountain seen rising above the pass, **Mount McDougall** (2591 m), was named after Reverend George McDougall and his sons John and David. It lies some 36 km away, beyond Highway 40 on the east side of the Kananaskis Valley.

George McDougall was a Methodist missionary stationed at Fort Victoria near Edmonton when he travelled to the Bow Valley to visit the Stoney Indians in 1864. He returned determined to establish a mission at Morley, but it was not until the fall of 1873 that his sons began living amongst the Stoneys. Reverend John built a mission that developed into a village of 500 people with a school and an orphanage, while David McDougall established a trading post at the Ghost River. The McDougalls brought with them 12 head of cattle, 11 cows and a bull, which were the first breeding herd in what is now the ranching country of southwestern Alberta.

From the beginning the Stoneys loved and trusted the McDougalls, so it was a sad day when Reverend George lost his life in a blizzard while on a late autumn buffalo hunt in 1876. His son continued his religious work amongst the Stoneys for 25 years.

To the right of Mount Allan and rising above **Wind Ridge** (2164 m), the northeast summit of **Mount Kidd** (2958 m) may be seen some 16 km farther away. When travelling east from Banff, this peak is best viewed from the top of the hill before one descends to the park gates. By the time this viewpoint is reached, only the top of the mountain is visible.

The northwest summit of **Mount Lougheed** (3105 m), often highlighted by stripes of snow sloping down to the right on the steep east face, is perhaps the most spectacular peak in this panorama.

The distant peaks on either side of Mount Lougheed are **Wind Mountain** (3153 m) and **Mount Sparrowhawk** (3121 m), backdrop to the Nakiska ski slopes on Mount Allan when seen from Highway 40.

Mount Sparrowhawk always appears very high and aloof from this viewpoint. In a view that includes natural names like Grotto, Wind and Pigeon, one would expect that the mountain would have been named after the small hawk that is a resident of Alberta. In fact, it was named after *HMS Sparrowhawk*, a destroyer that was lost during the Battle of Jutland during World War I.

The classic group, the **Three Sisters** (2936 m), is one of the most photographed and painted scenes in the Rockies and is more associated with the town of Canmore than with any other of the peaks visible from Harvie Heights.

Ship's Prow is not an official name, but one that is very descriptive of the steep cliffs below **Mount Lawrence Grassi** (2693 m). It is a popular and challenging rock climbing route. Lawrence Grassi started work in the local coal mines in the early part of the twentieth century, later becoming known as a mountain guide and trail builder.

On the extreme right of this panorama is **Ha Ling Peak** (2408 m), formerly known as Chinaman's Peak. Although the name Chinaman's was not official until 1980, the name goes back to 1886. Ha Ling, a Chinese cook at a mining camp, made a bet of 50 dollars he could climb the peak and return within six hours. Leaving a flag on the top as proof, he was back in camp in five-and-one-half hours, thereby winning the bet. In 1997, following pressure from the Chinese community who thought the name derogatory, the name Chinaman's Peak was removed and replaced by Ha Ling Peak the following year.

Although not particularly impressive from this viewpoint, the mountain is very noticeable from the Trans-Canada Highway as one approaches Canmore from the east as well as from the townsite itself.

Whiteman's Gap, the pass between Ha Ling Peak and the east end of Mount Rundle, was used extensively in the early 1800s as part of a route through White Man's Pass into British Columbia, the Columbia River valley and eventually Oregon. The road up to the gap, now an access into the Spray Lakes and Smith-Dorrien areas of Kananaskis Country, was built in 1948 by Calgary Power in order to reach the Three Sisters dam site. A high point of the **Goat Range** may be seen beyond the gap.

The steep cliffs of the east end of **Mount Rundle** (2846 m) rise to the right of Whiteman's Gap.

*Ha Ling Peak from Whiteman's Gap.
Photo Gillean Daffern.*

*Mount Lawrence Grassi from Quarry Lake.
Photo Gillean Daffern.*

The Three Sisters

One of the most photographed views in the Rockies is of the Three Sisters from the Trans-Canada Highway. They are also the peaks most associated with the community of Canmore, which has evolved from a railway siding and coal mining town to its current status as a thriving tourist-related community.

Although James Hector did not name the mountains, the geologist of the Palliser Expedition clearly appreciated the view from his campsite in the Canmore area. He wrote, "At dark we camped by some old Indian wigwams where the valley is wide and flat, and with fine patches of level prairie along the river for our horses. Just opposite our camp there is a mountain with three peaks which form a striking group."[133] It was a brother of Major Rogers, the discoverer of Rogers Pass in the Selkirk Mountains, who named the three peaks in 1883. He recalled, "There had been quite a heavy snowstorm in the night, and when we got up in the morning and looked out of the tent I noticed each of the three peaks had a heavy veil of snow on the north side and I said to the boys, 'Look at the Three Nuns.' They were called the Three Nuns for quite a while but later were called the 'Three Sisters,' more Protestant like I suppose."[134] The name "Three Sisters" first appeared on Dr. George Dawson's map of 1886 and it is quite likely it was he who thought that the name Three Sisters would be more appropriate.

The highest of the Three Sisters was first climbed in 1887 by J. J. McArthur. The lowest is a much more difficult ascent and was not climbed until 1925 by a party led by Canmore's most illustrious mountain man, Lawrence Grassi.

The Three Sisters. Photo Gillean Daffern.

Lawrence Grassi

Lawrence Grassi was a remarkable individual who emigrated from Italy in 1916 and based the rest of his life below the Three Sisters in the town of Canmore. He came to work in the coal mines and soon had an impressive record, not only as a coal miner but also as a climbing guide.

Grassi visited all areas of the Rockies, making many solo climbs, some of them undoubtedly first ascents that were never recorded. Wearing suspenders and old mining boots with hobnails and sometimes even rubber boots, he didn't look the role of the classic alpine guide. His favourite was probably the technically demanding Mount Louis, which he climbed 32 times.

His strength was legendary. In the Tonquin Valley southwest of Jasper, he carried a much heavier man on his back for 3.2 km down a steep mountain, across a glacier and over moraine to a waiting rescue party. An examination of the trails Grassi built reveals that huge stones were moved single-handedly to construct steps, bridges or stepping stones.

After he retired from the mines, Grassi spent several summers in the Lake O'Hara area where he worked as a park warden. His beautiful rockwork there will be used by generations of hikers to reach the high valleys of Lake Oesa and Lake McArthur.

Grassi loved the mountains. It is said he once headed off to Calgary for an eye examination but failed to arrive. Lawrence explained that when he got as far as Ghost Dam he looked back, and because the mountains looked so far away, he couldn't go any farther and had to return.

In a speech to the House of Commons supporting the naming of two lakes above Canmore after Lawrence Grassi, Dr. J. S. Woodsworth said, "Last summer I spent a month in a little mountain town in the Rockies. For me, the most interesting individual in the community was Lawrence Grassi, an Italian miner. In the course of a prolonged strike, instead of loafing about the village, he set off into the hills, axe on shoulder, to make trails to points of interest. It was a labour of love. He loved the mountains but enjoyed having others share their beauty. So day by day he pushed through the bush discovering the best ways of approach—blazing a trail, cutting out the underbrush, grubbing out stones and rocks, bridging little mountain streams...."[135] Dr. Woodsworth went on to say, "The world needs Grassis...men who will seek new paths; make the rough places smooth; bridge the chasms that now prevent human progress; point the way to higher levels and loftier achievements."[136]

It is fitting that Mount Lawrence Grassi be part of Canmore's backdrop. A walk along the trail that Lawrence Grassi built to Grassi Lakes will provide some insight into this most renowned of Canmore's citizens.

Andy Drinnan (l) and Lawrence Grassi, 1928. Courtesy Whyte Museum, V14 AC 192-P7.

Grassi's steps on the trail to Lake Oesa.

Stoney Squaw Mtn.   Mt. Norquay   Mt. Louis   Cascade Mtn.   Mt. Fifi

22 A View of Mount Louis

From Anthracite

Highway 1 at the Cascade Power Plant, 10.5 km west of Banff National Park boundary; 2.7 km east of the easternmost access to Banff townsite.

As one approaches Banff townsite from the east, one of the most spectacular peaks of the Canadian Rockies is briefly visible. Near the site of the former coal mining town of Anthracite, the highway turns to the west and Mount Louis appears in the distance, jutting abruptly toward the sky. From this point one is looking up the valley of Forty Mile Creek, which also turns to the west, permitting a view between Mount Norquay and the lower slopes of Cascade Mountain.

At 2682 m, **Mount Louis** is not a high peak nor does it have a glacier or snowfield. It is the vertically dipping limestone of Devonian age that gives the mountain its sense of remoteness and inaccessibility. Following the first ascent of the mountain, the now legendary guide Conrad Kain looked up at the peak and said to his client, "Ye Gods, Mr. MacCarthy, just look at that; they never will believe we climbed it."[137] From all angles, not just the one from

Anthracite, the mountain still appears today, at least to those who are not technical rock climbers, to be unclimbable.

During the summer of 1916, Kain and Albert MacCarthy had planned to spend a day horseback riding "for a day's picnic 'to view the scenery,'"[138] in the vicinity of Mount Louis. However, when Conrad began searching for a route on the lower cliffs, MacCarthy followed him up and this preliminary reconnaissance developed into the first ascent of the mountain.

Mount Louis is one of three similar-looking peaks of the Sawback Range. Mount Edith is the southernmost of the three but is hidden behind Mount Norquay from this viewpoint. To the north of Louis lies **Mount Fifi** (2621 m), somewhat similar to Louis but less impressive. In the background between Louis and Fifi are unnamed mountains of the Sawback Range.

Mount Louis is most striking in the winter. When all the surrounding mountains are covered with snow, Louis' vertical cliffs remain bare and make a dramatic contrast.

Edith, Louis and Fifi were all named one day in 1886 when Canada's first prime minister, Sir John A. Macdonald, and his wife were making a cross-country trip on the recently completed Canadian Pacific Railway. Louis Stewart, the park superintendent's son, took Lady Macdonald's attendant, Edith Orde, and her dog Fifi hiking to Edith Pass, which provides a view of the three peaks. Later a park surveyor named them after the two hikers and the dog.

There are many mountains in the Rockies named after people but this may be the only one officially named after a dog. In 1911 a bulldog named Hoodoo, even though he had to be hauled up the final cliffs by a rope, reached the summit of a mountain near Snake Indian Pass in Jasper National Park and was honoured by having the peak named after him. Sadly, the name was never officially adopted and the peak was named Monte Cristo Mountain in 1934, although no one knows why.

The view of Mount Louis and Mount Fifi is framed by **Mount Norquay** (2522 m) to the left and the lower slopes of **Cascade Mountain** (2998 m) to the right. John Norquay made the first ascent of the peak that carries his name. He was premier of Manitoba from 1878 until 1887.

Stoney Squaw Mountain (1868 m) is the low rounded feature in front of Mount Norquay. According to Ernest Ingersoll who wrote the *Canadian Guide Book* in 1892, the name honours an elderly Assiniboine woman whose husband lay ill for several months in their lodge at the base of the mountain. It is said she hunted sheep on and near the peak to sustain him as he recovered.

Mount Louis. Photo Don Beers.

Conrad Kain: "A Mountain Guide of Rare Spirit"

Of all the mountain guides who came to Canada in the late nineteenth and early twentieth centuries, Conrad Kain is probably the most famous. His autobiography entitled *Where the Clouds Can Go*, is a classic of Canadian mountain literature and tells the story of an early, difficult life in Austria, that was transformed when he came to Canada in 1909 to lead climbs at the Alpine Club of Canada's Lake O'Hara camp.

Although credited with 50 first ascents, including Mount Louis, his most significant was Mount Robson, the highest peak in the Canadian Rockies and one of the most spectacular mountains in the world, which he climbed in 1913 with Albert MacCarthy and William Foster.

Although renowned as a leader, climber and storyteller, Conrad Kain's personal attributes were the qualities for which he was most respected. A measure of the character of the man is the fact that he attempted to give credit to Donald "Curly" Phillips and the Reverend George Kinney for the first ascent of Mount Robson even while some were asserting that they had not quite reached the summit of Mount Robson in 1909 and that Kain's climb in 1913 should be regarded as the first ascent.

Mount Kain, a peak to the southeast of Mount Robson, honours his efforts on this mountain and many others.

As a professional mountain guide, Conrad Kain laid out the methods by which a guide should gain and maintain the confidence of his party: "First, he should never show fear. Second, he should be courteous to all, and always give special attention to the weakest member in the party. Third, he should be witty, and able to make up a white lie on short notice, and tell it in a convincing manner. Fourth, he should know when and how to show authority; and, when the situation demands it, should be able to give a good scolding to whomsoever deserves it."[139]

Sadly, Conrad Kain died at a young age, just six months after his fiftieth birthday. On that day he completed his last difficult climb, another ascent of Mount Louis. In a letter to Charles Thompson, the respected outfitter, Jimmy Simpson, wrote, "Conrad gave every ounce of his best at all times. He would die for you, if need be, quicker than most men think of living. No matter what his creed, his colour, or his nationality, he was measured by a man's yardstick, no other. We shall all miss him."[140]

Conrad Kain's gravestone carries the inscription, "A mountain guide of rare spirit."

Conrad Kain. Courtesy Whyte Museum, V14 AC192 P/4.

Cascade Mtn. · Palliser Range · Mt. Aylmer · Lake Minnewanka Valley · Mt. Inglismaldie · Mt. Girouard · Mt. Peechee · Mt. Ch... · Ste...

23 The View to the East

From Whiskey Creek meadows

Highway 1, 2.4 km east of the Mount Norquay junction; 1.6 km west of the easternmost access to Banff townsite.

Because three major valleys converge at Whiskey Creek meadows, it provides a number of excellent views including this panorama of the peaks to the east. The Cascade Valley approaches this area from the left, Lake Minnewanka lies in the valley directly ahead and the Bow River and the Trans-Canada Highway turn to the right and pass below the peaks on the right side of this panorama.

To the left, beyond the steep slopes of nearby **Cascade Mountain** (2998 m), the **Palliser Range** reaches its southern limit in mountains that descend to the valley containing Lake Minnewanka. **Mount Aylmer** looms beyond nearer, unnamed high ridges. At 3162 m, the peak rises over 300 m higher than any of the other mountains on the north side of the lake, its frequent snow cover testifying to this fact.

Mount Inglismaldie (2964 m), **Mount Girouard** (2995 m) and **Mount Peechee** (2935 m) form a massive interconnected group that is the northern end of the Fairholme Range lying immediately south of Lake Minnewanka.

George A. Stewart was superintendent of Rocky Mountains Parks, which later became Banff National Park. He named Mount Inglismaldie after the castle of the same name in Kincardineshire, Scotland, the ancestral home of the Earl of Kintore, who had visited this area in the 1880s.

Mount Girouard is the highest and most spectacular peak of the three. Having towers visible on the south side of the summit, it would seem to be the peak most castle-like. However, it was named 20 years later than Inglismaldie in honour of Colonel Sir Eduard Percy Girouard who was a railway builder in Africa during the expansion of the British Empire in the last decades of the nineteenth century. He was born in Montreal and was a graduate of the Royal Military College at Kingston.

The southernmost peak of the group is Mount Peechee. George Simpson, the first non-native to visit the Banff area, named the lake now known as Minnewanka after Peechee, the Métis who guided him through the mountains and along its shores in 1841. Some four decades later Dr. George Dawson noted that "Peechee Lake" had not appeared on maps and was not being recognized and decided to transfer the name to the mountain that rises above the midpoint of the lake.

A portion of **Mount Charles Stewart** (2809 m) may be seen above the trees at the right end of this panorama. This peak rises directly above Harvie Heights, just to the east of the park gates. Charles Stewart was the premier of Alberta from 1917 to 1921 and later became a cabinet minister in the federal government. The mountain is one of a very few in which both the first and last name of the individual are attached to the feature. There was already a Mount Stewart when it was determined, in 1928, that Mr. Stewart should be honoured. The authorities are reluctant to apply the same name to more than one mountain and perhaps appropriate political connections were made use of to bend the rules somewhat and allow Charles Stewart to have his mountain.

Bow River Rerouting

As one leaves this viewpoint travelling eastward, the highway turns gently to the left and it appears that the natural place for both it and the Bow Valley to go is to the left of Mount Inglismaldie and into the valley now occupied by Lake Minnewanka. Instead, both the highway and the Bow River make an abrupt 90 degree turn to the right.

It is believed that prior to the last major Ice Age some 20,000 years ago, the Bow River did in fact flow to the left of Mount Inglismaldie, through the valley now occupied by Lake Minnewanka and out into the foothills, following the route of the present Ghost River.

During the Ice Age the flow of a huge glacier through the valley, probably 2,000 ft. thick, would have undoubtedly made some major changes to the topography of the area. Then, as the glaciers receded, large amounts of debris would have been deposited at various points in the valley. It is theorized that a large moraine was left in the Minnewanka Valley that blocked the flow of the ancestral Bow River. A huge lake was then formed that eventually flowed into the valley occupied by the present-day Bow River. The Bow has since eroded the valley deeper into its present form.

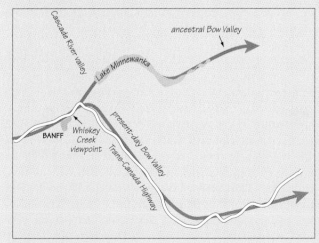

Major valleys near the Whiskey Creek meadows viewpoint.

Cascade Mountain

On August 15, 1858, the Palliser Expedition reached, "a beautiful little prairie at the base of the 'Mountain Where the Water Falls,' or the Cascade Mountain."[141] The "beautiful little prairie" became known as Whiskey Creek meadows and the mountain kept its name of Cascade, the peak most associated with the town of Banff. The waterfall is still flowing and the meadow, although not as peaceful a setting as it once was, looks much the same as it did when James Hector camped here.

Cascade Mountain looms over the meadow, so this is not the best spot from which to see the entire mountain. Probably the most photographed view is from Banff townsite itself where Banff Avenue seems to have been positioned to line up with the mountain.

While climbing the lower 600 m of Cascade Mountain, Hector enjoyed seeing various species of mountain wildlife, some of which he probably had not seen before. He recorded in his journals that a hummingbird flew against his face, that he was startled by a "flock of white objects (mountain sheep) darting away,"[142] that "among the blocks of rock the siffleurs [marmots] kept whistling in a very loud shrill note,"[143] and that he observed pikas, "one of the most comical animals I have seen…. It sits up on its hind legs and calls its note in the most impudent fashion."[144]

Pika. Photo Don Beers.

Cascade Mountain from the summit of Mount Rundle.

Mt. Rundle — Tunnel Mtn. — Sulphur Mtn. — Sanson Peak — Sundance Range — Eagle Mtn. — Healy Creek — Mt. Bourgeau

24 The View to the West

From Whiskey Creek meadows

Highway 1, 2.4 km east of the Mount Norquay junction; 1.6 km west of the easternmost access to Banff townsite.

Together with Cascade Mountain, all the peaks that form the left portion of this panorama surround the town of Banff.

View from Tunnel Mountain of Banff. Mount Bourgeau in the distance. Photo Gillean Daffern.

Mount Rundle (2846 m) is one of the classic mountains of the Canadian Rockies and the Trans-Canada Highway offers several spectacular views of it. One of the best is from Whiskey Creek meadows. Looming at the left edge of this panorama, the long, evenly sloped northwest ridge rises majestically to the mountain's summit overlooking the Bow Valley southwest of Banff.

The Bow River passes between Mount Rundle and the steep eastern cliffs of **Tunnel Mountain** (1692 m). This innocent looking mountain and these cliffs have been the scene of several tragedies involving people who walk up the easy trail from the townsite, then become careless while looking to the east and south from the clifftops.

When viewing this attractive little mountain from Whiskey Creek meadows, its resemblance to a resting buffalo is obvious. The name "tunnel" was derived from an incident that Charles Shaw, one of the surveyors for the Canadian Pacific Railway, considered to be one of the most extraordinary blunders in the history of his profession. A preliminary survey conducted through the Bow Valley assumed it would be best if the railway followed the river. Noting the difficulties associated with river crossings and the steep cliffs between the mountain and the northwestern edge of Mount Rundle, they recommended a tunnel. They failed to notice that if the railway simply passed around the northern slopes of the little mountain, there was nothing to hinder construction.

A favourite of many, Tunnel Mountain was ascended by James Outram in 1900 prior to his first ascents of higher and more challenging peaks such as Mount Assiniboine and Mount Columbia. He was most impressed, writing that, "the view will

Mount Rundle

"Mount Rundle is my bread and butter mountain. I never tire of painting it, for it is never the same. In deep shadow in the morning, it borrows a warm glow from the setting sun at the end of the day. Its colour runs the gamut from orange to cold blue-grey, with overtones of violet and intervals of green,"[145] wrote Walter Phillips.

Clearly a favourite with this famous artist who was known for his watercolours and coloured woodcuts, this classic peak is perhaps the most recognized mountain in the Canadian Rockies and has probably been on more calendars than any other. The viewpoint from which most photographs are taken is five km to the west with Vermilion Lakes in the foreground.

From Whiskey Creek meadows there is an excellent view of the rock layers that form its northeastern cliffs. Some "textbook" geology is very clearly defined. The layers that form the steep limestone cliffs at the top of the peak were named after the mountain itself and are known as the Rundle formation. Of Mississippian age, they were formed about 330 hundred million years ago. Below the Rundle, the gently-sloping layers of more easily eroded shale were named Banff Shale after the town below. The limestone cliffs below the Banff are Devonian in age. Known as the Palliser and Fairholme formations, they are made of limestone formed 350 million years ago. The Mississippian and Devonian rocks were carried along the Rundle Thrust Fault that lies below the Devonian and above the Cretaceous and Jurassic rocks, which are of a considerably younger age.

Mount Rundle is really a small mountain range, stretching southeast for some 12 km from the point one sees in this viewpoint to Whiteman's Gap above the town of Canmore.

Reverend Robert Rundle was one of Banff's earliest visitors. He passed below the mountain twice during the nine years he spent doing missionary work amongst the Cree and Assiniboine Indians during the 1840s. Becoming very involved in native culture, he learned to speak Cree and even wrote hymns in the language. James Hector originally chose a descriptive name for the peak, Terrace Mountain. But John Palliser, who had noted the influence of Rundle's work in the behaviour of the natives, was so impressed with the missionary that he decided instead to name the mountain in honour of Reverend Rundle.

The mountain was first climbed in 1888 by J. J. McArthur during his survey of the Bow Valley area.

Mount Rundle from Vermilion Lakes. Photo Don Beers.

Reverend Rundle. Courtesy Glenbow Archives, NA-659-43.

Mount Bourgeau

Eugene Bourgeau. Courtesy Saskatchewan Archives Board.

The view to the west from Whiskey Creek meadows features an outstanding peak described by James Hector as, "a truncated mountain, evidently composed of massive horizontal strata."[146] He named it for his colleague and friend, Eugene Bourgeau. The peak dominates the view enjoyed by those travelling west on the Trans-Canada Highway through the meadows.

The Bow Valley turns abruptly to the northwest at the foot of Mount Bourgeau and it is at this point that more snow begins to accumulate on the mountains. During early summer months, the summit cliffs of Bourgeau, seen rising behind a lower ridge, are often still covered with the previous winter's snow.

Eugene Bourgeau was the botanist on the Palliser Expedition of 1857-1860, his career having begun with his love of flowers in the French Alps where he tended his father's herds. Sir William Hooker, the first director of Kew Gardens in London, had received many specimens from distant lands through Bourgeau's work and referred to him as a "prince of botanical collectors."[147] It was on his recommendation that Bourgeau became a member of the Palliser Expedition. He was not a disappointment. Over his two years with the expedition he collected specimens from 819 species as well as a great quantity of seeds.

When Bourgeau left the expedition in 1859 to fulfill a previous commitment in London and in the Caucasus, he had obviously made an impression with Palliser and other members of the expedition. Palliser wrote that Bourgeau was, "always hard at his work in which his whole soul seems engrossed, and no matter what his fatigues or privations may be, his botanical specimens are always his first care. We were very sorry indeed to lose our friend, who was a great favourite with us all. In addition to his acquirements as a botanist, he united the most sociable, jovial disposition, ever ready not only to do his own work, but assist anyone else who asked him."[148]

Right: Mount Bourgeau from Vermilion Lakes.

Below: Mount Bourgeau summit, looking down on Whiskey Creek meadows. Photo Gillean Daffern.

never be forgotten."[149] But the person to remember most when looking at Tunnel Mountain is Anne Ness who climbed to the top most days for 40 years, totalling over 8,000 trips.

Nearly all of the 10 km-long ridge of **Sulphur Mountain** (2451 m), including **Sanson Peak** (2256 m) on its northern end, is visible from Whiskey Creek meadows. Hardly an outstanding peak, its claim to fame is the amount and variety of development that has occurred on its slopes and summits.

The hot springs that flow from its northeastern slopes are the source of its name and also prompted the creation of Rocky Mountains National Park, the forerunner to Banff National Park, and the Canadian national parks system. In 1875 two American fur hunters, Willard Younge and Benjamin Pease, spent a few weeks at Morley where the natives told them of the springs and gave them directions. After noticing a plume of steam rising above the spruce trees, they became the first non-natives to visit the site. Ten years later, when it appeared that the springs were to be exploited by a trio of entrepreneurs, Prime Minister John A. Macdonald created the world's third national park, not to protect the splendid natural environment that we think of today as Banff National Park, but rather that, "proper control of the lands surrounding these springs may be vested in the Crown"[150] and "reserved from sale or settlement or squatting."[151] Today, the Sulphur Mountain gondola takes visitors to the summit of the ridge from near the site of the hot springs.

In 1903, what is now known as Sanson Peak was chosen as the site for a weather observation facility. Norman Sanson was a meteorologist associated with the Banff Museum from 1896 until 1931. As part of his duties he climbed the mountain every week or two, a large contingent of Banff residents accompanying him on his one thousandth trip in 1931. In 1945, at the age of 83, he climbed the mountain to observe a solar eclipse from his favourite location.

In 1956, one of the more noticeable scars in Banff National Park was created by the construction of a road up the western slope of Sulphur Mountain to the summit of Sanson Peak. The location had been chosen by the National Research Council as the site of a cosmic ray research station that was later taken over by the University of Calgary and operated until 1978.

Beyond the slopes of Sulphur Mountain the northern end of the **Sundance Range** descends into the Bow Valley beyond Sundance Creek. It is thought that the native Indians used to perform rituals on the plateau above the falls on Sundance Creek.

Eagle Mountain (2820 m) may be seen beyond the lower slopes of the Sundance Range and to the left of the Healy Creek

valley where the mountain skyline actually descends into the forest. Healy Creek flows directly toward us from its headwaters eight km beyond **Mount Bourgeau** (2930 m). The access road to the Sunshine ski area lies in this valley.

Healy Creek was named by George Dawson after Captain John Jerome Healy, a multi-talented American who served in the Union Army during the Civil war. He entered Canada and operated the infamous Fort Whoop-Up prior to the arrival of the Northwest Mounted Police. After returning to the United States to become a sheriff in Montana, he reentered Canada and began prospecting in this area of the Rockies. Later he moved to Dawson City and operated a fleet of steamboats on the Yukon River.

From Whiskey Creek meadows, the Trans-Canada Highway heads southwest to the foot of Mount Bourgeau, where it turns almost 90 degrees around the southeastern end of the Sawback Range and begins travelling parallel to, rather than across, the trend of the ranges. An unnamed peak rises to the right of Mount Bourgeau and further views are cut off by the lower slopes of Mount Norquay.

Sulphur Mountain gondola. Photo Gillean Daffern.

Norman Sanson (front row, left) and friends at the weather station on Sanson Peak, 1931. Courtesy Whyte Museum, NA-66-1855.

Mt. Bell · Mt. Babel · Taylor Pass · Panorama Ridge · Mt. Temple · Haddo Peak · Mt. Niblock · Fairview Mtn. · Mt. St. Piran · Bath Glacier · Mt. Daly · Mt. Balfour · Waputik P

25 Mount Temple and Peaks of the Bow Valley

From Castle Junction

Highway 1 from the overpass at the junction with Highway 93.

The Haddo Snow Spot.

As you travel between Banff and Lake Louise, pause at Castle Junction to enjoy this view, which is dominated by Mount Temple, the highest peak in the Lake Louise area. The panorama also features Bath Glacier and a distant view of the glacier-draped Mount Balfour, an indication that, if you are travelling from the east, you are approaching the series of icefields that follow the Continental Divide from Lake Louise to Jasper.

The nearest mountain in this panorama is **Mount Bell** (2910 m), which lies immediately north of Boom Lake. The valley containing Consolation Lakes lies beyond the peak and it was during the 1910 Alpine Club of Canada camp in that valley that the name was chosen. Miss Nora Bell was a member of an ACC party that made the first ascent of the mountain during the camp.

Taylor Pass lies between Mount Bell and **Panorama Ridge** (2824 m). Through the pass one glimpses **Mount Babel** (3101 m), which stands at the eastern end of the Valley of the Ten Peaks above Moraine Lake.

Anyone who has walked along the long ridge known as Panorama Ridge will agree that this feature is aptly named. The views in all directions are outstanding.

Looming beyond Panorama Ridge is the peak that dominates the Lake Louise-Moraine Lake area, **Mount Temple** (3543 m). During the early 1880s, when the town of Silver City was thriving in the meadows near this viewpoint, the peak was referred to as Mount Lefroy. The confusion regarding the names of peaks in the Lake Louise area was straightened out by George Dawson in 1884.

Beyond Mount Temple rises **Haddo Peak** (3070 m). During the summer the mountain displays a distinctive circle of snow on slopes that can be seen from this viewpoint. The "Haddo Snow Spot" remains large and quite prominent into mid-August. Lord George Haddo was the eldest son of the Marquis of Aberdeen. Mount Aberdeen, 80 m higher, is adjacent to Haddo Peak but from this angle is hidden behind Mount Temple.

To the right of Haddo Peak, a twin-peaked outlier of Mount Temple forms the skyline.

Mount Niblock (2976 m) and **Fairview Mountain** (2744 m) appear close together. Fairview Mountain, however, rises on the other side of Lake Louise from Mount Niblock and **Mount St. Piran** (2649 m).

The smoothly-contoured Fairview Mountain was a favourite of the early mountaineers who often used it as a warm-up for their more serious climbs. A broad, vertical stripe of snow seen in early summer would have made the mountain very distinctive on the approach to Laggan (as Lake Louise Station was known at the time). In his book *The Glittering Mountains of Canada*, J. Monroe Thorington, one of these early mountaineers wrote, "When the train had passed the square-topped tower of Pilot Mountain, it was always Fairview that we looked for. We learned to recognize its outlines far away; long before Storm Mountain and the wooded saddle of Vermilion Pass were near; long before the opening of the Valley of the Ten Peaks drew our eyes to the towering heights of Deltaform and Neptuak and Temple. Perhaps it was only because we knew the little mountain so well; but little heights always affect the mountain-lover in such fashion. A small peak as a rule is the best viewpoint because there is still something left to look up to.... And so it is with Fairview. Year after year we have come back to it; perhaps as a convenient training walk, but more likely on account of the sheer beauty with which it is surrounded."[152]

In the distance the long ridge of **Mount Daly** (3152 m) is 45 km from the viewpoint. Charles Fay suggested the name in 1898 to honour Joseph F. Daly, president of the American Geographic Society. Dr. Fay went on to make the first ascent of the peak in 1903.

Bath Glacier, which lies below Mount Daly, is the first icefield that can be seen when approaching the mountains from the east. This glacier is significant in that it is the southernmost extent of what is a nearly continuous series of icefields and glaciers that stretch north to Jasper townsite. In 1967 Don Gardner, Chic Scott, Neil Liske and Charlie Locke made a ski traverse from the Yellowhead Pass to Kicking Horse Pass using these icefields and glaciers. This pioneering trip took 21 days and has only been repeated by one other party.

Beyond the northern slopes of Mount Daly, the northern slopes of **Mount Balfour** (3272 m) may just be seen if one looks carefully. Binoculars are helpful. A massive, ice-draped peak, Mount Balfour lies seven km beyond Mount Daly. It is the highest peak of the Waputik Range that lies between the Yoho Valley and the Upper Bow Valley to the north of the Trans-Canada Highway. Although this distant view is intriguing, the mountain is best seen from the Hector Lake viewpoint on the Icefields Parkway, 18.8 km north of the Trans-Canada Highway.

It is interesting to note that Mount Balfour is the first peak on the Continental Divide to be seen whether one is approaching the interprovincial border from the east or the west on the Trans-Canada Highway. When travelling from Banff, the mountain becomes visible about eight km east of Castle Junction. If approaching the Divide from the west it is part of the Ottertail Creek bridge panorama, 8.8 km west of Field.

It was named by James Hector of the Palliser Expedition after his mentor Professor John Hitton Balfour, who was both a professor of botany at Glasgow University and the dean of the medical school at the University of Edinburgh. Dr. Balfour had provided considerable encouragement and support to the expedition.

Waputik Peak (2736 m) lies near the southern end of the Waputik Range, which forms the western side of the Bow Valley from Lake Louise to Hector Lake. George Dawson chose the name because of the great numbers of mountain goats seen on its slopes. Waputik is the Stoney word for white goat.

Top: A portion of the panorama from Panorama Ridge (l-r) Mount Tuzo, Deltaform Mountain, Neptuak Mountain, Curtis Peak, Wenkchemna Peak, Mount Hungabee, Eiffel Peak.

Bottom: Glacier-draped Mount Balfour in winter from Bow Peak.

Mount Temple

Mount Temple. Photo Don Beers.

Clearly the most massive and the highest of the mountains of the Lake Louise area, Mount Temple is the first of the high peaks near the Continental Divide that one sees driving west along the Trans-Canada Highway. The view of the mountain from the vicinity of Castle Junction was described by Walter Wilcox in an account of the first ascent read to the Appalachian Mountain Club in Boston on March 12, 1895. "One who travels west from Banff up the valley of the Bow will see in front of him, shortly after leaving Cascade Siding, a tall helmet-shaped peak rising in a series of inaccessible cliffs to a snow tipped summit. But it is not until Laggan is reached, and the western face of the peak is seen—now to the southeast—that its height or beauty is adequately realized, although from all points it dominates the landscape."[153]

From the Bow Valley the mountain offers three quite different views to the traveller, each of which features huge, steep cliffs. The view from Castle Junction makes clear the fact that this is a mountain different in height and character from those to the east. Rising another 719 m above Panorama Ridge, Mount Temple reaches an elevation of 3543 m. As well, its rock appears darker and more purplish and its upper cliffs are always highlighted by snow. From the Moraine Creek bridge on the Trans-Canada Highway—a most impressive viewpoint even though the summit cannot be seen—the mountain appears at its narrowest.

The view from Lake Louise is the classic one of Mount Temple and, again quoting from Wilcox's speech of March 12, 1895, "From a base fifteen hundred feet higher than Laggan, this western face rises in one unbroken wall of nearly four thousand feet. A plateau above the latter is occupied by a magnificent area of glacier and neve, sweeping down in curving folds from the summit to the top of the wall, while the overhanging seracs above, and the fine powder on the scattered ledges below tell of many a thundering avalanche of ice. This is Mount Temple."[154]

In 1894, Walter Wilcox, Samuel Allen and L. F. Frissel made the first ascent of Mount Temple utilizing the southwest ridge. Despite the mountain's inaccessible appearance from the various viewpoints in the Bow Valley, this so-called "Tourist Route" is so easy that Ken Jones, the first Canadian-born alpine guide, claims it is possible to lead a milk cow to the top. Ken is of course joking, but technically it is an easy climb. However, there are risks involved both from falling rock and, if the route is lost, steep cliffs and avalanches. In 1955 seven people were killed on this route in Canada's most costly mountaineering accident. The cliffs of the north face were not climbed until the 1960s.

The mountain was named by George Dawson in honour of Sir Richard Temple, an economist who was the leader of a "British Association" field trip to the Canadian Rockies in 1884. Primarily interested in India, this was Sir Richard's only visit to Canada. Dr. Dawson was working in the area during 1884, but it is not known whether the two met. Perhaps they did and somehow Sir Richard made an impression on Dawson, who then chose to name one of the most spectacular peaks in the area in his honour.

Mt. Babel · Mt. Bident · Mt. Quadra · Mt. Fay (east ridge) · Mt. Fay (west ridge) · Tower of Babel · Mt. Little · Mt. Bowlen · Tonsa · Mt. Perren · Mt. Allen · Mt. Tuzo · Deltaform Mtn.

Consolation Lake valley

26 The Valley of the Ten Peaks

"Not even Lake Louise can boast of so noble a galaxy of guardian mountains as is furnished by the range of the Ten Peaks and the craggy and imposing pile of Mount Temple."[155] *Hugh Stutfield and Norman Collie were on horseback and obviously took the time to savour this outstanding view when they passed this way in 1902. These days, most visitors travelling the road are anxious to get to Moraine Lake, but it is well worth the time to stop here and enjoy the panorama of a dozen high peaks tightly packed into a narrow viewing angle. Consolation Valley lies below the peaks on the left side of the view and the Valley of the Ten Peaks, with Moraine Lake, lies in the valley to the right. Mount Temple rises immediately behind the viewpoint.*

Mount Bident (3084 m) and **Mount Quadra** (3173 m) rise from a spectacular glacier lying above steep cliffs at the southern end of the valley containing Consolation Lakes. Mount Bident's name is derived from the peak's similarity to a double tooth. Mount Quadra's name is also descriptive, and refers to its four individual tops along the summit ridge.

Featuring a spectacular, near vertical east face, **Mount Babel** (3101 m) takes its name from a pinnacle called the **Tower of Babel** (2310 m), the top of which is over 700 m below the summit of the mountain. Mountaineer Walter Wilcox named the pinnacle because it reminded him of the story in the bible in which the Tower of Babel reached to the heavens. It was a huge rockfall from the Tower of Babel that formed the dam that holds back Moraine Lake. When Wilcox named the lake he thought the rocks had been carried forward by a glacial advance and left as a terminal moraine.

"Beyond the nearer range of mountains could be seen, through two depressions, a more distant range, remarkably steep and rugged, while one particularly high peak was adorned with extensive snowfields and large glaciers. No scene has ever given me an equal impression of inspiring solitude and rugged grandeur."[156] This was Walter Wilcox's reaction to his first look at the mountains in the **Valley of the Ten Peaks**. In 1894, his companion, Samuel Allen, had chosen to name the peaks from east to west using the numbers from the Stoney Indian language as follows: Heejee, Nom, Yamnee, Tonsa, Sapta, Shappee, Sagowa, Saknowa, Neptuak and Wenkchemna. A number of Stoney Indians had been hired to look after the horses used by Wilcox and his group and Allen must have learned the numbers from them. All but three of the peaks have subsequently been renamed to honour a variety of individuals. The first eight of this impressive lineup may be seen from the Moraine Lake viewpoint.

From the Moraine Lake road
9.3 km west of the Lake Louise road; 3 km east of the Moraine Lake parking lot.

The Tower of Babel. Photo Glen Boles.

Gertrude Benham, Professor Fay and the Kaufmann Brothers

Professor Charles Fay. Courtesy Whyte Museum, V14 ACOP-802.

Born in England, Gertrude Benham was reported to have made 130 ascents in the Alps before her only visit to the Canadian Rockies in 1904. Arriving in June, it was her intention to spend the summer climbing in the Rockies, then travel to New Zealand in October. She certainly had a busy summer.

With Hans and Christian Kaufmann as her guides she reached the summits of many of the major peaks in the Rockies including Victoria, Lefroy, Stephen, Assiniboine and Mount Balfour. Then she travelled to the Selkirks where she climbed a number of peaks including Mount Sir Donald.

Probably her most remarkable achievement was a day that saw Benham and the Kaufmann brothers setting out from Lake Louise at midnight, crossing Abbot Pass between Mount Lefroy and Victoria (2922 m), descending to Lake O'Hara, ascending Cataract Valley, then climbing to the summit of Mount Stephen (3199 m) by a previously unclimbed ridge. By lantern light they descended to the town of Field, arriving at 3:00 am. Thirty five km of travel involving a total elevation gain of a staggering 2800 vertical metres was involved in this very long (27 hours) day's effort.

An all-round lady, she also did embroidery and knitting, made her own clothes, painted and collected wildflowers. She died at sea at the age of 71 while returning from a solo trip across Africa.

By 1904, when the paths of Gertrude Benham and Charles Fay briefly crossed, the professor was already an established

mountaineer who had spent several successful seasons in the Rockies. Apparently the Geographic Board of Canada had asked Fay to select a mountain that he would like to be named in his honour. Heejee Peak (#1) in the Valley of the Ten Peaks was chosen and Professor Fay was determined to make the first ascent of the mountain that was to carry his name.

But Gertrude Benham had her eye on this spectacular peak as well. On July 19 she and Christian Kaufmann climbed the icy Hourglass Couloir between Peaks #3 and #4 and reached a summit that they took to be Heejee. Upon their return to Moraine Lake it was pointed out to them by Walter Wilcox that the mountain they had climbed was, in fact, not Heejee.

The determined Miss Benham and Christian Kaufmann resolved to again ascend the couloir and make the first ascent of Heejee the next day, but Professor Fay and Hans Kaufmann were planning to make the first ascent that day as well. Both parties set out, but Professor Fay and Hans Kaufmann found difficult snow conditions and rockfall on their route above Consolation Lakes and were forced to abandon the attempt. Meanwhile, Benham and Christian were successful.

Professor Fay was very annoyed with this turn of events, alleging later in a letter to Charles Thompson that he would likely have been able to complete the first ascent of his mountain had Hans Kaufmann not insisted on attempting the route via Consolation Valley. The Kaufmann brothers had a reputation for playing jokes. Whether or not they conspired to allow the lady to make the first ascent is not known, but if they did it is thought that Miss Benham was an innocent party to the conspiracy. Disappointed, Fay asked that he be honoured by the naming of a different mountain until he found out that his alternate mountain, Shappee, had already been climbed, again by Gertrude Benham and Christian Kaufmann. At this point the professor reluctantly accepted having his name attached to Heejee and completed the second ascent of the peak on August 5. His guides were not the Kaufmanns, but Christian Hasler and Frederick Michel.

It is interesting to note that Professor Fay's grandson completed the first ascent of the northeast ridge of Mount Fay in 1961.

Mount Fay. Photo Don Beers.

Although both sides of the upper portion of **Mount Fay** (3235 m) (#1) can be seen, the actual summit is hidden behind Mount Babel. Mount Fay features a beautiful, symmetric summit overlooking the Fay Glacier when viewed from the north. It was renamed in honour of Professor Charles Fay, a president of both the Appalachian Mountain Club and the American Alpine Club and one of the most distinguished mountaineers of the late nineteenth and early twentieth centuries. A professor of modern languages, Fay was one of a party of four attempting Mount Lefroy in 1896 when P. S. Abbot became the first mountaineer to be killed in the Canadian Rockies. Fay returned the next year to participate in the first ascents of both Mount Lefroy and Mount Victoria. He made a total of 25 trips from his home in the eastern United States to climb in the Canadian Rockies.

Mount Little (3088 m) (#2) and **Mount Bowlen** (3072 m) (#3) loom above the visitor at Moraine Lake. The thick edge of the Fay Glacier, which lies in front of Mounts Fay, Little and Bowlen, may be seen both from the lakeshore and from this viewpoint. George F. Little was a climber from Maine and made the first ascent of the mountain in 1901. He was with Charles Fay and P. S. Abbot when the latter was killed on Mount Lefroy. Honourable J. J. Bowlen was Alberta's lieutenant-governor during the 1950s and Peak #3 was named in his honour in 1958.

Tonsa Peak (3057 m) (#4), is one of the two mountains in the valley that has not been renamed. An ice-filled gully known to mountaineers as the 3-3.5 Couloir lies between Tonsa and Bowlen. In the past it was used by climbers to access the Neil Colgan Hut. After some accidents on this route it is no longer recommended.

In 1950, Walter Perren became one of the last two alpine guides brought to Canada from Switzerland by the Canadian Pacific Railway. In 1955 he joined the National Park Warden Service where he developed search and rescue methods and supervised training until 1959. Recognized as the father of modern rescue techniques in the Canadian Rockies, peak #5 (Sapta) was renamed **Mount Perren** (3051 m) in his honour.

Shappee Peak (#6) was renamed **Mount Allen** (3310 m) in 1924 after Samuel Allen who participated with Walter Wilcox and others in the early exploration of the Lake Louise-Moraine Lake area.

One of the first mountains in the Canadian Rockies to be named after a lady mountaineer is **Mount Tuzo** (3246 m) (#7), renamed in 1907. Miss Henrietta "Hettie" Tuzo was the first to climb this peak. A charter member of the Alpine Club of Canada, Miss Tuzo had climbed several peaks in the Rockies and Selkirks when she and guide Christian Kaufmann made the ascent in 1906.

They climbed the 3-3.5 Couloir, then crossed a snowfield behind peaks #4, #5 and #6 en route to the bottom of their peak. During the descent they narrowly avoided an avalanche as they watched it cover their tracks. Hettie's son, John Tuzo Wilson, became a well-known Canadian geologist, particularly in the area of continental drift and plate tectonics.

Only the tip of the highest peak of the 10 can be seen from the Moraine Lake road viewpoint. The mountain known originally as Saknowa was renamed **Deltaform Mountain** (3424 m) by Walter Wilcox in 1897 after he was impressed with the peak's similarity to the Greek letter Delta. The summit cliff features a thick horizontal band of light-coloured rock that contrasts with the darker colour of the rest of the peak.

Top: Mount Tuzo (left) and Deltaform Mountain from the Valley of the Ten Peaks. Photo Gillean Daffern.

Bottom: Tonsa, Mount Perren and Mount Allen from Moraine Lake. Photo Don Beers.

27 The Classic View of the Canadian Rockies

From Chateau Lake Louise

The entrance to the Victoria dining room.

Norman Collie. Courtesy Whyte Museum, V497 PA51-17.

"As God is my judge I never in all my explorations saw such a matchless scene,"[157] was how Tom Wilson recalled the day in 1882 when, accompanied by his Indian guide Gold Seeker, he became the first non-native to see this extraordinary view. With the exception of the recession of the Victoria Glacier, the view visitors enjoy over a century later hasn't changed.

Fairview Mountain (2744 m), which rises to the left of the lake, is one of the most climbed peaks in the Canadian Rockies. My only quarrel with the name is that the view from the summit is much better than just "fair." Ken Jones, the first Canadian-born alpine guide in the Rockies, often says that the best views aren't necessarily from the highest mountains and Fairview is a good example of this. When one considers that the other peaks in the panorama tower 720 m above Fairview Mountain and that Lake Louise lies over 1000 m below the summit, then the panorama from the Chateau is put into perspective. Fairview was originally named Goat Peak by Walter Wilcox and Samuel Allen who were among the first to explore the valleys and peaks in the Lake Louise area. Their native guide had pointed out goats on the mountain.

Mount Lefroy (3423 m) and **Mount Victoria** are the peaks that combine to make the backdrop to Lake Louise such a "matchless scene." At 3464 m, Mount Victoria is the higher of the two by 41 m. Both feature steep cliffs with large glaciers on their upper slopes.

General Sir John Henry Lefroy was an astronomer who was particularly interested in studying the magnetic declination from various locations in Canada. A mountain was named in his honour by James Hector of the Palliser Expedition in 1858, 24 years before Tom Wilson reached the shore of the lake. It appears, however, that Hector was referring to Mount Temple when he assigned the name Lefroy. When he reached the summit of Kicking Horse Pass from the British Columbia side, he would certainly have noticed Mount Temple and recognized it as one of the dominant peaks in the area, a mountain that seems to "stand alone." After some further confusion, during which the mountain that we now know as Mount Victoria was called Mount Lefroy, George Dawson named Mount Temple and formally attached the name Lefroy to the peak we see rising behind the shoulder of Fairview Mountain.

J. Norman Collie

The view from Chateau Lake Louise is dominated by Mount Victoria and Mount Lefroy, both of which were first climbed by parties that included this distinguished mountaineer who was clearly the epitome of the Victorian gentleman.

Born in 1859, Collie began his climbing career on the Isle of Skye, later making first ascents in the Alps and Caucasus, even climbing with a British expedition in the Himalaya. In 1897, when he accepted Professor Charles Fay's invitation to join the Appalachian Club for a summer of climbing in the Canadian Rockies, he was considered one of the most highly regarded British mountaineers.

The previous year Charles Fay had been one of four Appalachian Club members attempting Mount Lefroy when the first climbing fatality in the Canadian Rockies occurred, resulting in the death of Philip Abbot. Abbot's father had asked Professor Fay to make arrangements for a "Memorial Climb" the following year. The Alpine Club of London was asked to participate and were represented by Norman Collie and H. B. Dixon, together with guide Peter Sarbach. Exactly one year after the accident the party reached the summit. After a day's rest, Collie and Sarbach led the party that made the first ascent of Mount Victoria. Their route traversed the mountain's long summit arête from left to right.

Collie returned to the Canadian Rockies another five summers, making numerous ascents during exploratory trips into areas northwest of Lake Louise. In 1898 he and Hermann Woolley completed the first ascent of Mount Athabasca and from the summit were the first to see the Columbia Icefields. In 1903, Collie, together with his companion Hugh Stutfield, co-authored *Climbs and Exploration in the Canadian Rockies*, a book that is now considered to be a classic in literature related to the Rocky Mountains. His last visit was in 1911 when he made his 21st first ascent in the Canadian Rockies. Being the first to explore much of the Rockies, he took the opportunity to name in excess of 30 peaks.

Academically, Norman Collie was extremely successful, both as a respected teacher and as a researcher. He completed important work in organic chemistry and did extensive research in other fields of chemistry that resulted in the first fluorescent light and the taking of the first x-ray for medical diagnostic purposes. For this important work he was the recipient of numerous awards and honourary degrees.

His biographer, Dr. William Taylor, summarized Collie as "a fascinating character who excelled at science, mountaineering, exploration, geography, photography, art, and whatever else he turned his hand to."[158]

Top: Mount Victoria from Fairview Mountain. Photo Tony Daffern.

Bottom: The Mount Lefroy first ascent party, 1897. Courtesy Whyte Museum, V701-LC10.

Mount Whyte (left) and Mount Niblock from Mount St. Piran. Photo Gillean Daffern.

Lefroy and Victoria, then descend to Lake O'Hara. The portion of this route that lies below the overhanging glaciers of Mount Victoria was named "The Deathtrap" by early travellers because of the threat of avalanches. Today's visitors are often able to hear and in some cases see the avalanches from the Chateau.

The high ridge of Mount Victoria forms a part of the Continental Divide that continues to the north to **Mount Collier** (3215 m). Joseph Collier was a British physician who, together with his brother George, was guided to the summit in 1903 by Christian Kaufmann. Samuel Allen had previously referred to the peak as Mount Nichols after the Reverend H. P. Nichols, with whom he had climbed the mountain in 1893. To the right of Mount Collier, a somewhat more picturesque peak remains unnamed.

Mount Whyte (2983 m) and **Mount Niblock** (2976 m), which are connected by a high ridge, are both about 500 m lower in elevation than their neighbours on the Divide. They are quite striking from the Bow Valley below the lake but are most prominent when seen as the backdrop to Lake Agnes, which lies to the right of the appropriately named **Beehive** (2270 m). Sir William Whyte was a native of Scotland who held several positions with the CPR during the construction of the railway. John Niblock was the western superintendent for the CPR and, together with Whyte, was one of the earliest promoters of tourism in the Canadian Rockies. As a railway superintendent, John Niblock had some influence over the naming of the numerous stops on the various railways that were being built in western Canada during the late nineteenth century and named a stop on the line south of Calgary after his wife Clare. By 1895, when the boxcar at the site was replaced with a frame building, the stop had become well known as Clare's home or Claresholm.

The magnificent panorama from Chateau Lake Louise is completed by the smooth slopes of **Mount St. Piran** (2649 m) to the right. Willoughby J. Anstey, who was the first manager of Chateau Lake Louise, named Mount St. Piran after his birthplace on the north coast of Cornwall in southwestern England. Edward Whymper, the famous British mountaineer known for his first ascent of the Matterhorn, visited the summit and was so impressed with the view that he recommended building a path to the top. The **Little Beehive** (2210 m) rises below the eastern slopes of Mount St. Piran.

There is a good view of Mount Lefroy from the point where Hector's route from the pass would have reached the Bow River, but the peak is not as prominent as Mount Temple.

Mount Victoria is a long, high ridge featuring two summits one km apart. The southern peak is the highest, rising from the so-called "sickle" to its left. Both Lefroy and Victoria were first climbed in 1897 by parties led by the first alpine guide to climb in the Canadian Rockies, Peter Sarbach of St. Niklaus, Switzerland.

J. J. McArthur named the mountain in 1897 to honour Queen Victoria who reigned over the British Commonwealth and Empire for 64 years until her death in 1901. The mountain had previously been known as Mount Green after Reverend W. S. Green, a member of the British Alpine Club who visited the Rockies and the Selkirks in 1888. Green's book *Among the Selkirk Glaciers*, aroused much interest in the "Canadian Alps." It is said that Green's visit marked the birth of mountaineering in Canada.

Most of the hundreds of thousands of people who visit the area each year would be surprised to know there is a pass at the end of the apparent dead-end valley beyond the lake. Alpinists are able to follow the Victoria Glacier to Abbot Pass, which lies between

The Lake Louise Club

By 1890 the first small Chalet had been built near the shores of Lake Louise. In 1894 Yale College students Samuel Allen of Chicago, Walter Wilcox of Washington and three others paid 12 dollars per week for accommodation, meals, and the use of horses and a boat. Allen and Wilcox had visited the area before and had failed in attempts to climb Mount Victoria and Mount Temple. But they had big plans for the summer of 1894 and returned with a better equipped expedition that included other students from Yale. They referred to themselves as the Lake Louise Club and were bent on exploring, climbing and mapping in what was then uncharted wilderness.

Although some in the group were inexperienced in the techniques of mountaineering, they set out to climb Mount Lefroy. A large boulder was dislodged, striking Louis Frissell and seriously injuring him.

Following this near disaster, the club focused on lower-altitude explorations, during which they discovered Paradise Valley and Wenkchemna Valley (the Valley of the Ten Peaks). They also completed first ascents of two easier peaks, Mount Aberdeen and Mount Temple where, "Many a hearty cheer rent the thin air as our little party of three reached the summit, for we were standing where no man had ever stood before, and… at the highest altitude yet reached in North America north of the United States boundary."[159]

Despite the successful ascent of Mount Temple, the group's general inexperience had been demonstrated on Mount Lefroy and through the summer their limitations regarding glacier travel and cooking (one of the group is said to have claimed he could still remember one stomach ache 40 years later) led to other near disasters. But they persevered and when the club members returned to their homes in the eastern United States, they had explored over 100 sq. km of country around Lake Louise.

As well, the group named many of the lakes and mountains in the area, made a detailed map and measured the depth of Lake Louise. A major contribution was *Camping in the Canadian Rockies*, which was written by Walter Wilcox. The first major book about the Rockies, it was to inspire many others to explore and climb in the Canadian Rockies.

Bottom left: From left to right, Yandell Henderson, L. F. Frissell, G. H. Warrinton and Walter Wilcox. Courtesy Whyte Museum, NA 66-2251.

Bottom right: Samuel Allen at Opabin Pass. Courtesy Whyte Museum, V701 LC-4.

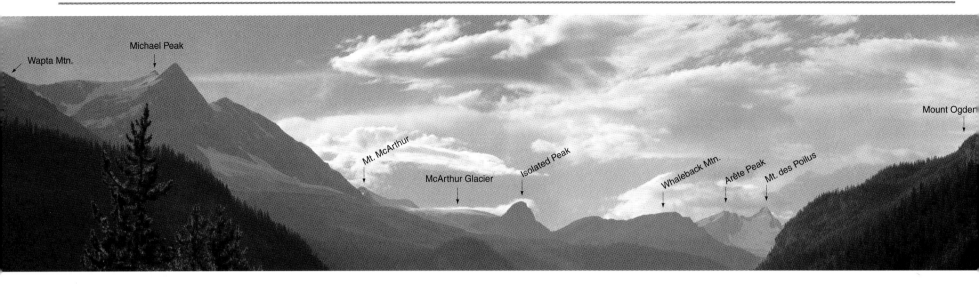

Wapta Mtn.

Michael Peak

Mt. McArthur

McArthur Glacier

Isolated Peak

Whaleback Mtn.

Arête Peak

Mt. des Poilus

Mount Ogden

28 A View into the Yoho Valley

From the Big Hill
The Spiral Tunnels viewpoint on Highway 1, 8.9 km west of the Alberta/British Columbia border; 7.7 km east of Field.

Spiral Tunnels map. Photo P. R. Howarth.

"The valley, as much as could be seen from the slope of the pass, offered a decidedly hostile and repellent aspect and apparently no one was ever sufficiently interested to endeavour to probe its mysterious depths."[160]—Trail to the Charmed Land *by Ralph Edwards*

In 1948 Dan McGowan wrote, "In that great chain known as the Canadian Rockies there are many lofty mountains but only one Big Hill."[161] These steep slopes, which form the western side of the Kicking Horse Pass, were a major challenge during the construction of the Canadian Pacific Railway and continue to cause difficulties even today. When the railway was first completed in 1884, the tracks headed straight down from the summit of the pass to Field at a grade of up to 4.5 per cent. The dangers inherent in this steep descent were recognized and three safety switches were incorporated and constantly manned to divert runaway trains and cars. In 1909 the tracks were realigned when the Spiral Tunnels were constructed, thus reducing the grade to 2.2 per cent. Although an additional 6.4 km of track was required, two locomotives could be used instead of four and the speed of the trains was able to increase from eight to 40 km per hour. The Trans-Canada Highway now follows, more or less, the route taken by the original railway line.

The tunnels, whose construction was an engineering marvel in the early part of the century, continue to fascinate visitors today. This viewpoint was built to allow visitors to watch the trains entering and leaving the lower tunnel, often at the same time.

But the eyes of mountain enthusiasts are invariably drawn beyond the railway to this wonderful view into the "mysterious depths" of the legendary Yoho Valley.

Train starting the descent from Kicking Horse Pass in 1898. Lantern slide by H. Woolley. Gillean Daffern collection.

J. J. McArthur

James Joseph McArthur was a Dominion land surveyor who worked in the Rockies from 1886 to 1893, completing a topographic survey of the mountains along the Canadian Pacific Railway's main line from Canmore to the summit of the Gold Range. He mapped 5000 sq. km at a scale of 1:20,000 with a contour interval of 100 ft. In the course of this detailed work, he made some of the earliest first ascents in the Rockies, including such well-known peaks as Rundle, Bourgeau, Stephen and the highest of the Three Sisters. In a single year, 1891, McArthur travelled some 640 km and ascended 43 peaks in excess of 2500 m. A bulky 20 lb. camera and 15 lb. transit were carried to each summit.

The ascent of Mount Stephen was one of McArthur's more challenging. He wrote of a 30 m ice-filled couloir near the top where he felt that a single slip would mean death and how worried he was as to how they would descend through this dangerous spot. When they finally reached the summit ridge they had to crawl along it to the highest point, almost 2000 m above the valley below. After this tremendous effort, smoke from forest fires prevented any photography.

A. O. Wheeler, a colleague of McArthur's who spent much of his professional life surveying the Continental Divide through the Rockies, wrote about him with the greatest of admiration. He noted the contrast between the great struggles and hardships endured during his summer-long surveys, in the most difficult of weather and over challenging terrain, and the brief, unassuming notes in the government record books describing his travels and accomplishments.

For many years J. J. McArthur was the authority on the Rockies west of Calgary. As well as Mount McArthur, a lake in the Lake O'Hara area—one of the most beautiful in the Rockies—was named in his honour.

J. J. McArthur, 1909. Courtesy National Archives of Canada, PA-42178.

Mount McArthur with McArthur Glacier at right.

Jean Habel

Jean Habel. Courtesy Whyte Museum, NA 35-3.

Arête Peak and Mount des Poilus. Photo Dr. John D. Birrell.

Ralph Edwards, Jean Habel's guide and outfitter in the Yoho Valley, wrote, "The professor was no meek follower in other men's footsteps. Not on your life! He believed in striking out for himself and, regardless of the opinion of others, following out his theories to their culmination in either victory or defeat."[162]

Inspired by views of what he named Hidden Mountain from the Big Hill in 1896, Jean Habel returned the following year to "explore the regions to a point as high as possible upon this peak."[163] A tall, dignified mathematics professor from Berlin, Habel was highly regarded in mountaineering circles. As well as making trips to the Canadian Rockies, he climbed and explored in the Alps and Andes, which were not extensively known at that time. Like some other European visitors, he had difficulty relating to the packers and outfitters he was forced to work with and depend upon.

Probably at the suggestion of Tom Wilson, he travelled to Emerald Lake and reached the Yoho Valley by way of Yoho Pass. The descent into the valley and indeed his entire 17-day exploration of it was limited by bad weather and difficult travelling conditions in the lush growth found on the western side of the Continental Divide.

Although in later years Tom Wilson vehemently insisted that he had reached the Yoho Valley on a prospecting trip in 1884, Habel is generally given credit for being the first to see Takakkaw Falls and certainly was the first to reach the head of the river and the Yoho Glacier. The party's first venture onto the glacier was interrupted when Fred Stephens, one of the outfitters, fell into a crevasse and had to be rescued. Two days later the group ascended the glacier again and succeeded in reaching an outlier of Mount Balfour. Although Habel's party was close enough for a good view of his Hidden Peak, they did not attempt to climb it, because Mount Balfour, apparently, had became the professor's new mountaineering focus. Short of provisions, the party abandoned their climbing plans and followed the Yoho River to its confluence with the Kicking Horse near the present-day Trans-Canada Highway.

In 1901 Habel returned to the Canadian Rockies and journeyed as far north as present-day Jasper National Park, becoming the first to reach the headwaters of the Athabasca River and see the north face of Mount Columbia. Unfortunately this trip, like his explorations in the Yoho Valley in 1897, was plagued by poor weather and he was unable to attempt the mountain.

Like many others, he became fascinated with Mount Columbia and during the following winter contracted with Tom Wilson to take him on an expedition to the peak via the Columbia River. However, Jean Habel died suddenly before he could return a fourth time to attempt the climb.

Takakkaw Falls. Photo Gillean Daffern.

In 1896, Jean Habel, a German mountaineer, was entranced by a distant, glacier-draped, pyramid-shaped peak "flashing and then disappearing in the distance"[164] as his train descended the Big Hill and like the thousands who have seen this view since, he was drawn to explore this magnificent valley. "The Yoho," as it is sometimes called, features spectacular, glacier-fed waterfalls the most well known being the 380 m-high Takakkaw Falls and the unique Twin Falls.

The lower slopes of **Wapta Mountain** (2778 m) are visible on the left side of the panorama. Lying immediately north of the ridge that contains the Burgess Shale fossil beds, it is one of the mountains that forms the backdrop to Emerald Lake. In summer the slopes below the cliffs are a bright green. The snow slides that keep them bare of trees descend all the way into the valley, leaving piles of snow next to the Yoho Valley road until mid-August.

"Wapta" is the Stoney word for river, but the meaning of the word has been ignored in the naming of features in Yoho National Park where there exists Wapta Lake, Wapta Icefield, Wapta Falls and Wapta Peak.

In the late nineteenth century the easiest access to the Yoho Valley was from Emerald Lake and through Yoho Pass, which lies just beyond Wapta Peak. Jean Habel passed this way when he became the first person to explore the valley in 1897.

Michael Peak (2696 m), rising beyond Yoho Pass, can be identified by a small snowfield lying on its southern slopes. On the opposite side of the mountain is a much larger glacier that lies along the northeastern side of the President Range. Michael Peak is unusual in that it isn't a peak at all according to the topographical maps, but simply a small high point from which the President Range begins its descent into Yoho Pass.

The distant **Mount McArthur** (3015 m) is a very special feature of this view, the mountain being just visible beyond the slopes of Michael Peak. You can't see the summit from the wooden walkway. Look for it from the mid-point of the parking area. The **McArthur Glacier**, which drapes the summit and extends for some distance to the east, is most impressive, dazzling white on sunny summer days.

Contrasting with Mount McArthur is the sharp, black profile of **Isolated Peak** (2845 m) that looms to the right of the glacier. When viewed from the upper part of the Yoho Valley, the mountain seems to stand alone, and this is the reason for its name.

British mountaineer Edward Whymper spent a considerable amount of time in the Yoho Valley, exploring, climbing and planning the trail system for the CPR. During one of his visits he named **Whaleback Mountain** (2627 m), the reason for his choice of name being understandable from the Big Hill viewpoint. Though not a high feature, the ridge forms the smooth skyline resembling the back of a whale to the right of Isolated Peak.

Mount des Poilus (3161 m), the mountain that caught Jean Habel's eye from the train in 1886, may be seen beyond and to the right of the Whaleback Mountain. Glacier des Poilus covers its southwestern slopes and an extensive area at its base. **Arête Peak** (2760 m) to the left of Mount des Poilus is a narrow ridge with steep slopes on both sides. The Interprovincial Boundary Commission assigned this name probably because they were impressed with the arête that connects the mountain with Mount des Poilus.

Jean Habel had named the mountain he saw from the train "Hidden Peak" because it seemed to disappear and then reappear as he descended the Big Hill in 1886. The following summer he spent 17 days exploring the Yoho Valley, in part attracted by the mysterious mountain. In 1900, Norman Collie named the peak Mount Habel in honour of the Yoho's first visitor who had died in the meantime. The name was not to stick.

One week following the armistice that ended the First World War, 11 peaks in the Kananaskis area were named after prominent French military leaders who had served during the conflict. *Les Annales*, a French publication, had suggested that one mountain be named, "for the great hero of the age, the humble and fascinating poilu"[165] (the lowest ranking soldiers of the French Army who had battled the invading Germans).

Arthur Wheeler was asked to recommend a peak and the fact that he chose to rename Mount Habel undoubtedly had something to do with the fact that Jean Habel was a German citizen. However, almost 70 years later Jean Habel's name was again placed on a mountain in the Canadian Rockies. Author Graeme Pole's suggestion that a peak on the Continental Divide just north of Yoho National Park be named Mount Habel was accepted by the authorities in 1987.

The slopes of **Mount Ogden** (2695 m) form the right side of the panorama. Within it the lower spiral tunnel loops some 887 m through the mountain with an elevation change of about 15 m.

Isolated Peak from Whaleback Mountain.

Tocher Ridge · Mt. Carnarvon · Mt. Marpole · Emerald Peak · The President · The Vice President · Michael Peak · Mt. Balfour · Mt. Burgess · Fossil Ridge · Mt. Field · Mt. Ogden · Mt. Dennis · Mt. Stephen · Mt. Duches

29 Mount Stephen and the Peaks above Emerald Lake

From the Ottertail River bridge

Highway 1, 8.8 km west of Field; 21.3 km east of the Yoho National Park boundary.

As the forests of the Kicking Horse Valley dip down into the Ottertail River, one is treated to a broad panorama of attractive peaks. For those travelling from the west, the view includes the first glimpse of a high peak on the Continental Divide, some 27 km to the east.

The reddish-tinged slopes of **Tocher Ridge** (2393 m) limit the view on the left side of the panorama. Interestingly, the Ottertail River flows between this ridge and Mount King at the southern end of the Van Horne Range to meet the Kicking Horse River on the opposite side of the valley from this viewpoint. The Amiskwi River flows in the valley to the right of Tocher Ridge from its headwaters at the northern tip of Yoho National Park.

Mount Burgess from Emerald Lake.

In 1919 a permanent warden staff was implemented for Yoho National Park, with preference given to servicemen returning from the First World War. One such was veteran Jock Tocher, who came to Field to visit his sister and fell in love with the mountains. He was in the first group of wardens, serving until his retirement in 1960. Remembered as a teacher and one who cared deeply about his job and the park, he was honoured with the naming of this ridge.

The peaks from **Mount Carnarvon** (3040 m) on the left to Mount Burgess on the right border a deep, wooded basin in which lies Emerald Lake, the largest lake in Yoho National Park. Flowing directly toward the viewer from the lake is the Emerald River, whose broad valley allows one to see almost to the base of the **President Range**.

The sharp spike that is Mount Carnarvon dominates the left side of the panorama, not because of its altitude but because it is four km nearer than the more distant peaks of the President Range. Named by James Hector as he led his party up the valley shortly after the kicking horse incident, it honours H. H. H. Molyneux, Earl of Carnarvon and undersecretary for the colonies at the time of the Palliser Expedition.

"Matterhorn"-shaped mountains are formed when glaciers carve bowl-shaped cirques into a mountain mass from three or more sides, leaving sharp, pyramidal-shaped peaks. Mount Carnarvon is one of the best examples of this type in the Rockies.

At an elevation of 2150 m, Hamilton Lake lies in the small, hanging valley between Mount Carnarvon and **Emerald Peak** (2545 m). An attractive unnamed peak and **Mount Marpole** (2997 m) lie beyond the ridge joining the two nearer mountains.

Emerald Peak, although part of the skyline from Ottertail River bridge, is a much lower mountain than any of the others in this panorama. It lies immediately northwest of Emerald Lake.

The high peaks of the President Range dominate the view at the head of Emerald Basin, a high valley beyond Emerald Peak and to the north of Emerald Lake. The snowy summit of **The President** (3138 m) is 136 m higher than **The Vice President** (3066 m), which is covered by the extensive Emerald Glacier. The high col connecting the two is known as President Pass.

Edward Whymper, of Matterhorn fame, was one of the first mountaineers to explore the area of Yoho Park to the north of the railway. He travelled to Canada as the guest of the Canadian Pacific Railway and in 1904, perhaps as a thank you, named The President after the railway's president, Thomas Shaughnessy and The Vice President after its vice president, David McNicoll. He also named Mount Marpole after Richard Marpole, an executive with the Canadian Pacific Railway at the time of his visits to the Rockies.

The barely noticeable high point at the southeastern end of the President Range is **Michael Peak** (2696 m). Whymper suggested the name in honour of his friend Arthur Michael, a chemistry professor from Boston who was a prominent member of the American Alpine Club and participated in the first ascents of Mount Lefroy and Mount Victoria in 1897.

In 1901, James Outram, led by guides Christian Kaufmann and James Pollinger, made the first ascents of The President and Vice President while completing a traverse of the President Range. At that time The President was known as Emerald Mountain and Michael Peak as Angle Peak.

One of the highlights of this panorama is the view through Yoho Pass to the massive **Mount Balfour** (3272 m) on the interprovincial border. The highest peak visible from Ottertail bridge, it lies 11 km beyond the pass. A small portion of the Waputik Icefield may be seen on the upper slopes of the mountain. Flowing out of this icefield is the Daly Glacier, which provides the water for Takakkaw Falls.

Mount Burgess (2599 m) was known informally as the "Ten Dollar Mountain" for a period of time when it became one of the best known peaks in the country. Beginning in 1954, this peak, with Emerald Lake in the foreground, was featured on the back of the 10 dollar bill. Seventeen years later its image was superseded by one of Sarnia's petrochemical plants. It forms the right side of the amphitheatre containing Emerald Lake and from this angle is much less attractive. A. M. Burgess was a deputy minister of the Interior.

Fossil Ridge connects Wapta Peak (hidden behind Mount Burgess) to **Mount Field** (2643 m), which lies immediately north of the town of Field. The Burgess Shale fossil beds have been

Mount Balfour.

The Vice President and President from the Whaleback. Photo Dr. John D. Birrell.

Mount Stephen from just west of the town of Field.

excavated from quarries on the ridge, which are located above the highest vegetation midway between the two peaks. The area has been declared a World Heritage Site.

Beyond Mount Field, the Yoho River flows from the north into the Kicking Horse River. Rising beyond the Yoho Valley, **Mount Ogden** (2695 m) is visible. The lower portion of the Spiral Tunnels loops within the mountain named for J. G. Ogden, a vice president and auditor with the CPR.

The two peaks at the right side of this panorama lie to the south of the Kicking Horse River. The nearest, **Mount Dennis** (2539 m), is only seven km away and was named in 1916 after Lt. Col. John S. Dennis, a surveyor who in 1869 was involved in igniting the Riel Rebellion.

The surveying of what the Métis felt was their lands was instrumental in their transfer to Canadian jurisdiction from the Hudson's Bay Company. Fearing the changes, the Métis formed a committee that was successful in halting the surveys, but then went on to seize Fort Garry. While a "List of Rights" prepared by Louis Riel was being discussed by both the English- and French-speaking people of Red River, Dennis and another Canadian put up armed resistance. They subsequently surrendered to Riel and were placed in prison while the Métis leader went on to form a provisional government. Dennis later became surveyor general of Canada and shortly before his death in 1885 was involved in mineral exploration near Castle Junction in Banff National Park.

In the distance and to the right of Mount Dennis one can see the spectacular southeastern summit ridge of **Mount Stephen** (3199 m) with its distinctive horizontal layering. This is the mountain that looms almost 2000 m above the town of Field.

George Stephen was a former president of the Bank of Montreal when he was named the first president of the Canadian Pacific Railway in 1881. The mountain was named in his honour in 1886. Mr. Stephen, in turn, was named Baron Mount Stephen in 1891, so in this case the mountain was named after the man and the man was named after the mountain.

The first ascent of Mount Stephen in 1887 was probably one of the most difficult of the many first ascents made by surveyor J. J. McArthur. Accompanied by his assistant T. Riley, he climbed the 1946 vertical metres burdened by heavy surveying equipment.

The lower slopes of **Mount Duchesnay** (2927 m) limit the views on the right side of this panorama. Edward J. Duchesnay was the assistant general superintendent of the CPR's western division. He surveyed a line for the CPR to the Yukon that was never built. He was killed by a rockfall in a tunnel near Spuzzum, BC in 1901.

Charles Walcott and the Fossils of the Burgess Shale

The first fossil bed in Yoho National Park is said to have been discovered by Otto Klotz who was working for the Canadian Pacific Railway. His discovery was made on the slopes of Mount Stephen. Later his fossils came to the attention of two geologists from the Geological Survey of Canada, George Dawson and R. G. McConnell. This, in turn, brought the news of the discovery to Charles D. Walcott, secretary of the Smithsonian Institute in the United States. Dr. Walcott was a leading authority on the paleontology of the Cambrian era and he decided to visit the site in 1907. The geology of the area, and in particular the fossils, fascinated him to the point where he worked in the Canadian Rockies every season until 1925.

The highlight of his career occurred in 1909 as he rode below the long ridge connecting Wapta Mountain with Mount Field. A block of shale had tumbled down the slope onto the trail and was blocking it. Walcott dismounted and was about to tip the slab out of the way but instead reached for his rock hammer and split the slab open. The fossils in this slab and thousands of others from the Burgess Shale formation have challenged the skills of paleontologists ever since.

The following year Walcott returned accompanied by his sons Stuart and Sidney, and together they examined all the layers on the ridge above the point where the original rock had been found, eventually finding the fossiliferous band.

For the next 30 days they quarried the shale and slid samples down the ridge to the trail where they were loaded onto packhorses and taken down to the CPR station at Field. Eventually some 65,000 specimens on 30,000 slabs of rock were delivered to the Smithsonian Institute.

Although Dr. Walcott spent a considerable amount of time at the quarry, he also travelled widely in other areas of the Rockies. Some of his numerous scientific publications feature spectacular panoramic photographs of mountains taken from passes or from high on mountain slopes.

Following his death in 1927, Walcott's samples, photographs and notes remained in storage until a new generation of paleontologists became interested in them in the late 1960s.

The key to the remarkable preservation of the animals of the Burgess Shale was the Cathedral Escarpment, a 150 m-high submarine cliff that existed in the seas covering this area 515 million years ago during the Cambrian era. Creatures of the era lived in the shallow water above the escarpment, but during major storms great quantities of mud and creatures were swept over the cliff to the bottom far below. At this level there was no light, little dissolved oxygen and virtually no life. The fossils were thus left undisturbed by scavengers. A second factor critical to the preservation of soft body parts was that carcasses were coated with a thin film of clay forced into all parts of the animal's body during the tumble down the escarpment. This covering inhibited the decomposition by bacteria.

Many of the creatures are unique and not related to any others known to have lived before or since. Among the more bizarre is Aysheaia, which is thought to have fed on primitive sponges of the era. Another, Opabinia regalis, was a fantastic five to 10 cm-long beast with five eyes and a mouth on the end of a long tube. It was propelled by paddle-like legs that allowed the animal to hover near the bottom of the sea floor.

The fossil beds have been declared a World Heritage Site by UNESCO, the United Nations Educational, Scientific and Cultural Organization.

In 1996, a prominent peak on Mount Burgess was named Walcott Peak to honour the geologist who decided to split that slab of shale that had fallen across the trail rather than just tipping it out of the way.

John Gibbon, Dr. Charles Walcott and Tom Wilson, 1924. Courtesy Whyte Museum, V701 LC-98.

(Top to bottom) Aysheaia, Opabinia and Leanchoilia. Drawing Ron Ellis.

30 Headwaters of the Ghost River

From Benchlands

Highway 940, 12.4 km northwest of the junction with Highway 1A.

Benchlands is a small community with an outstanding mountain view situated, suitably, on benches above the Ghost River. Beautifully framed between tree-covered foothills, the panorama features a variety of interesting front range mountains and one distant, beautiful and often snowclad peak.

Saddle Peak (2831 m) on the left side of the panorama is one of three peaks in the southern Rockies with this name. The most well known is a small mountain that overlooks the village of Lake Louise. A gentle "saddle-back"-shaped pass to the west of it inspired the earliest travellers in the area to name it in 1894. It even features a stirrup-shaped pattern of snow that lasts into the early summer. A second Saddle Mountain is located in the Livingstone Range west of Nanton. Much more saddlelike in shape, this small mountain has two summits of almost equal elevation separated by a smoothly contoured connecting ridge.

The Saddle Peak seen from Benchlands, however, was not named for its resemblance to a saddle at all, but rather because someone abandoned a saddle below the peak. Some years later in 1916 the saddle was found and the peak named.

Adjacent to Saddle Peak, **Orient Point** (2636 m) lies farther to the northeast, with the South Ghost River to the south and the Ghost River to its north. Although about 200 m lower in elevation, it seems to loom in front of the higher Saddle Peak. Marking the

most easterly extension of Banff National Park, it is geographically in quite a prominent location and was probably used to "orient" early travellers to the whereabouts of Devil's Gap, a well-known passage through the Front Ranges of the mountains. The fact that it is named a point rather than a mountain or peak is further evidence of its significance to early visitors.

The Ghost Lakes are located in Devil's Gap at the eastern end of the valley between Mount Costigan and Orient Point. Beyond lies the eastern end of Lake Minnewanka.

Mount Costigan (2980 m) is the dominant peak in the centre of the Benchlands panorama. It was named after the Honourable John Costigan, a New Brunswick parliamentarian and senator who often visited the area.

Right: Orient Point from the South Ghost. Photo Gillean Daffern.

George Simpson

Although not obvious from the Benchlands viewpoint, the route between Orient Point and Mount Costigan, and through the valley containing Lake Minnewanka, is a natural one from the prairies into the heart of the Rockies. In fact, the first European to visit the site of present-day Banff townsite travelled this way.

As governor of the Hudson's Bay Company, Sir George Simpson was probably the most powerful man in British North America at the time. He was combining business with adventure when he passed this way in August, 1841, with 22 men and 45 horses, for although Simpson was interested in expanding the HBC's fur empire, he was also on a trip around the world.

The party was guided by a Métis named Peechee who is commemorated by the peak that lies to the south of Lake Minnewanka's midpoint. Simpson wrote that his party was the first one composed of non-natives to travel this route into the mountains that is now known as Devil's Gap. He described the slopes adjacent to the valley as, "a gentle ascent of six or eight hundred feet, covered with pines, and composed almost entirely of the accumulated fragments of the adamantine heights above; and on the upper border of this slope there stood perpendicular walls of granite, of three or four thousand feet, while among the dizzy altitudes of their battlemented summits the goats and sheep bounded in playful security."[166]

Simpson's party continued on to what has become Banff townsite, built a raft to carry the horses and baggage across the Bow River, then travelled through the Continental Divide by way of what is now known as Simpson Pass. The party then followed the Columbia River to the Pacific Ocean. Reaching Asia, he crossed Siberia, Russia and Europe to complete his trip around the world.

George Simpson. Courtesy Glenbow Archives, NA-841-164.

Looking west into Devil's Gap toward the eastern end of Lake Minnewanka; Phantom Crag at right. Photo Gillean Daffern.

Devil's Head. Photo Gillean Daffern.

The most distant peak visible from Benchlands is part of the Palliser Range and lies to the right of, and 13 km beyond Mount Costigan. **Mount Aylmer** (3162 m) is an impressive, pyramid-shaped mountain and because it is almost 200 m higher than Mount Costigan, it often has snow cover when the nearer and lower peaks are bare. With an elevation of 3162 m, it is the highest peak north of the Bow River for a considerable distance. From the Benchlands viewpoint, a good portion of the mountain is visible because one is looking directly up the valley of the Ghost River, which takes a very straight route through 13 km of front range mountains.

Mount Aylmer is one of those few mountains that was named by the person who made the first ascent. As part of his professional duties as a surveyor, J. J. McArthur climbed the mountain in 1889 and officially named it in 1890 after his hometown of Aylmer, Quebec. Aylmer is located at Lac Deschenes on the Ottawa River, some 10 km southeast of Hull.

The most striking of the peaks seen from Benchlands is **Devil's Head** (2997 m). Its distinctive shape results from 250 m-high cliffs on the north, east and south sides combined with a fairly flat-topped summit. This creates a mountain that, consistent in profile, is easily identified from any easterly viewpoint. Following a snowfall, the near vertical cliffs remain black while the surrounding peaks are white, which makes this mountain even more eye-catching. Evidence of its prominence is the fact that the mountain and its name were mentioned several times in Peter Fidler's 1792 journal, the first peak to be referred to by name by a white visitor to the Rockies. The name Devil's Head is a translation of the Stoney Indian name based on the mountain's shape.

Black Rock Mountain lookout.
Photo Gillean Daffern.

W. S. Drewry, an assistant to J. J. McArthur, attempted to climb the mountain in 1891 while in the area surveying, but was turned back by the precipices below the summit. These challenging cliffs must surely have been noticed by all the early mountaineers as they journeyed by train to make first ascents in the more spectacular main ranges of the Rockies during the early part of this century. However, Devil's Head's somewhat isolated location and distance from the railway combined to delay the first ascent until 1925 when J. W. A. Hickson and L. S. Crosby, guided by Edward Feuz Jr., climbed the mountain from the west.

Although 324 m lower than Devil's Head, **Black Rock Mountain** (2910 m) appears to be its equal in elevation from this viewpoint. This is because Black Rock is located some eight km closer to Benchlands. This location is unusual because the mountain is not part of the general front range of the mountains, but rather rises alone some five km to the east with no other mountains to the north or south of it.

Black Rock Mountain's special location was noticed by the Alberta Forest Service when it was choosing locations for its initial series of fire lookouts during the late 1920s. A relatively high mountain set somewhat east of the main front range provides an ideal viewpoint of forested foothills to the north, east and south, and in 1929 a wooden lookout building was built at the very summit and tethered to the site by cables. During the summer months it was manned by lookouts who communicated with the forest rangers below by a telephone cable. For the 30 years it was in operation the lookout was supplied by packhorses. In order to build a horse trail up steep scree slopes that provided a route through cliff bands near the summit, an impressive amount of rockwork had to be done.

Today, the lookout still stands on what is probably the most exposed building site in Canada and the horse trail remains as a popular hiking trail, both testifying to some fine workmanship by men who must have been very aware of the difficulties involved in building and servicing a residence on top of a mountain.

The lookout was closed in 1952, replaced by two others at lower elevations that were easier to service.

The block-shaped mountain beyond and to the right of Black Rock is unofficially unnamed, although it has been referred to as **Castle Rock** (2972 m) since at least 1910. Castle-like in its appearance from the east and north, it is 175 m higher than Devil's Head.

31 The Backdrop to the Village

Three high mountains towering over the hotels form a spectacular backdrop to Kananaskis Village. Just south of the village junction is the best place to view these three as well as some other nearby peaks.

The Fortress (3000 m), one of the most aptly named peaks in the Rockies, is the peak in the distance on the left side of the panorama.

Mount Kidd (2958 m) is the "Pilot Mountain" of the Kananaskis Valley. The Pilot Mountain in the Bow Valley between Banff and Castle Junction was named by George Dawson for its location on the outside of a major bend in the Bow Valley that makes the peak visible for long distances both up and down the valley. Mount Kidd is similarly situated, being visible from both the northern entrance to the Kananaskis Valley near the Trans-Canada Highway and from the Kananaskis Lakes area to the south.

The massive character of the mountain with its two separate peaks is best seen from the vicinity of Rocky Creek, 11.3 km south of this viewpoint. From the Kananaskis Village junction one can see only the north and highest peak. In 1981, the **Mount Kidd fire lookout** was constructed on the grassy slopes of the ridge to the right of the mountain. Although it was the most recent addition in the series of fire lookouts established in the late 1920s to help protect Alberta's forests, it was only occupied until 1992. The building was removed in 1997.

Stuart Kidd originally lived near Calgary but according to his son could not resist the attraction of the mountains and so moved to Morley in 1907, where he operated the Scott and Leeson Trading Post. Kidd became fluent in the Stoney language and was made an

From near Kananaskis Village junction

Highway 40, 0.5 km south of Kananaskis Village junction; 4.3 km north of Evan-Thomas Creek.

Left: The two peaks of Mount Kidd from near Rocky Creek. The tightly folded layers are near the northern end of the Lewis Thrust Fault. Photo Gillean Daffern.

Top left: Stuart Kidd (l) with Con "Dutch" Bernhard, packer and guide, c. 1920. Courtesy Glenbow Archives, NA-2451-7.

Top right: The top of Mount Bogart showing above Ribbon Peak. The view from Kovach Pond. Photo Gillean Daffern.

honourary chief, probably the first white to be so honoured, and given the name of "Tah-Osa," which means "Moose Killer." Part of his business was outfitting survey parties that worked in the Kananaskis Valley area. One of these was led by geologist D. Bogart Dowling, who chose Kidd's name for the mountain.

Bogart Dowling himself is honoured by **Mount Bogart** (3144 m), which is located 4.5 km beyond Mount Kidd and rises almost 200 m higher. Snow lingers longer on its summit than on any other peak in the panorama. Ribbon Creek, which flows toward the viewpoint between forested slopes, has its headwaters between the two mountains. The lower peak to the right of Mount Bogart is unofficially referred to as **Ribbon Peak** (2880 m) and tends to hide Mount Bogart from some angles.

Connected to Mount Bogart by a long, high ridge is **Mount Sparrowhawk** (3121 m). A large snow cornice forms each winter on the east-facing slope of the ridge just to the left of Sparrowhawk. Lingering into late summer, it is sometimes the only snow to be seen from this viewpoint.

Mount Allan. Photo Gillean Daffern.

On the right side of the panorama are the smooth grassy slopes of **Mount Allan** (2789 m). Dr. J. A. Allan, who in 1912 became the first professor of geology at the University of Alberta, was responsible for locating much of the coal reserves in the province. Appropriately, a coal mine operated from 1947 until 1952 on the lower slopes of the mountain named in his honour. The Kananaskis Exploration and Development Company mine was initially a strip mine, but later developed into an underground operation complete with a railway and cars. In 1948 the miners' families came to join the workers and a number of tar paper shacks and log cabins were built below the mine on the north bank of Ribbon Creek. As the village grew to a population of almost 200 people, it was given the name Kovach after Joe Kovach, the district forest ranger.

Slumping coal markets forced the closure of the mine and today only some crumbling stonework and foundations remain in the forest that has overgrown the old townsite. On the slopes of Mount Allan, the mine scar appears as a lush meadow following reclamation of the site.

Mount Allan is also the site of the Nakiska ski area, where the 15th Olympic Winter Games alpine skiing events were held in 1988. The highest point of Mount Allan that can be seen from this viewpoint is known as Olympic Summit.

Dr. J. A. Allan. Photo Gillean Daffern.

HMS Sparrowhawk and Mount Sparrowhawk

Mount Sparrowhawk from Mount Kidd lookout site. Photo Gillean Daffern.

Although her crew performed valiantly, *HMS Sparrowhawk*'s role in the Battle of Jutland during the First World War was not one to bring fame and honour to the Royal Navy. She was one of a flotilla of 11 destroyers proceeding through a very dark night with absolutely no idea of where the enemy was and with only a very vague idea of the position of other British ships. In the course of the battle, the destroyers turned to fire torpedoes and as a crew member of the Sparrowhawk related, "the helm was put over and orders passed to fire the remaining torpedo. The *HMS Broke*, ahead of us, had also put her helm over but, just as we were both turning, she was hit forward, and when she should have eased her helm and steadied to fire a torpedo, as we were doing, I saw that she was still swinging to port with her helm jammed, and coming straight for our bridge at 28 knots. I remember shouting a warning to everyone to hold on, and to the forward gun's crew to clear the forecastle, just as she hit us."[167]

HMS Contest, following in the night, failed to see the damaged Sparrowhawk and sliced off her stern, leaving the crippled ship to lie where she was, unable to steam. At dawn, the Sparrowhawk's crew was horrified when a German light cruiser appeared. Bravely they prepared to engage the much larger enemy warship with their only remaining operable gun while "dead in the water." Much to their relief the enemy ship did not open fire, but "settled down forward, then stood on her head and sank."[168] She was the Ebling, which had been severely damaged in an earlier engagement and had been trying to reach the Danish coast. An hour later *HMS Marksman* appeared and took the Sparrowhawk in tow, but when both hawsers broke, the unfortunate Sparrowhawk was ordered sunk by British gunfire.

Mount Sparrowhawk honours the brave crew and this rather unfortunate ship.

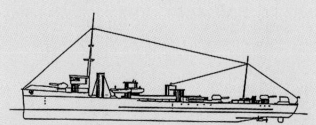

HMS Sparrowhawk.

32 The Mountains of the Kananaskis Range

From the Evan-Thomas Creek bridge

Highway 40 at the bridge over Evan-Thomas Creek, 4.8 km south of the Kananaskis Village junction; 7 km north of the Rocky Creek bridge.

This panorama, featuring five peaks of the Kananaskis Range, is perhaps the most spectacular view seen during the drive up the Kananaskis Valley. Only the central portion of the range may be seen from the Evan-Thomas bridge. Mount Lawson and Mount Kent at the southern end of the range and Mount Engadine at the northern end are not visible.

The Wedge. Photo Gillean Daffern.

The leftmost mountain in the view is **The Wedge** (2652 m), a distinctive and attractive little peak named for its similarity to a carpenter's wedge. The lower slopes of the mountain clearly show the extent of the most recent forest fire. The darker-coloured forest is made up of spruce trees that survived the fire while the lighter-coloured trees are a younger, lodgepole pine forest that started growing immediately following the fire.

The lower, rounded mountain to the right of The Wedge is **Limestone Mountain** (2180 m), one of two mountains with this name. The other is located in the Front Ranges near the Ram River.

Mount Inflexible (3000 m) is the distant peak in the centre of the panorama. *HMS Inflexible* was a battle cruiser that participated in the Battle of Jutland during the First World War.

The three-peaked mountain to the right of Mount Inflexible was named **Mount James Walker** (3035 m) in 1977. A remarkable individual, Colonel James Walker travelled west with the North West Mounted Police, managed the Cochrane Ranche, established a sawmill near the mouth of the Kananaskis River, was elected chairman of a committee to oversee what was to become Calgary prior to its incorporation, was a school trustee and a charter member of the city's hospital board, acquired the property that became Stampede Park, organized a special patrol during the 1885 rebellion, set up the first telephone system in the city, drilled a natural gas well on his east Calgary property, and in his later years led a battalion of the Canadian Forestry Corps serving in England and Scotland during the First World War. Competing against 3,000 other nominees, he was voted Calgary's "Citizen of the Century" during the city's centennial year in 1975.

The view from Evan-Thomas bridge is clearly dominated by **The Fortress** (3000 m). The names of virtually all mountains in the Rockies begin with "Mount" or end with "Mountain" or "Peak." It is in keeping with the distinct character of this peak that its name is different in that it begins with "The."

From this viewpoint the vertical cliffs of The Fortress rise symmetrically to the flat-topped summit, making it one of the most picturesque and aptly named peaks in the Kananaskis Valley. Once known as The Tower, it was renamed because of possible confusion with a peak known as The Towers located in the Mount Assiniboine area to the west of Wonder Pass.

To the right of The Fortress, the peak with the narrow, steep-sided summit is not officially named, although it is referred to as **Gusty Peak** (3000 m). It was named in 1972 by the party that claimed the first ascent in snow and very high winds.

Mount Galatea (3185 m) is the highest mountain visible from the Evan-Thomas bridge. *HMS Galatea* was the flagship of the First Light Cruiser Squadron during the Battle of Jutland and was the first ship to open fire in the battle. The first ascent was made by Katie Gardiner with guide W. Feuz in 1930.

The Fortress.

Katie Gardiner

Katie Gardiner completed 33 first ascents in the Canadian Rockies—more than any other woman. Only three men, other than professional guides, exceeded her total.

Travelling alone on the CPR, Katherine Gardiner arrived for her first season of climbing in the Canadian Rockies in 1929. She was no stranger to climbing and exploration. The daughter of a distinguished British climber who was the first to reach the summit of Mount Elbruz in the Caucasus, she had often accompanied him on his annual climbing trip to the Alps. Upon her arrival in Banff she contacted Walter Feuz, the youngest of a family of alpine guides brought over from Switzerland by the CPR, and together with two packers they explored the country between the Bow Valley and Crowsnest Pass.

Impressed by the guiding services of Feuz and finding the area to her liking (in particular, the opportunity for first ascents), she returned for the next two seasons. Always accompanied by Feuz, she completed a total of 14 first ascents in the Kananaskis area.

Ken Jones, who has been a guide in the Rockies since the 1930s, remembers meeting Katie Gardiner at Shadow Lake in Banff National Park. He was to lead Miss Gardiner and two friends on an ascent of Mount Ball and initially wondered what he had gotten himself in to as his client was very clumsy on the trail and looked "as though she could trip over her own shadow."[169] To Jones' relief, however, she was very capable when the trail was left behind and the rock climbing began.

In subsequent years Gardiner continued climbing in Canada, visiting the spectacular Bugaboo area of the Purcell Range in 1935 with Ken Jones and Walter Perren. When in their fifties, Gardiner and guides Edward Feuz and Christian Hasler climbed Mount Robson, the highest peak in the Rockies and considered a very difficult ascent. Upon their return to Lake Louise when it was suggested that it must have been a tough climb, Ed Feuz replied, "Hard? Why with Katie Gardiner along, it was a piece of cake."[170]

Katie Gardiner. Courtesy Whyte Museum, M67 Box 7 Album 4.

Mt. Fox Mt. Foch Mt. Sarrail Mangin Glacier Warrior Mtn. Waka Nambe Mt. Northover Mt. Lyautey Mt. Indefatigable Mt. Invincible Mt. Warspite Mt. Black Prince Mt. Smith-Dorrien Mt. Murray

33 The Peaks above the Kananaskis Lakes

From the Old Elpoca Creek bridge

Valleyview trail, 5.9 km south of the northern junction of the trail with Highway 40.

Mount Joffre from Highway 40.

Before the development of Kananaskis Country and the construction of Highway 40, this bridge was part of the dusty gravel road known simply as "The Forestry Road." The old bridge over Elpoca Creek is at a considerably higher elevation than the new highway bridge, which can be seen below. This, together with the steep canyon below the bridge that eliminates the possibility of tree growth, provides an elevated, unobstructed panorama of Kananaskis Lakes and the mountains beyond.

Although not a particularly high mountain, **Mount Fox** (2973 m) is situated in a prominent location immediately west of Elk Pass, which at an elevation of less than 2000 m is the lowest pass through the Rockies between Crowsnest Pass and Vermilion Pass.

A Mount Fox was named by Captain Palliser of the Palliser Expedition and shown on his 1860 map, but like Mount Head in the lower Highwood Valley, the mountain now designated as Mount Fox was almost certainly not the mountain that Captain Palliser had in mind. A more likely explanation is that Palliser was referring to the group of mountains now known as the British Military Group. It is not certain who Captain Palliser had in mind when the name was chosen. A likely individual was Sir Charles Fox, a prominent British railway designer who built lines in Africa, Asia, Europe and eastern Canada. Mount Fox is the only peak of the dozen identified in this panorama whose name is not related to the First World War.

The view features glimpses of both Upper and Lower Kananaskis Lakes, which separate the mountains of the Spray Range to the north from the peaks to the south of the lakes.

Above the upper lake a portion of the **Mangin Glacier** is visible. The southernmost significant accumulation of ice in the Rockies, this large snowfield rises to the summit of Mount Joffre, the dominant peak in this area. Hidden from this viewpoint by Mount Foch and Mount Sarrail, it is the highest of the French Military Group that honours, to quote Arthur Wheeler of the Boundary Survey, "distinguished generals who have rendered such names immortal through their splendid service to France in the great war now in progress."[171] The Group forms an anomaly on the Continental Divide as it curves northeastwards from the summit of Mount Joffre, so that for approximately 13 km one travels east from Alberta into British Columbia.

Mountain enthusiasts should be sure to stop on Highway 40, two km north of the junction with Kananaskis Lakes Trail, for a glimpse of Mount Joffre. The mountain is only visible for a very limited distance between the slopes of Mount Sarrail on the north and Mount Indefatigable on the south. Rising majestically some 24 km away, Mount Joffre's height and significance are very apparent. At 3450 m, it is the highest mountain between Mount Assiniboine and the U.S. border. Marshall Joffre was commander in chief of the French Army during 1916.

Mount Foch (3180 m) was named after Marshall Ferdinand Foch, supreme commander of allied forces during the latter stages of the Great War. In March of 1918 a massive German offensive threatened Paris and the channel ports and it was at this point that Foch was appointed Generalissimo. Known as the Somme Offensive, it was not immediately stopped, but it is thought doubtful that any other commander could have held the Allies together as he did or recovered the military initiative as quickly. At 3180 m, Mount Foch is the highest peak of this panorama.

The second of the French Military Group visible from the Old Elpoca Creek bridge viewpoint is **Mount Sarrail** (3170 m), named for the general who commanded the French Third Army.

Warrior Mountain (2973 m) and **Mount Northover** (3048 m) are located on the Continental Divide to the north of the French Military Group, Mount Warrior lying above the lower portion of the Mangin Glacier. *HMS Warrior* was a Royal Navy cruiser that was put out of action by enemy gunfire during the Battle of Jutland in 1916. It was taken in tow by *HMS Engadine* but the fires aboard Warrior reached the magazine and it exploded and sank. Lieutenant A. W. Northover was serving with the 28th Battalion of the Canadian Expeditionary Force in 1917 when he was killed in action.

Although 15 km distant, the small but spectacular tower-like feature named unofficially **Waka Nambe** (2880 m) may be seen between Warrior Mountain and Mount Northover. The name is an Indian word meaning "Great Spirit Thumb" or "Hand of God" and is a refreshing break from the World War One era names of its neighbouring peaks.

Below Warrior Mountain and Waka Nambe one can see Fossil Falls, a large waterfall on Aster Creek that descends from Aster Lake and the glaciers above into the valley between **Mount Lyautey** (3082 m) and the steep northwestern slopes of Mount Sarrail.

Mount Lyautey is a massive mountain lying east of the Divide and some distance away from the other mountains that honour French military leaders. General Louis Hubert Gonzalve Lyautey was the French minister of war.

From this viewpoint there are striking similarities between **Mount Indefatigable** (2670 m) and **Mount Invincible** (2670 m). Their summits have similar profiles and their eastern slopes are both steep near the summit ridges. The less steep slopes below the cliffs hold snow in a similar manner, this highlighting indicating the layers of rock are oriented in the same direction. Additionally, both mountains are 2670 m in elevation.

These similarities must have been noticed by members of the Boundary Commission who named them after two warships that came to similar ends during the Battle of Jutland. *HMS Indefatigable*, part of the Second Battle Cruiser Squadron, was struck by five shells from the German battleship Vonder Tann and exploded. Only two of the 1,015 crewmembers aboard survived. *HMS Invincible* was Admiral Hood's flagship as he led the Third Battle Cruiser Squadron into the battle. Initially Hood's ships were successful in landing some heavy blows on enemy ships, but then his flagship was destroyed by enemy gunfire with the loss of 1,026 men.

Mount Indefatigable is situated at the southern end of the Spray Mountains, which form the western side of the Smith-Dorrien Valley and disappears into the distance at the right end of the panorama. **Mount Warspite** (2850 m) and **Mount Black Prince** (2932 m) were named after cruisers during the Battle of Jutland. Nicknamed "The Old Lady," *HMS Warspite* survived the First World War and went on to serve in the Second World War. *HMS Black Prince* was destroyed by German battleships, going down with all 750 of its crew members.

The rounded profile of **Mount Smith-Dorrien** (3155 m) looms behind a nearer ridge and casts an impressive presence over the valley of the same name. General Sir Horace Lockwood Smith-Dorrien was a British soldier who was involved in the Zulu and Boer wars in Africa before commanding the British Second Army. He later became the governor of Gibraltar.

Mount Murray (3024 m) rises smoothly to the right of Mount Smith-Dorrien. General Sir A. J. Murray was the chief of the Imperial General Staff in 1915 and commanded forces in Egypt.

Behind the northern ridge of Mount Murray and beyond French Creek, the peak of **Mount Burstall** (2760 m) is the most distant mountain visible from the Old Elpoca bridge. Lieutenant General Sir E. H. Burstall commanded Canadian troops during the First World War.

Mount Warspite.

General Foch. Courtesy The Story of 25 Eventful Years in Pictures.

Elpoca Mtn.

Gap Mtn.

Pocaterra Ridge

Mt. Kent

Mt. Wintour

34 Geology of the Opal Range

From Highwood Pass
Highway 40 at Highwood Pass, 17.3 km south of the junction with the Kananaskis Lakes Trail; 38.6 km north of the junction with Highway 541.

Gap Mountain from the north. Photo Gillean Daffern.

At an elevation of 2206 m, Highwood Pass is the highest point in Canada reached by a paved highway. There are a number of good reasons to pause at the top of the pass, one of which is to enjoy the view to the north, which, although somewhat restricted, features the distant peaks of the Kananaskis Range and some very interesting and instructive geology.

To the north Highway 40 follows the valley of Pocaterra Creek as it descends toward Kananaskis Lakes. To the left of this valley is the unofficially named **Pocaterra Ridge** (2667 m), brilliantly green in early summer and featuring some classic avalanche slopes. Both were named after George Pocaterra who was a frequent visitor to this part of the Rockies in the first five decades of this century.

The southernmost peak of the Kananaskis Range may be seen in the distance between the northern slopes of Pocaterra Ridge and Gap Mountain. *HMS Kent* was a battle cruiser that fought alongside *HMS Glasgow* and *HMS Cornwall* in the Battle of the Falkland Islands during the First World War. During this engagement the Kent sunk the German cruiser Nurnberg.

Gap Mountain (2667 m), which rises in the centre of this panorama, was named in 1978 because of its location above the

gap where Pocaterra Creek flows between the Opal and Elk ranges. George Pocaterra originally called this peak Mount George after himself and at the same time assigned the name Mount Paul to the much more impressive mountain that forms the right side of this panorama. Paul Amos was a Stoney Indian who travelled with Pocaterra and was his blood brother.

Gap Mountain is located at the southern end of a long ridge that forms the eastern edge of the Kananaskis Valley for some 20 km. Often cut by steep canyons, the ridge has only one other named high point: **Mount Wintour** (2700 m). Two of the peaks that form the summit of this long, narrow mountain may be seen in the distance to the right of Gap Mountain, which is its equal in elevation. Captain Charles Wintour was in command of the 4th Destroyer Flotilla of the Royal Navy during the Battle of Jutland in 1916. During the action the flotilla broke out of fog to find themselves confronting a group of German battleships. Captain Wintour went down with his flagship, *HMS Tipperary*.

Vertically dipping strata form the spectacular **Elpoca Mountain** (3029 m) to the right. The fact that the mountain rises above Elbow Pass accounts for its name. The "El" portion of Elpoca stands for the Elbow River, which flows east from the pass, while "Poca" represents Pocaterra Creek, which flows to the west.

George Pocaterra

Many of the features in this panorama are named after one of the most interesting characters to visit this area of the Rockies. Born in a valley in the Italian Alps, George Pocaterra attended university in Switzerland and was fluent in four languages. After coming to Canada as a young man, he established the Buffalo Head Ranch in the Highwood Valley, which was eventually purchased by his close friend Raymond Patterson in 1933.

As well as ranching, Pocaterra was involved in trapping, hunting, coal exploration and in the general exploration of the area. Some of the trips undertaken with Raymond Patterson are described in Patterson's best known book, *The Buffalo Head*.

While becoming familiar with untravelled areas in southern Alberta, Pocaterra made friends with the Indians. He was very proud of learning their native languages and folklore, and was eventually made blood brother to a Stoney named Spotted Wolf, with whom he travelled the old Indian trails.

The country that George Pocaterra particularly loved changed extensively with the development of the Kananaskis

Lakes to produce electrical power. Pocaterra later wrote, "I was probably the first white man to see the beautiful lake district from the south. The most beautiful mountain scenery in the world, as far as I am concerned, was at these lakes, but now it is completely spoiled by the power dams, and the drowning of the marvellously beautiful islands and exquisitely curving beaches, the cutting down of the century old trees, and the drying up of the twin falls between the two lakes and of the falls below the lower lake."[172]

The valley to the east of Elpoca Mountain contains Piper Creek, at present an unofficial name. Norma Piper, a coloratura soprano very active in Calgary's operatic community, became George Pocaterra's wife in 1936. Evidence of the breadth of George Pocaterra's interests is the fact that he acted as stage manager for the operatic company with which she sang.

George Pocaterra crossed Highwood Pass numerous times in the early 1900s, generally from horseback, and it is safe to say he enjoyed the view.

George Pocaterra. Courtesy Glenbow Archives, NA-695-80.

Thrust Faults and Front Range Geology

Highwood Pass is an excellent spot from which to gain an understanding of the rock types and the geological processes that resulted in the formation of the Front Ranges of the Rocky Mountains.

There are two main types of rocks involved, the youngest of which were formed during the Mesozoic era. Primarily sandstones and shales, these rocks were deposited during the age of the dinosaurs from 225 million years ago until 65 million years ago. They are comparatively soft and easily eroded, tending to wear away relatively quickly and leaving rounded, smoothly-graded slopes. Pocaterra Ridge is entirely composed of Mesozoic rocks as are the slopes between Gap Mountain and Elpoca Peak.

Limestone is the dominant rock type of the Paleozoic era rock layers that underlie the Mesozoic rocks. These rocks were deposited in seas from 570 million years ago until the

Mesozoic era began 225 million years ago. During Paleozoic time life evolved from very simple forms to include fish, amphibians and reptiles. Gap Mountain and Elpoca Mountain are made of Paleozoic limestone.

The mountains were formed by thrust faulting, which involves fractures along which great slabs of rock slide and are piled on top of one another. In this area the movement along the thrust faults occurred over a period of about 30 million years. It was caused by great compressional forces associated with the collision of the Pacific oceanic plate and the North American continental plate.

In the case of the mountains seen from Highwood Pass, two layers of Paleozoic limestone were tilted steeply upward to the point where some of the layers are actually vertical. The slopes between Gap Mountain and Elpoca Mountain separate the Lewis thrust sheet from the Rundle thrust sheet.

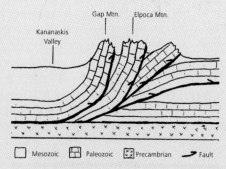
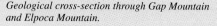

Geological cross-section through Gap Mountain and Elpoca Mountain.

Mt. MacLaren · Gunsight Pass · Mt. Strachan · Mt. Muir · Weary Creek Gap · Mt. McPhail · Horned Mtn. · Mt. Bishop · The Hill of the

35 The Mountains of the Upper Highwood Valley

From near Cat Creek
Highway 40, 7.4 km north of the
junction with Highway 541;
31.3 km south of Highwood Pass.

Mount Muir. Photo Gillean Daffern.

*This beautiful group of peaks is best seen from the top of a
hill 1.7 km north of Cat Creek. The contrast between the
steep grey cliffs of cleanly defined peaks rising behind
forested and grass-covered hills makes this panorama
special. From this point one can see 13 km of the
Continental Divide to the west of the Highwood Valley.*

Mount MacLaren (2850 m), on the left side of the panorama, is
too close to get a good look at from this viewpoint but its
complex topography is evident. The high pass between it and
Mount Strachan is known as **Gunsight Pass** because of its "V"
shape when viewed from certain vantage points. To its right rises
Mount Strachan (2682 m), named after Lieutenant Harcus
Strachan in 1918.

Mount Muir (2758 m) is the northernmost peak in the High
Rock Range, which stretches from the Crowsnest Pass. The
mountains to the north are part of the Elk Range, which terminates
beyond Highwood Pass. Geologically, there does not seem to be
anything of significance at the point where the range forming the
Divide changes name. However, topographically there is a
difference. In the Elk Range to the north the mountains form more
of a continuous wall whereas in the High Rock Range to the south
the mountains are generally separate entities with passes and cols
between them.

Alexander Muir is the only composer to have had a mountain in
the Canadian Rockies named in his honour. He wrote the music
and lyrics for *The Maple Leaf Forever*[173] in 1867, the year of

Canadian Confederation. Soon the song became the unofficial
Canadian national anthem. The predominant view of the times
that the country was of "British-only" origin with a Scottish, Irish
and English heritage is clear from the opening verse:

> In days of yore, from Britain's shore,
> Wolfe the dauntless hero came,
> And planted firm Britannia's flag,
> On Canada's fair domain.
> Here may it wave, our boast, our pride,
> And joined in love together,
> The thistle, shamrock, rose entwine,
> The Maple Leaf Forever.

Written originally in French, our present national anthem *O
Canada* was first performed in Quebec in 1880, the English lyrics
not being written until 1908. At the time of the First World War
and the Interprovincial Boundary Survey, *O Canada* was
becoming the best known patriotic song in the country, but
"traditionalists," as it appears survey commissioners Arthur
Wheeler and Richard Cautley may have been, obviously still held
The Maple Leaf Forever in high regard.

The pass that separates Mount Muir and Mount McPhail was
named **Weary Creek Gap** after Weary Creek, which flows from
the pass into British Columbia. From this vantage point the pass is
hidden behind a high grassy ridge that stretches east from the steep
cliffs of Mount Muir. It has also been named the Elk Trail Pass by
the Stoney Indians who have a legend telling how elk from the
Bow to the Crowsnest travelled through this pass from the more
heavily hunted Alberta side to the Elk Valley in British Columbia.

The History of the Upper Highwood

The Highwood River valley has been through several stages of use and abuse in the relatively short time that the white man has had influence. Logging, occasional devastating fires and explorations on horseback dominated the period prior to the Second World War.

John Lineham (Lineham Creek is 4.5 km north of the viewpoint) came to Alberta from Montreal in the early 1880s and in 1903 began operating a logging company in the Highwood Valley. Winter camps of 35 to 40 men were maintained along the river with 10 to 12 teams of horses. Piled at points where they could easily be rolled into the river, the logs were floated to High River during the spring high water. About 25 men followed the logs downstream using boats, peevies, teams, and if necessary, dynamite to undo logjams. Most years someone would drown in the river. Rough trails were built into the main valley and subsidiary valleys to accommodate the logging operation that continued until the Highwood Fire of 1910.

The year 1910 was extremely dry in the mountains of southern Alberta as a group of surveyors were laying out the boundaries of areas to be logged. They were camped on the banks of the Highwood near the mouth of Picklejar Creek when a gust of wind blowing across their camp fire sent a few sparks into the tinder-dry forest. Before the fire was out, the Highwood, Sheep and Elbow river valleys had been burned and the fire had spread east to the Chain Lakes area and south into Montana. At night the flames were clearly visible from Okotoks. This resulted in the formation of a Forestry Department who established the present boundaries of the Forest Reserve.

Logging continued on a reduced scale though the 1920s and 1930s until the Phillips Fire of 1936 again devastated much of the valley. During these early years Raymond Patterson, George Pocaterra and others explored the valley. Patterson's classic book, *The Buffalo Head*, records some of his memories at this stage of the valley's history. Following the Phillips Fire, a road was constructed through the valley and over Highwood Pass to assist in the proper management of what was left of the forest.

After the Second World War, coal exploration and off-road-vehicle use by hunters, fishermen and other recreationists prevailed in the valley. Coal seams found within the Kootenay formation of the Cretaceous geologic time period attracted mining interests during the 1960s. Bulldozers cut numerous trails to expose the strata for examination and provide access to drill sites. By the mid 1970s the main road up the valley was frequently hidden in clouds of dust, while off-road vehicles were running rampant over the old logging trails to the point where wildlife and other visitors were suffering.

Since 1978 the valley has been part of the Kananaskis Country recreation area. Wildlife management and foot-powered recreation are the most important considerations. The dusty old road is now a modern highway and although it is closed for over six months of the year, the valley now sees many times the number of visitors as in previous years.

Log jam on the Highwood River. Courtesy Glenbow Archives, NA-695-33.

John Lineham. Courtesy Glenbow Archives, NA-1230-19.

Also known as The Pyramid" for obvious reasons, **Mount McPhail** (2883 m) rises spectacularly to the north of Weary Creek Gap and at 2883 m is the highest peak in this panorama. It was named for N. R. McPhail, a member of the surveyor general's staff who was killed in action in 1917. The cirque at the base of its northeastern face contains a beautiful and very deep lake. R. M. Patterson felt he was the first white man to visit the lake and eloquently described its discovery in his book *The Buffalo Head*, which should be read by anyone interested in the history of this valley.

There are only a few mountains in this area of the Rockies that are named because they resemble some thing, and **Horned Mountain** (2667 m) is one of them. The "horn" sticking out on the right-hand side is easily seen from this location.

Beyond the gentle slopes of **The Hill of the Flowers**, named by Patterson, lies **Mount Bishop** (2850 m), which honours the most famous of Canadian War World I fighter pilots, Billy Bishop VC. In the early summer a distinct capital "T" is formed by melting snows on the mountain's southern slopes.

"The Courage of the Early Morning"

The subtitle above is the title chosen by W. A. Bishop for his father's biography. The phrase was used by a Montreal publisher in a tribute to William Avery "Billy" Bishop VC, Canada's top flying ace in World War One. Known as a flamboyant extrovert, Bishop shot down a total of 72 enemy aircraft, including three on a daring solo dawn attack on a German airfield for which he was awarded the Victoria Cross.

Captain Bishop's combat report for this day is as follows: "I fired on seven machines on the aerodrome, some of which had their engines running. One of them took off and I fired 15 rounds at him from close range (60'') and he crashed. A second one was taking off, I opened fire and fired 30 rounds at 150 yds. range, he crashed into a tree. Two more were then taking off together. I climbed and engaged one at 1000' finishing my drum, and he crashed 300 yds. from the aerodrome. I changed drums and climbed E. A fourth Hun aircraft came after me and I fired one whole drum into him. He flew away and I then flew 1000' under 4 Scouts at 5000' for one mile and turned W. climbing. The aerodrome was armed with one or more machine guns. Machines on the ground were 6 Scouts (Albatross type I or II) and one two-seater."[174]

Bishop's squadron commander comments were added to the bottom of the report: "Cap't Bishop had been encouraged to catch the Hun aircraft referred to in VII Corps Daily Intelligence Summary No. 151. His method was not quite what I intended. He was several times at a height of 50 ft. over this enemy aerodrome at least 17 miles E. of the lines. His machine is full of holes caused by machine gun fire from the ground."[175]

During the Second World War, Billy Bishop, serving as an Air Marshall, played an important role in the British Commonwealth Air Training Plan by inspiring a new generation of pilots to serve their country in the air at its time of need.

Captain Billy Bishop and his Nieuport B1566. Courtesy National Archives Canada, PA-001651.

The Hill of Flowers from Weary Creek Gap. Photo Gillean Daffern.

The Hill of the Flowers

In the mid-1930s Raymond Patterson and his wife Marigold rode up the slopes of the large hill that, from this vantage point, appears to be below the southern slopes of Mount Bishop. Patterson had climbed the hill 10 days earlier and noted that, "if this hot weather held, the whole summit of this butte was going to be a solid carpet of flowers—a blaze of colours that would outshine anything I had ever seen, even in this Highwood country."[176]

Patterson's prediction was correct and he wrote that as he and Marigold approached the top of the hill, "the summit of the hill opened up, and we saw that it was one living, shimmering carpet of many colours: here, by God's truth, were flowers beyond all imagining—flowers such as we had never seen. It was the kingdom of the flowers, the garden of the gods."[177] He goes on to describe the scene in detail, noting that the plants that grew here, the potentillas, forget-me-nots, dwarf asters, moss campion, saxifrages and many others, "had to hug the gravel and take cover from the wind—but how they liked it and how they grew!"[178]

Raymond Patterson felt that the Rockies were the worst-named range in the world and in his opinion, "If you look carefully at the map you can find there, enthroned in stone, a collaborator, a traitor to his country, sundry generals of dubious merit, and a demagogue who, for his own ends, wrecked a way of life which had taken centuries to perfect—to cite only a few of these ill-named mountains."[179] It is interesting to speculate as to the mountains and individuals he was referring to.

He felt that the "old voyageurs of the North West Company, if they had chanced to pass this way, would have called it, quite plainly and simply, La Butte des Fleurs—The Hill of the Flowers."[180] Raymond and Marigold Patterson knew it by that name following their day on The Hill of the Flowers as have, I'm sure, all those who have read *The Buffalo Head*.

In the fall of 1990 I spoke with Marigold Patterson in Victoria, B.C. and mentioned The Hill of the Flowers. She straightened up, her eyes sparkled, and she recalled the day instantly saying, "It was marvellous, a sea of flowers."[181] She then proceeded to list the names of many of the flowers that she could still, 55 years later, visualize on that hilltop on the other side of the Rocky Mountains.

The Canadian Cavalry Attacks Enemy Machine Guns

Lieutenant Strachan. Courtesy National Archives Canada, PA-2515.

Most people think the ground action of the First World War was restricted to trench-type warfare and it surprises many to learn that Canadian cavalry saw action.

Harcus Strachan was serving as a lieutenant with the Fort Garry Horse in France during the fall of 1917. The following account of the action for which he was awarded the Victoria Cross appeared in the *London Gazette* on December 18, 1917: "He took command of the squadron of his regiment when the squadron leader was killed. Lt. Strachan led the squadron through the enemy line of machine-gun posts, and then, with the surviving men, led the charge on the enemy battery, killing seven of the gunners with his sword.

"All the gunners having been killed and the battery silenced, he rallied his men and fought his way back at night through the enemy's line, bringing all unwounded men safely in, together with 15 prisoners.

"The operation - which resulted in the silencing of an enemy battery, the killing of the whole battery personnel and many infantry, and the cutting of three main lines of telephone communication two miles in rear of the enemy's front line - was only rendered possible by the outstanding gallantry and fearless leading of this officer."[182]

Another report of this amazing story appeared in *The Register of the Victoria Cross* and reads: "The men went forward at the gallop to an objective dear to any cavalryman's heart. A battery of field guns lay before them. A good horse, firm ground, and guns to be taken - a cavalryman wants no more. The Canadians charged down upon them, and in a moment were among the guns, riding the gunners down or sabring them as them stood.... There was a brief melee of plunging horses and stumbling artillerymen. Then the business was finished."[183]

Top: Lieutenant Harcus Strachan leading his squadron of cavalry. Courtesy National Archives Canada, PA-002515.

Bottom: Mount Strachan. Photo Gillean Daffern.

Mt. Evan-Thomas   Mt. Packenham   Mt. Hood   Mt. Brock   Mt. Blane   The Blade   Mt. Burney   Mt. Wintour

36 Opal Range

From Lower Kanaskis Lake

Smith-Dorrien/Spray Trail, 2.9 km northwest of the junction with Kananaskis Lakes Trail.

H. L. A. Hood. Courtesy The Story of 25 Eventful Years in Pictures.

A small, picturesque lake situated just below the dam at the north end of Lower Kananaskis Lake provides the foreground for this view of the southernmost six peaks of the spectacular Opal Range. Consisting of a total of eight mountains, the range stretches 20 km from Elpoca Mountain at the south end to Mount Evan-Thomas in the north.

The range forms the eastern side of the Kananaskis Valley for a considerable distance but, with the exception of a few limited views, is largely hidden from Highway 40 by a high ridge immediately west of the main Opal Range. However, from this viewpoint on the Smith-Dorrien Trail one can look over this ridge and enjoy a good view of this spectacular range whose strata has been thrust into a near-vertical orientation. This makes for challenging climbing for mountaineers, the first recorded ascents not being made until the 1950s.

George Dawson named the range after he discovered many small cavities lined with quartz and coated with what he thought was a thin film of opal.

Six km south from the northwestern end of the range, **Mount Evan-Thomas** (3097 m) is the first named feature and from this angle has a broad summit with two rounded peaks. Of the eight peaks in the range, this is the first of seven to honour people or ships associated with the Battle of Jutland. In fact, the northernmost four—Mount Evan-Thomas, **Mount Packenham** (3000 m), **Mount Hood** (2903 m) and **Mount Brock** (2902 m)—are all

Mount Blane. The Blade to right. Photo Tony Daffern.

named for rear admirals who commanded battle cruiser squadrons. Rear Admiral H. Evan-Thomas commanded the Fifth Battle Cruiser Squadron, Rear Admiral W. C. Packenham the Second, Rear Admiral H. L. A. Hood the Third and Rear Admiral O. Brock the First. Battle cruisers were more lightly armoured than battleships but were faster, had larger guns, and often exceeded them in size. However, the battle cruisers were not particularly successful against the German battleships and at the end of Churchill's appointment as First Lord of the Admiralty, few were under construction.

Rear Admiral Hood's flagship was *HMS Invincible*. (The mountain honouring the ship may be seen behind you if you are at the viewpoint.) The rear admiral was killed when his flagship was sunk during action with German battleships.

Clearly, the most spectacular peak of the Opals from this viewpoint is **Mount Blane** (2993 m). The near vertical strata is very apparent as is a distinctive notch with an isolated summit on the mountain's south ridge known as "**The Blade**" (2943 m). This gives it character that some of the other peaks are lacking from this angle. As one drives from this viewpoint toward the junction with Kananaskis Lakes Trail, Mount Blane remains in view and at the junction with Highway 40, it is possible to look up King Creek valley and get an excellent close-up look at this peak.

According to the official government records, Mount Blane was named after Sir C. R. Blane, commander of the battle cruiser *HMS Queen Mary*, which was part of Rear Admiral Brock's squadron and was destroyed in the battle. However, the captain in command at the time was named C. R. Prowse. It is not known why Commander Blane was chosen to be honoured in this way and not Captain Prowse.

An unnamed high point rises just to the right of Mount Blane. Farther south, the summit of **Mount Burney** (2934 m) may just be seen over the northern slopes of **Mount Wintour** (2700 m), which hides the southernmost two peaks of the Opal Range. Vice-Admiral Sir Cecil Burney, who was commander of *HMS Marlborough*, led the First Battle Squadron during the battle.

Mount Wintour is an interesting mountain from this viewpoint, its steep slopes cut by numerous steep drainages that create fascinating snow highlights in the spring. Its vertical cliffs are best seen from Highway 40, just south of the junction with Kananaskis Lakes Trail. Captain C. J. Wintour went down with his ship during the Battle of Jutland.

Rear Admiral Hugh Evan-Thomas. Drawing by Francis Dodd. Courtesy Jellicoe.

Mount Wintour from the Rock Wall Interpretive Trail. Photo Gillean Daffern.

The Battle of Jutland

The Battle of Jutland. Courtesy The Story of 25 Eventful Years in Pictures.

The Battle of Jutland was the only major naval confrontation between the British and Germans during the First World War. The German Navy was facing the greatest battle fleet the world had ever seen when it challenged the Royal Navy in 1916. After the smoke had cleared the British had lost six cruisers and eight destroyers while the Germans had lost one battleship, five cruisers and five destroyers.

The tactical victory is said to have gone to the Germans as they had inflicted double their own losses in terms of tonnage against a greatly superior opponent. In addition, the British lost over twice as many men as the Germans. However, the German fleet was forced to retreat and never again ventured forth from its protected harbour of Helgoland. Thus, it is argued, the British were victorious as Britannia continued to rule the waves for the duration of the Great War. At any rate, this great battle at sea did little to change the ratio of strength between the two fleets or the strategic situation of the war.

The power of the guns and explosions, the massiveness of the ships, and the devastation wreaked upon their crews is evident from the recollections of those who watched the destruction of two battle cruisers, Rear Admiral Hood's flagship *HMS Invincible* and *HMS Queen Mary*.

An officer watching the battle from another ship recalled being inspired by the sight of Rear Admiral Hood (aboard *HMS Invincible*) leading his squadron of battle cruisers into the battle with every gun in action. Initially Hood's ships were successful in landing some heavy blows on enemy ships but suddenly the evershifting low cloud and mist began to favour the enemy and German shells began to strike the Invincible. As Hood's flagship was struck flames shot up, then there was a huge, fiery explosion that was followed by a billowing column of dark smoke that swelled up hundreds of metres in the air. When the smoke cleared the battle cruiser was gone. The North Sea is relatively shallow where the Invincible was struck with the result that the ship created her own tombstones for her 1026 dead. She was split almost exactly in half. The two ends then sunk and rested on the bottom, so that they stood up almost vertically with the stem and stern standing an appreciable distance out of the water.

HMS Queen Mary came under the concentrated fire of two enemy battleships, the Derfflinger and the Seydlitz. Her final moments were described by Von Hase of the Derfflinger, "First of all a vivid red flame shot up from her forepart. Then came an explosion forward which was followed by a much heavier explosion amidships. Black debris flew into the air and immediately afterwards the whole ship blew up with a terrific explosion; a gigantic cloud of smoke rose, the masts collapsed inwards and the smoke hid everything."[184] An officer aboard *HMS New Zealand* reported, "We passed the Queen Mary about 150 yards on our port beam, by which time the smoke had blown clear, revealing the stern from the funnel aft afloat and the propellers still revolving, but the forward part had already gone under. When we were abreast, this after portion rolled over and blew up. Great masses of iron were thrown into the air and things were falling into the sea around us. Before we had quite passed, the Queen Mary completely disappeared."[185] Of the crew of 1,275, all but seven were killed.

Although it seems almost tedious at times to have so many mountains in the same area named after ships and people involved in the Battle of Jutland, it is easy to imagine how this monumental sea battle and the others of the Great War could have had a powerful impact on the people of the day. Most of those involved in the surveying of the Interprovincial Boundary would have had relatives and friends directly involved and these great battles would not have been far from their minds as they did their work in the peace and tranquillity of Alberta's Rocky Mountains.

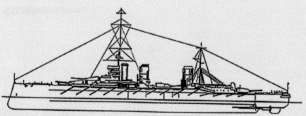

HMS Queen Mary.

37 A View of Mount Assiniboine

The forest closes in on Smith-Dorrien Trail to the south of Spray Lakes. However, this small, circular pond provides an opportunity to see the mountains to the west. The best viewpoint is 100 m south of the turnoff to the Buller Lake picnic site. This is a very special viewpoint in that it is the only vehicle-accessible location in Alberta from where one can see Mount Assiniboine.

The location also provides an interesting view of the Spray Mountains that lie to the west of the Smith-Dorrien Trail to the south of this viewpoint. The highest of these is **Mount Birdwood** (3097 m), named after Field Marshall Sir William Riddell Birdwood who was the first commander of the Australian and New Zealand Army Corps during World War One. He was involved in the ill-fated Gallipoli Campaign and later led the so-called ANZAC forces in France. The Gallipoli action is remembered in the song *And the Band Played Waltzing Matilda*, which is often heard on Remembrance Day, particularly in Australia.

In the distance beyond Mount Birdwood and Mount Smuts lies the unofficially named **Snow Peak** (2789 m).

Mount Smuts (2938 m) and **Mount Shark** (2786 m) are the other two peaks of the Spray Group. General Jan Christian Smuts was a soldier and statesman who became prime minister of South Africa from 1919 to 1924 and from 1938 to 1948. The mountain was named in 1918 and commemorates his role in the First World War. *HMS Shark* was a destroyer of the Royal Navy that was torpedoed and sunk during the Battle of Jutland in 1916.

Rising in front of and between Mount Smuts and Mount Shark is **Tent Ridge** (2545 m), an unofficial name but appropriate given the shape of the feature.

Where the right-hand ridge of Mount Shark dips into the trees, one is looking up the Currie Creek valley and through a pass of the Blue Range. The two peaks just visible through the trees are 14 km west of Mount Shark, beyond the Continental Divide. **Mount Brussilof** (3005 m) is named after a successful Russian general during the First World War who went on to hold important military commands under Josef Lenin. *HMS Alcantara* (2840 m) was another British warship involved in the Battle of Jutland.

Mount Morrison (2896 m) and **Mount Turner** (2813 m) are part of the Park Ranges and lie beyond the Spray River that flows into Spray Lakes Reservoir. The two mountains stand together between the valleys of Bryant Creek to their north and Currie Creek to their south. This is no coincidence. Lieutenants Morrison and Turner fought side by side in 1900 with the Royal Canadian Dragoons under the command of Brigadier-General Horace Smith-Dorrien during the South African War.

The Dragoons were a cavalry unit that had been ordered to cover the retreat of a British "search and destroy" column that was operating in the Komati River basin. The retreat was a slow operation as the column's baggage train was made up of wagons pulled by oxen. With only a single colt machine gun, the Dragoons were not in a strong position to defend the column. Lieutenant Morrison wrote, "I turned in my saddle and…. Square across our rear a line of Boers a mile long was coming on at a gallop over the

From Buller Pond
Smith-Dorrien/Spray Trail, 27.4 km north of Kananaskis Lakes Trail; 17.7 km south of Spray Lakes Dam.

Lieutenant Turner. Courtesy The Register of the Victoria Cross.

plain, firing from their horses. It looked like the spectacular finale in a wild west show. They were about 1500 yards away, but coming on rapidly and shooting at our gun, most of them, to try and stop it…. I thought indeed we saw our finish."[186]

Two troops of the Dragoons, one under the command of Lieutenant Turner, dismounted to try to hold off the attack. For his part in the action Lieutenant Turner was awarded the Victoria Cross, the citation reading, "When the guns were in danger of being captured, Lt. Turner, although he had already been twice wounded, dismounted and deployed his men at close quarters and drove off the enemy, thus saving the gun."[187]

During the First World War, Lieutenant-General Sir Richard E. W. Turner commanded the Canadian troops who held their positions during the first poisonous gas attacks at Ypres in 1915. Later, he became responsible for the training of all Canadian troops in Britain.

Retiring as a major general, Sir Edward W. B. Morrison DSO had a successful career in journalism, becoming editor-in-chief of the *Ottawa Citizen* from 1898 to 1912. He was awarded the Distinguished Service Order for his service in Africa and later became the officer commanding the Canadian Artillery during the First World War.

Twelve km beyond Mount Turner and 800 m higher looms the undisputed monarch of the southern Rockies, **Mount Assiniboine** (3618 m). From this location, the topography allows one to look up Bryant Creek valley and the major valley containing Marvel Lake and Gloria Lake to the mountain. For mountain enthusiasts it is a special treat to be able to see the top 700 m of what is sometimes referred to as the "Matterhorn of the Rockies."

There is another roadside view of Mount Assiniboine, but it requires a drive of well over 100 km from Buller Pond to a point on Highway 93 in Kootenay National Park where the peak is visible from the west.

To the right of Mount Assiniboine is **Mount Magog** (3095 m). The glacier that lies below both peaks is visible on Mount Magog but in the case of Mount Assiniboine is hidden behind a high ridge.

Although it is interesting to see from one roadside location mountains honouring an Australian general, a South African general, a Russian general, and two Canadian major-generals, the history behind the naming of the northernmost three peaks of this panorama provides welcome relief from what can become a somewhat wearisome array of warships and individuals related to the "Great War."

Mount Assiniboine was named in 1883 by Dr. George Dawson after the Assiniboine or Stoney Indians who hunted in the Canadian Rockies. The name means, "those who cook by placing hot stones in water."

Og, Gog and Magog are all individuals mentioned in the Old Testament of the Bible. Both English and Celtic mythology also tells of Gog and Magog who were giants. Lakes in the area of Mount Assiniboine are named after all three, but only Og and Magog are the names of mountains.

Cone Mountain (2896 m), which completes the panorama to the right, rises to the north of Bryant Creek valley beyond the west end of Spray Lakes Reservoir. The name describes its profile, which is not seen from the Buller Pond viewpoint, but rather from the Spray River valley.

Badge of the Royal Canadian Dragoons. Courtesy We Stand on Guard.

Mount Birdwood. Photo Gillean Daffern.

Mount Assiniboine

"The monuments of Cheops and Chephren dwindle into nought before this gigantic architectural cliff of nature."[188] These words were written by the Catholic priest and explorer Pierre-Jean de Smet in 1845 while he was camped at what is now known as White Man Pass. De Smet was probably the first non-native to see the mountain and he, like everyone who has seen it since, was obviously very impressed.

James Outram, the first man to reach the summit of Mount Assiniboine, summarized the significance of this well-known, though not frequently seen mountain when he wrote, "Its massive pyramid forms a conspicuous landmark from almost every considerable eminence for scores of miles around, towering fully 1500 feet above its neighbours, and by its isolation no less than by its splendid outline commanding attention and admiration."[189]

Although it cannot be seen from any of the heavily travelled highways, Mount Assiniboine has become one of the most recognized mountains of the Rockies. This is undoubtedly because of its distinctive pyramidal shape as well as the lovely glacier and lake that lie below it when viewed from its most photographed angle. But from this viewpoint the "Matterhorn-like" shape does not present itself, and it is the mountain's height and massiveness that are most impressive. The east-facing cliffs of Mount Assiniboine rise over 1700 m above the valley below.

It is located on the Continental Divide, with Banff National Park to the east and Mount Assiniboine Provincial Park to the west. With an elevation of 3618 m, Mount Assiniboine is the highest mountain south of the Columbia Icefields.

It was named in 1885 by George Dawson who first saw it from Copper Mountain on the south side of the Bow Valley west of Banff. The Assiniboine were a branch of the Sioux Nation, which hunted in the area.

It was in 1893 that Tom Wilson led the first group to the base of Mount Assiniboine. Robert L. Barret was the client and he undoubtedly was hoping to make the first ascent, but no attempt was made to climb the mountain, probably because the trip was undertaken late in the season. Following unsuccessful attempts by several parties, the mountain gained a reputation for difficulty. When it was heard that Edward Whymper, the

The east face of Mount Assiniboine from Buller Pond.

famous English climber who made the first ascent of the Matterhorn, was to visit the Rockies with his own Swiss guides, there was talk he would attempt Assiniboine even though he was 62 at the time. But finally James Outram, together with Swiss guides C. Bohren and Christian Hasler, were successful in 1901.

Mount Assiniboine from Lake Magog.
Courtesy Whyte Museum, NA 71-557.

Mt. Rose · Cougar Mtn. · Mt. Rae · Forgetmenot Mtn. · Banded Peak · Outlaw · Forgetmenot Ridge · Mt. Cornwall · Mt. Glasgow · Mt. Remus · Mt. Romulus · Nihahi Ridge

38 The Peaks of the Elbow River Headwaters

From west of Priddis
Highway 22, 9.4 km west of the junction with Highway 22X; 10.5 km east of the junction with Highway 66.

John Rae. Courtesy Glenbow Archives, NA-1252-2.

It can be argued that the most enjoyable mountain panoramas are the ones that surprise you, that appear almost instantly as you hike over a high pass or drive over the crest of a hill. This view into the headwaters of the Elbow River valley is one of these. It's well worth the time to stop at the top of the hill to take a careful look at what can be seen.

Mount Rose (2515 m) is part of a small group of peaks that stands in front of the main front range between the Sheep and Elbow rivers. Although the origin of the name is listed as unknown, it likely relates to Alberta's provincial flower, the wild rose. **Cougar Mountain** (2863 m), which lies six km beyond Mount Rose, was named prior to 1928. Again, the specific reason for the name is not known, but it probably received the name following a cougar-related event that took place on the mountain.

Mount Rae (3218 m), the northernmost mountain of the Misty Range, is the high, distant peak eight km west of Cougar Mountain. Its northern slopes feature a small glacier below which lies Elbow Lake, the source of the Elbow River. Only the upper portion of its steep eastern cliffs can be seen from this viewpoint, its distinctive notch and triangular-shaped peak being very apparent. This massive, block-shaped mountain is the highest that may be seen from the prairies.

While in the employ of the Hudson's Bay Company, Dr. John Rae conducted four major expeditions into the uncharted Canadian Arctic and in the course of these journeys walked the incredible distance of 36,000 km. Whereas other explorers of the era were of the opinion that it was important to conduct their exploration in dress and manner of Victorian gentlemen, John Rae adapted to the Inuit techniques of living off the land. He was the first to bring back to England the news of Sir John Franklin's fate, although his information that the expedition's members had ended their days eating human flesh was not well received. James Hector named the mountain after Dr. Rae just four years later.

A small range of four mountains dominates the centre portion of the panorama. From Mount Rae the Elbow River flows between Cougar Mountain and the easily identified **Banded Peak** (2934 m), which is the southernmost of the group of four. To the right lies a somewhat similar peak unofficially referred to as **Outlaw** (2850 m), the gentler slopes of **Mount Cornwall** (2970 m) and then **Mount Glasgow** (2935 m).

Mount Glasgow has the distinction of being the first mountain in the Canadian Rockies named by a non-native. In 1792, Peter Fidler took bearings on it and called it Pyramid.

The long, low ridge that lies in front of this range and a small summit at its south end are named **Forgetmenot Ridge** and **Forgetmenot Mountain** (2332 m) after the beautiful blue flower, the Forgetmenot, that grows throughout the foothills and mountains of the Alberta Rockies. The Elbow River flows in a northerly direction behind the ridge to its confluence with the Little Elbow River.

The Marquis of Lorne sketched this group of four peaks during an ambitious, cross-country trip he made during his years as governor general of Canada (1878-1883). An engraving of the sketch was made by Edward Whymper, the man who first climbed the Matterhorn and who visited the Rockies several times in the early years of the twentieth century.

The block-shaped **Mount Romulus** (2832 m) is the northernmost peak seen from this location. Its lower neighbour, **Mount Remus** (2688 m), lies just in front of it and is difficult to identify. Both mountains are located just to the north of the Little Elbow River, just across the valley from Mount Glasgow. Romulus and Remus were the legendary founders of Rome.

The southern end of the eight km-long **Nihahi Ridge** (2545 m) begins below the summit of Mount Romulus and extends to the right side of the panorama. Nihahi means "rocky" in the Stoney language, the name probably being derived from the cliff band that lines the eastern side of the ridge.

Mount Rae. Photo Gillean Daffern.

Snow Highlighting

If one has the opportunity to watch a particular panorama on a regular basis, one of the most interesting aspects is the changing snow patterns. Aside from the general rule that the higher mountains receive more snow than the lower ones, there are also other variables. The mountains of the Elbow Valley provide some excellent examples.

Probably the major factor is the varying angle of slopes associated with strata. Soft layers such as shale erode much faster than hard layers such as limestone. A mountain with a number of soft and hard layers will provide opportunities for snow to accumulate along the gently sloped, softer layers and, therefore, to highlight the layering of the rocks.

The band on Banded Peak is a dramatic example of this form of highlighting. Positioned near the top of the mountain is a steep cliff that is most obvious in winter after a fresh fall of snow, the dark cliff accentuated against much gentler slopes that are white.

The steep cliffs of Mount Romulus also remain snow-free. However, they have the effect of causing a large cornice to form along the east or lee side of the cliff tops. This results in a horizontal white line of snow that becomes quite thick over the winter. Very distinctive when viewed from the foothills and plains, the cornice remains well into late spring.

The small range from Banded Peak to Mount Glasgow for some reason seems to attract falls of early and late season snow. Even in the late spring and early summer, rain may fall on nearby mountains, but this group will be white with fresh snow. There must be some meteorological reason for this but it is not a simple one.

The "Cornwall Snowpatch" is generally the last accumulation of winter snow to melt in this area of the mountains. Very noticeable from the prairies to the east, it is a near circular shape of snow on the eastern slopes of Mount Cornwall just below the summit.

The cliffs that make the band on Banded Peak.

Mount Romulus.

The Battle of the Falkland Islands

HMS Glasgow. Courtesy Jane's War at Sea *1897-1997.*

Mounts Cornwall and Glasgow are two of over a dozen peaks in the Kananaskis area named after British warships of World War One. Wheras most were ships that had participated in the Battle of Jutland in 1916, *HMS Cornwall* and *HMS Glasgow* were both cruisers that played a significant role in the 1914 Battle of the Falkland Islands.

German naval forces had been raiding commercial shipping in the south Atlantic and a much larger Royal Navy formation was dispatched to the area. The battle, although not a complete victory, freed Britain's trade and troop transport routes in that part of the world from the threat of surface raiders for the duration of the war.

The *Cornwall* and *Glasgow*, together with *HMS Kent*, were pursuing three German warships that were trying to escape the main battle and seek refuge in Tierra del Fuego. Choosing to concentrate their attention on the German light cruiser Leipzig, *HMS Glasgow* engaged first, attempting to slow down the fleeing German ship and allow the *Cornwall* to catch up and assist. The *Glasgow* suffered some hits but the tactic was successful and soon *HMS Cornwall* came into range and her fire struck the Leipzig's foretopmast and carried it away. *Cornwall* then turned to starboard and pounded the enemy vessel with all of its heavy guns. The two English ships then engaged their wounded quarry from opposite sides, their combined fire becoming more and more effective as they slowly closed the range. Out of ammunition, the Leipzig fired its last two torpedoes, but the British had by then retreated out of range. The British ships then reapproached the Leipzig to see if the Germans had "struck her colours," but since her ensign was still flying, opened fire once more. Her flag still flying, the Leipzig heeled over to sink rapidly by her bows. The British ships could rescue only 18 of the 286 sailors and Captain Ellerton of *HMS Cornwall* later recalled that he regretted that an officer as gallant as Captain Haun of the Leipzig was not one of them.

Banded Peak, Outlaw, Mount Cornwall and Mount Glasgow from the east. From a sketch by the Marquis of Lorne called "The Rocky Mountains from our camp on Elbow River." Engraving by Edward Whymper.

Thunder Mtn.   Tornado Mtn.   Livingstone Gap   Livingstone Range

39 The View through the Gap to Tornado Mountain

River valleys that cut through mountain ranges often provide a window through which we can see distant peaks. As one travels along Highway 22 between Longview and Highway 3, the Livingstone Range forms an unrelenting wall of Paleozoic limestone to the west. Fortunately, there is a wonderful window along this 110 km stretch of road where one can see through the Livingstone Gap to distant mountains that are on the Continental Divide.

The Oldman River flows southwest along the western side of the Livingstone Range, then abruptly turns to the east through Livingstone Gap to enter the foothills and eventually pass under a bridge on Highway 22. From this viewpoint, if the weather is favourable, one is treated to a spectacular view through the window to **Tornado Mountain** (3236 m), some 41 km to the west.

As a member of the Palliser Expedition, Lieutenant Blakiston was travelling south through the valley that now contains Highway 22 in August of 1858 when he, too, paused at the river and enjoyed the view to the west. Lieutenant Blakiston described and named the Livingstone Range, writing in his journal, "The gap through which I had seen this mountain (Tornado Mountain) was in the eastern or near range, of very regular form, extending, with the exception of this gap, for a distance of five and twenty miles without a break. The crest of the range was of so regular a form that no point could be selected as a peak. I therefore gave the whole the name of 'Livingstone's Range,' it is a very marked feature when seen from the plains outside."[190]

Dr. David Livingstone was a British explorer, geographer and missionary who for 32 years travelled through Africa from the Cape to the equator and from the Atlantic to the Indian Ocean. In doing so, he laid the foundation for British title in many parts of the continent. Understandably, fellow explorers such as John Palliser and his contemporaries revered Dr. Livingstone and Palliser is said to have felt privileged to have sat beside him at a meeting of the Royal Geographic Society.

With an elevation of 3236 m, Tornado Mountain is the highest point in Alberta between Mist Mountain, near Highwood Pass, and the American border. Because it towers 160 m higher than any other peak in its vicinity, it is easily identified from the prairies,

From the Oldman River bridge
Highway 22, 87 km south of Longview; 24.7 km north of the junction with Highway 3.

Livingstone Lookout. Looking south across Livingstone Gap to Thunder Mountain. Photo Tony Daffern.

particularly when the summit is snowclad. Tornado Pass lies immediately to the west of the mountain at the headwaters of Dutch Creek.

Thunder Mountain (2335 m) is part of the Livingstone Range that lies to the south of the Livingstone Gap. In 1792, Peter Fidler climbed to the summit, thus completing the first ascent of a mountain in the Canadian Rockies. It was named by Morrison Bridgland in 1915, probably because of storms near the summit of the mountain.

A fire lookout is located on top of the long, high ridge five km north of the Gap. It is manned during the early summer with the primary goal of spotting grass fires to the east rather than forest fires to the west.

Classic Alberta foothills ranching country provides the foreground to this panorama.

Top: The Livingstone Range, south of Livingstone Gap; Centre Peak is the high point.

Bottom: The upper north ridge of Thunder Mountain, looking toward the summit. Photo Gillean Daffern.

Livingstone Gap

A visit to Livingstone Gap, 18 km west of the Oldman bridge on Highway 519, entails a very scenic drive to an area with much geographic and historic significance. The spectacular, narrow canyon through which the Oldman River flows was said to have been the playground of Napi, the trickster God of the Blackfoot people.

Peter Fidler was the first European explorer to visit southern Alberta, travelling south along the same path as Highway 22 now takes between the Livingstone Range and the Porcupine Hills. His journal, written in 1792, describes a game that the Indians said had been invented by Napi. Fidler witnessed the "Hoop and Dart" game being played on a flat area in the Gap. Eleven elders of the tribe sat on 11 piles of stones to act as umpires as players rolled a hoop and attempted to throw arrows through it.

When George Dawson visited the Gap in 1884, he found one large cairn over two m high and two smaller ones. They seemed to have no use as landmarks and having apparently been there for a long time, Dawson concluded they had been built over the years by Indians placing a stone upon them as they entered the mountains via this route. Nearby, on a flat piece of ground he noted the remains of two rectangles formed of large stones. He learned from the Indians that this area was called the Old Man's Playing Ground and that the Oldman River derived its name from the location.

The reason why the Oldman River created its spectacular S-shaped course through the Livingstone Range is not clear. Generally when a river cuts through the mountains in a direction perpendicular to the trend of the ranges it does so at a point where sub ranges begin or end and often where there is some faulting. In the case of the Livingstone Gap there is no break, geologically, in the Livingstone Range and thus no obvious reason for the Oldman River to cut through the range at this point.

Geologists believe there must have been an ancestral Oldman River whose waters eroded a valley through rock layers that were younger and more easily eroded than the present rocks

Livingstone Gap. Photo Doug Elias.

of the Livingstone Range. When the river finally eroded down to the level of what is now the top of the Livingstone Range, the river must have been able to maintain its course, despite the difficulty of having to cut through the harder limestones. Over the years the river cut deeper and deeper, and with further sculpturing by glaciers that would have flowed through the Gap during the ice ages, the modern form of the Gap evolved.

David Livingstone. Courtesy Livingstone.

Tornado Mountain

Lieutenant Blakiston was very impressed with the high distant peak he saw from this viewpoint in 1858 and recorded in his journal, "I was now looking through the gap in the near range through which the river issues, I saw a very decidedly dome-shaped mountain. It afterwards proved to be, when seen from the plains, and also from the top of a mountain in the Kootanie Pass, the highest and almost the only peak rising above the others in this part of the mountains. After the distinguished British naturalist, I named it Gould's Dome."[191]

John Gould was an ornithologist who wrote large, lavishly illustrated books including a five-volume work entitled *Birds of Europe*. Blakiston was very interested in natural history and must have, at some point, been impressed by Gould's work.

The mountain remained Gould's Dome for 57 years until it was renamed by R. W. Cautley of the Boundary Commission in 1915. His associate, Arthur Wheeler, was most impressed by

the mountain and wrote that, "the precipices of Tornado Mountain rise fully 2500 feet and the gigantic rock buttresses that stand out, separated by huge, cavernous chimneys, are awe inspiring."[192] The survey team members made the first and second ascent of the mountain. Their report reads, "Tornado Mountain is a storm centre of the locality and, on the occasion of two ascents, the party had narrow escapes; first, through a cloud-burst accompanied by sheets of hail, which caused the mountain to run wild, torrents of water cascading down its slopes in every direction, and rockfalls, loosened by the water, crashing on all sides; on the second occasion, a fierce electrical storm encircled the summit and severe shocks were felt by members of the party. For days at a time dark thunder clouds, rent by vivid flashes of lightning, were seen to gather around the summit, and similar storms were encountered while on other adjacent heights."[193] Wheeler wrote: "I never saw a mountain break loose like that before.... Still mountains are mountains, and you must take them as you find them."[194]

These experiences generated the idea to rename the mountain Tornado. The peak four km to the south, also visible from the Oldman River bridge, was given the name Gould's Dome even though it is not dome shaped at all. It is some 205 m lower in elevation and considerably less impressive. We can only speculate as to whether Thomas Blakiston would have approved of the name change.

Although the summit of Tornado Mountain is a beautiful sight, the view of the surrounding area from the summit shows considerable devastation. To the west lies the massive surface coal mining operations of the Elk Valley. To the south and east, large areas of old growth forest have been clear-cut in the Dutch Creek valley and more recently in the headwaters of Hidden Creek. However, the environs of Tornado Pass that lie immediately west of the peak have been spared and from this viewpoint the "gigantic rock buttresses and cavernous chimneys" are still most impressive.

Tornado Mountain. Photo Glen Boles.

Mt. Hoffman — Mist Mtn. — Gibraltar Mtn. — Mt. Burns — Bluerock Mtn. — Missinglink Mtn.

40 A View to Mist Mountain

Shortly after entering Kananaskis Country on the Sheep River Trail, one is treated to an excellent view of several of the mountains at the headwaters of the Sheep River.

The most spectacular feature is the east face of **Mist Mountain** (3140 m), which is framed on the left by an unnamed high point of the Highwood Range before the view is cut off by the tree-covered **Mount Hoffman** (1829 m). Mr. Hoffman served as a member of Arthur Wheeler's survey party and later became the proprietor of a hotel in Olds, Alberta.

Although the east summit of **Gibraltar Mountain** (2665 m) is clearly seen from this viewpoint, the steep north face that is the reason for its name is not visible until one drives farther west to the Bluerock recreation area at the western end of Highway 546.

The Sheep River flows between Gibraltar Mountain and the somewhat closer Mount Burns from its headwaters below the summit of Mount Rae.

Multi-summited **Mount Burns** (2936 m) is named after Pat Burns, one of the "Big Four" who organized the first Calgary Stampede in 1912. Together with A. E. Cross, A. J. McLean and George Lane, $100,000 worth of financing was arranged and the event was billed as "The Greatest Outdoor Show on Earth." Burns was very successful as a pioneer of both the ranching and meat packing industries. However, to the south of Mount Burns lies the site of one of Pat Burns's less successful business ventures. Around the turn of the century, Julius Rickert discovered coal in the valley

and was able to interest Pat Burns in the project. With the influx of one million dollars in capital, "Pat Burns Coal Mines Limited" began operations in 1913. There were plans for a railway to the site and part of the right-of-way was cleared, but by the 1920s the demand for coal declined and the project was abandoned.

Pat Burns made many trips through the foothills to his mine when the means of travel was by horseback. His employees wondered, at times, why he went so often. In his book *Pat Burns, Cattle King*, Grant MacEwan suggests that, "there was a subtle reason, simply his love for the foothills, and in making a pack trip to Upper Sheep Creek he was finding the best possible release from business pressures and catching the summer and autumn glories of the back country."[195]

Bluerock Mountain (2789 m) is easily recognized from the prairies, partly because it lies about five km to the east of the main front range. It features a long east-facing escarpment that from the summit stretches a considerable distance to the south before descending into the low forested hills. Because Bluerock is closer to a viewer on the prairies, it appears a darker blue than more distant peaks.

Further views to the right are interrupted by the tree-covered **Missinglink Mountain** (1935 m). Missinglink is a very strange name for a mountain in Alberta to have, the "Missing link" usually referring to a gap in the evolutionary development of homo sapiens. Although official records list the reason for the name as being unknown.

From the Sheep River valley
Highway 546, 8.2 km west of the Kananaskis Country boundary. After entering Kananaskis Country on Highway 546, the view of the mountains is quite limited until the road descends to a bench directly above the Sheep River and turns to the northwest. One km later, the road makes a 90 degree turn toward the mountains. A good sized parking area just prior to the turn is an ideal location from which to enjoy this wonderful view of the peaks at the headwaters of the Sheep River.

George Dawson, Mist Mountain and the Misty Range

George Dawson. Courtesy National Archives Canada, PA 26689.

Clearly, the highlight of the drive up the Sheep River valley is the view of Mist Mountain, a peak of the Misty Range that is the highest and most spectacular group of Front Range mountains in the southern Rockies. Located directly west of High River, they are the highest mountains visible from the prairies at any point in the province. Mount Rae and Mist Mountain are particularly prominent in the view from the city of Calgary.

Geographically, the range is very short with a length of only 17 km. But what the range lacks in length it more than makes up for in altitude, with three peaks—Mount Rae, Storm Mountain and Mist Mountain—exceeding 3000 m, very high for mountains so close to the foothills.

The range is made up of Carboniferous-age rocks between 286 and 345 million years old. Very fossiliferous, they contain numerous species, the most outstanding of which is the solitary horn coral. Cone-shaped, it grew to a length of 10 cm with a diameter of up to five cm.

The Misty Range, as well as Storm Mountain and Mist Mountain, were named by Dominion geologist George Dawson in 1884 after he experienced a prolonged period of bad weather below the western slopes of the range during his survey of the area. A second good reason for the name, and one probably not known by Dr. Dawson, is that it features a warm spring that causes mists to rise above it during the winter months.

Mist Mountain is a most attractive mountain from both the Sheep River viewpoint and from the prairies to the east. The vertical ribs of the east face are often highlighted by snow well into the early summer when it has melted off the nearer and lower mountains. Even without snow-highlighting, the ribs often cast interesting shadows across the face.

During the 1940s Donald King and a group of friends from High River explored and climbed in the Highwood and Sheep valleys. They began a tradition, which lasted for several summers, of camping on the summit of a mountain west of their hometown and, at a pre-arranged time and date, shooting flares into the night sky. Hundreds of people in the area would assemble on hilltops and other suitable sites to watch the show, which occurred precisely on the second as planned. At 11:00 pm on July 7, 1946, the launch site was the summit of Mist Mountain—the first recorded ascent of the mountain.

Gibraltar Mountain

Gibraltar Mountain. Photo Gillean Daffern.

When this peak is viewed from Bluerock recreation area, its similarity to the famous Rock of Gibraltar at the entrance to the Mediterranean Sea is striking. The 700 m-high, near vertical and in some places overhanging cliffs of the north face are most impressive. The slopes below these cliffs receive very little direct sunlight and are completely covered in a healthy accumulation of moss.

In the summer of 1918 the mountain was the scene of a tragic accident. Three young men who were working at Pat Burns's coal mine in the valley below climbed to the top of the mountain, which at that time was known locally as "Sheer Cliff." One of them, a visitor from the west coast named Patterson, was approaching the cliff edge when a gust of wind blew him over the precipice. The body was never found. Over four decades later a trunk containing his personal belongings was discovered in a corner of one of the old mining town's buildings when it was about to be burned down.

While there are easy ways to get to the summit of Gibraltar Mountain, the north face is a real mountaineering challenge. It was first climbed in 1971 by Bill Davidson and Jim White who took eight-and-one-half days to complete what was the first extended aid climb in the Canadian Rockies.

ON MISTY MOUNTAIN

I climbed to the top of a mountain,
Mounted God's stair to the skies;
I looked to the east with amazement,
Westward I stared in surprise;
I stood on the spire of a nation,
Held half a world in my eyes.

When suddenly a cloud settled over,
Quickly the vapours rolled in
So silent, and eerily soundless,
Setting directions a-spin;
The sun was a full moon of crimson
Bright where the curtain held thin.

Somewhere to the east sprawled the prairies,
Westward a peak-studded wall;
As shroudlike the white mists enveloped
My world in their foggy, wet pall;
I stood in the middle of nowhere,
Gazing at nothing at all.

Beyond the Hills[196] by Donald King, is a book of poetry inspired by his group's explorations and climbs. This poem was written after his experiences on Mist Mountain.

Mist Mountain at the headwaters of the Sheep River.

41 The Peaks of the Highwood Range

From Eden Valley

Highway 541, 22.8 km west of Longview; 21.3 km east of the junction with Highway 40.

The cross on Holy Cross Mountain. Photo Dan Fox.

Legend has it the Highwood River valley west of Sullivan Creek was named Eden Valley by Dr. George Dawson in 1883. A very well-travelled man, Dr. Dawson is also thought to have said it was the most beautiful valley he had ever seen.

Another story is that in 1897 a Mrs. Pflaughaupts rode up the Highwood River valley in a wagon and was very impressed with the country and the views. She and her husband established the Eden Valley Ranch, and thereafter the valley between Sullivan Creek and the Front Ranges became known as Eden Valley.

In the foreground of the panorama is the Stampede Ranch, one of the earliest ranches in this classic foothills ranching country. It was established in 1884 by Jim Meissinger who operated it until 1920 when the ranch was purchased by Guy Weadick, who named it the Stampede Ranch.

Weadick was born in New York and first came to Alberta in 1908 as the manager of a Wild West Show. A master showman at fancy and trick roping, he promoted and managed the first Calgary Stampede in 1912 before establishing the dude ranch business at the Stampede Ranch. The first Alberta-made movie, starring Hoot Gibson, was made here.

The **Bull Creek Hills** (2149 m) form the left edge of this panorama and with an elevation of 2150 m, they are very high hills. Although the name was well-established locally because of the fact the hills lay at the head of Bull Creek, the name was not made official until 1980. Four years later, in a rather bizarre turn of

events, the creek after which they were named was renamed Cutthroat Creek at the suggestion of a provincial fisheries biologist. So now there is no longer (officially at least) a Bull Creek for the Bull Creek Hills to stand beside.

The view of the mountains from the Eden Valley is somewhat obstructed by high foothills, but several interesting peaks may be seen. Immediately right of the Bull Creek Hills rises **Holy Cross Mountain** (2650 m), so-named because of the clearly defined cross that generally appears in the spring as the snow is melting off the east-facing slopes. The appearance of the cross is dependent upon the snow conditions of the previous winter and it only lasts a couple of weeks at best. The peak lies just north of Highwood Gap, at the point where the Highwood River passes through the Front Ranges into the foothills. George Pocaterra named the mountain in the early 1900s soon after arriving from his birthplace in the Italian Alps.

Mount Head (2782 m) lies to the north of a long, high saddle that connects it to Holy Cross Mountain, the two mountains being similar in height. The lower, eastern summit of Mount Head appears on the right from this viewpoint and from it a high, jagged ridge leads to the western summit that overlooks the upper Highwood River valley.

Lying midway between Mount Head and Mount Pyriform is **Patterson's Peak** (2728 m), named in March 2000 after Raymond Patterson. After purchasing the Buffalo Head Ranch from his friend George Pocaterra in 1933, Patterson travelled extensively in

The Naming of Mount Head

The history behind the naming of Mount Head is complex and somewhat unclear. What is known is that John Palliser placed the name "Mount Head" (in rather large letters) on his 1865 map, but did not refer to its specific location in his written report. However, he obviously felt that it was a significant point because it is the only named mountain on his map between the Bow Valley and Crowsnest Mountain just north of Crowsnest Pass. The name was placed on the Continental Divide at what appears to be the location of what is now known as Mount Tyrwhitt, which is only a minor high point near the northern end of the High Rock Range at Highwood Pass.

It seems probable that Palliser was not referring to the mountains that we now know as Mount Head or Mount Tyrwhitt. It is thought he may have applied the name to the large group of mountains at the head of the Kananaskis and Highwood rivers or perhaps to Mount Joffre, the peak that dominates this group. Palliser would have seen these peaks as he traversed North Kananaskis Pass in 1858.

With a copy of the map in hand, George Dawson travelled up the Highwood River in 1884, making a more detailed survey of the area. He realized that the mountain seen from Eden Valley was not significant enough to have been the only peak named on Palliser's map between the Bow Valley and Crowsnest Mountain. He also noted that the map showed the mountain to be located just northwest of the northern extremity of the Livingstone Range. Dawson determined that what we now know as Mount Head was the closest mountain to the point labelled Mount Head (at least relative to the Livingstone Range on Palliser's map) and so decided that, "There is no reason why the name should not be preserved in connection with the mountain, even if it be not that originally intended."[197]

However, the status of Palliser's report was such that on many small-scale maps of the Canadian Rockies printed as late as the 1920s Mount Head appears on the Continental Divide and is the only named peak between Kicking Horse Pass and the international boundary.

The mountain honours Sir Edmund Head, governor general of Canada at the time of the Palliser Expedition. John Palliser's father was an old friend of Sir Edmund's who encouraged Palliser and even gave him a retriever dog to take on the expedition. It is a most intriguing coincidence that there is a distinct head shape on the northeastern ridge of the lower, eastern summit when viewed from the foothills to the east. If Palliser's assistant, Thomas Blakiston, noticed "the head" when he travelled along the route of the present Highway 22, he made no mention of it in his journal. The presence of this head, gazing toward the northern skies, seems a very logical explanation for the mountain's name to those who have not read this interesting history.

Mount Head from Flat Creek, showing "the head." Photo Gillean Daffern.

the Highwood River valley area until the early 1940s. He made the first ascent of Mount Head and very likely was the first to climb Holy Cross Mountain as well.

In his books *The Buffalo Head* and *Far Pastures*, Patterson describes his explorations and adventures in the Highwood, Kananaskis and Elk river valleys. He also wrote extensively of his explorations in northwestern Canada, his account of the Nahanni River being a classic.

Holy Cross Mountain, Mount Head and Patterson's Peak are part of the Highwood Range that extends north to Gibraltar Mountain above the Sheep River.

From this viewpoint it is easy to see why the Dogtooth Range was so-named. It features **Mount Pyriform** (2621 m) whose name is descriptive, pyriform being a scientific term meaning pear-shaped. Snow often accentuates a small, horizontal cliff band near the summit. The peak to the south of Mount Pyriform is quite prominent from this angle, but is unnamed.

Junction Mountain (2682 m) can be seen on the right side of the panorama. The headwaters of Junction Creek, which flows north to the Sheep River, lie to the west of the mountain.

Flat Creek flows from the southern slopes of Junction Mountain to join the Highwood River just east of Stampede Ranch. Together with its tributaries, Wileman Creek and Head Creek, Flat Creek drains virtually all of the area below the peaks visible from the Stampede Ranch viewpoint.

Patterson's Peak

In his book *Far Pastures*, Raymond Patterson recalled driving up the Highwood Valley with Mary Pope, a visiting dude from England. They had a flat tire right at the top of Sullivan Hill, just east of Sullivan Creek. He wrote, "That flat couldn't have chosen a better time or place. This was Mary's arrival in the foothills and the Eden Valley of old Dr. Dawson burst on her suddenly in all its autumn glory."[198]

After the tire was changed, Patterson was telling her the names of the mountains and included Patterson's Peak. The ranch guest was most impressed, saying, "So you've got a mountain named after you. How marvellous! Tell me all about it, now, while we look at it."[199] Patterson explained with a grin, "That peak's nameless on the map. It's an orphan mountain and I just adopted it. If you ride up Flat Creek… you can leave your horse and clamber on up the valley to a lake that's hidden behind that mountain."[200]

Raymond Patterson claimed the mountain with some justification having had some personal experience on the peak. On a June morning, a year or two previous to hosting Pope, he had left the ranch before dawn on what became an unsuccessful solo attempt to climb the mountain. Renovations were being made to the Patterson home and with the disruptions and construction crew working, there were "too many people around and not a moment's peace…. So, without saying anything to anybody, I got up in the dark one morning and got my own breakfast and got out of the place while the bunch was still enjoying its beauty sleep—just kissed the outfit good-bye for one whole perfect day."[201]

Patterson rode 19 km up Flat Creek to the small lake below the northwest slopes of the mountain and, "…after lunch I took it into my head to climb that peak."[202] In *Far Pastures*, Patterson details how his progress was stopped about halfway to the summit by overhanging rock and how he eventually plummeted out of control down a steep snowslope before gently sliding onto the rocks at the bottom.

He concluded his story by telling Mrs. Pope, "All in all it was a memorable day and I still feel I have a sort of squatter's right to that mountain."[203]

Top: Raymond Patterson. Photo Palmer Lewis. Courtesy Marigold Patterson.
Bottom: Patterson's Peak (centre) from Sullivan Hill.

42 The Courcelette Group

As one approaches the narrow section of the Highwood River valley where it cuts through the Front Ranges, the mountains of the Continental Divide begin to loom above the nearer tree-covered ridges. To the left, a spectacular group of peaks lies to the south of Fording River Pass. To the north of the pass, two interconnected, lower mountains mark the point where westward progress by car is blocked.

Baril Peak (2998 m), the closest of the group on the left side of this panorama, honours M. C. L. Baril, a Dominion land surveyor who was killed in action on November 9, 1915.

Mount Cornwell (2972 m) and the peaks of **Mount Courcelette** (3044 m) exhibit distinctive horizontal bedding planes that are often highlighted by snow. Because all of the peaks in this group are considerably higher than others in the area, and because one is viewing the northern slopes, they often have snow cover.

John Travers Cornwell was only 15 years old when he was awarded the Victoria Cross, the Commonwealth's highest award for bravery in action against the enemy. Mount Cornwell was named in his honour in 1918.

Lying entirely in British Columbia beyond the Continental Divide, Mount Courcelette is the highest mountain of the High Rock Range with the exception of Tornado Mountain some 38 km to the south. The mountain is, to some extent, a small range with six distinct high points along its six km length. From this viewpoint one is only able to see Courcelette's northern outlier and the northern summit. The highest point, just 37 m higher than the northern summit, lies one km to the southwest and is hidden behind Mount Cornwell.

With an elevation of 2299 m, Fording River Pass lies to the right of Mount Cornwell and to the left of Mount Armstrong. The pass derives its name from the Fording River, which flows below the pass to the west and was named by George Dawson after his party found it necessary to ford it a number of times.

Formerly known as Table Mountain because of its long, flat top, **Mount Armstrong** (2823 m) was officially named after J. D. Armstrong of the surveyor-general's staff who was killed in action in 1917. Mount Armstrong's west face features a number of vertical ridges that are often highlighted by snow and by sun and shadow.

Mount MacLaren (2850 m) lies immediately north of Mount Armstrong. It is a complex peak with several individual summits, three that lie on the Continental Divide and a fourth that is entirely in British Columbia. Brigadier-General Charles H. MacLaren graduated from Osgoode Hall Law School in 1905 and went on to command a brigade of Canadian artillery during the First World War.

The high, rocky ridge that rises in front of Mount Armstrong and then slopes steeply to form the southern side of Highwood Gap is officially unnamed but has been known by at least three different names over the years. In the early 1890s "Mackenzie and Mann" had a logging camp on Cataract Creek and this is probably the source of the name Mount Mann, which was used prior to the 1920s. It is also known as The Battleship and **Grizzly Mountain** (1905 m). While riding in the area, Ross Edey and his father Merv saw a grizzly standing on its hind legs on top of the highest point of the ridge.

From the eastern approach to Highwood Gap
Highway 541, 11.6 km east of the junction with Highway 40; 32.4 km west of Longview.

Baril Peak from Rye Ridge. Photo Gillean Daffern.

John Cornwell VC

John Cornwell VC. Courtesy The Boy Hero.

John Trevers Cornwell was a 15 year-old member of a gun crew aboard HMS Chester, a Royal Navy cruiser that was severely damaged during the Battle of Jutland in 1916. His teacher described him as "an ordinary English boy"[204] whose "one great desire was to be a sailor."[205] In October, 1915, he enlisted as "Boy, 2nd Class" in the Royal Navy. He was referred to as, "a good boy, quick and ready, and always spick and span."[206]

Cornwell was soon promoted to "Boy, 1st Class" and on May 31, 1916, was aboard the cruiser HMS Chester as it sailed into the greatest sea battle of the First World War. As part of the crew of the forward six-inch gun it was his duty to set the gun to the range telephoned to him from the fire control. In a letter to John Cornwell's mother, Captain Lawson of the Chester described the "Boy Hero of the Battle of Jutland's," actions when he wrote, "The wounds which resulted in his death were received in the first few minutes of the action. He remained steady at his most exposed post at the gun, waiting for orders. All but two of the ten crew were killed or wounded, and he was the only one who was in such an exposed position. But he felt that he might be needed, and indeed he might have been; so he stayed there, standing and waiting, under heavy fire, with just his own brave heart and God's help to support him."[207]

Cornwell's ship was also honoured. Mount Chester is part of the Kananaskis Range and may be seen from the Smith-Dorrien/Spray Trail.

Mount Cornwell and Cornwell Cirque.
Photo Gillean Daffern.

Courcelette and the Battle of the Somme

Courcelette is a village in France that was the scene of heavy fighting by Canadian Forces during the Battle of the Somme. There was no other battlefield in the Great War that witnessed more killing per square yard than the Somme. The day the battle began, July 1, 1916, proved to be a disaster unequalled in the annals of British military history—some 57,500 men killed, wounded or missing in just a few short hours.

As part of the Battle of the Somme, Courcelette was attacked by the Canadian Corps on September 15. Seven of the newly-invented British tanks were allocated to the front and played an important role as the enemy was said to have felt quite powerless as they crawled along the top of the trenches filling them with continuous machine-gun fire. Later in the day the Canadians, with the assistance of one of the tanks, captured the village. There were 11 counterattacks the next day, but the prize was held.

The horror experienced by those who fought at Courcelette was typical of this war. A survivor recalled, "All around our men were falling, their rifles loosening from their grasp. The wounded, writhing in their agonies, struggled and toppled into shell holes for safety.... On my front and flanks soldier after soldier was tumbling to disablement or death, and I expected my turn every moment. The transition from life to death was terribly swift."[208]

When the Battle of the Somme ended on November 24, it had cost the Canadian Corps 24,029 men. In total the British lost an astonishing 600,000; the French 180,000 and the Germans 300,000. When this distinctive, twin-peaked mountain was being mapped by the Interprovincial Boundary Survey in 1918, the sacrifices of the Canadian regiments that fought in the Battle of the Somme were honoured.

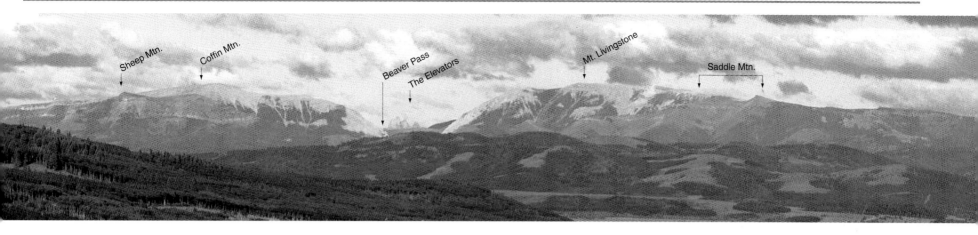

43 A View into the Upper Oldman Valley

Highway 533 heads southwest from Nanton over Timber Ridge, a high forested area of the northern Porcupine Hills, to eventually connect with Highway 22 at Chain Lakes. As the highway reaches its highest point on the ridge near the A. E. Cross Historic Site, the views to the west open up, but it is not until one reaches the top of a low hill 0.4 km east of the Monkman Ranch gate (just east of the intersection with the Stavely Road) that a most interesting panorama suddenly presents itself.

A spectacular set of distant mountains is framed between two quite similar and nearer mountains of the Livingstone Range to form this attractive view. **Coffin Mountain** (2429 m) to the left of **Beaver Pass** is named because it resembles a "sarcophagus" or stone coffin. **Mount Livingstone** (2422 m) to the right of the pass is named in honour of the famous British explorer of Africa, David Livingstone. **Sheep Mountain** (2271 m) lies in front of Coffin Mountain, and the mountain known locally as **Saddle Mountain** (2240 m) rises in front of Mount Livingstone.

Through Beaver Pass one may see the peaks known as **The Elevators** (2911 m). Part of the High Rock Range that forms the Continental Divide, the peaks are situated 21 km beyond the pass on the west side of the upper Oldman River valley. They are named after prairie grain elevators, a resemblance that is most striking when the peaks are viewed from a few kilometres south of Claresholm on Highway 2.

George Dawson, who was the assistant director of the Geological Survey of Canada at the time, made a special note in his journals about these peaks when he travelled up the Oldman River to its headwaters in 1883. His August 10 entry noted that he, "took a photo of grand, rugged peaks of limestone though with rather poor light."[209]

The Elevators from the Oldman River valley. Photo Glen Boles.

From the Monkman Ranch Hill

Highway 533, 31.5 km west of the junction with Highway 2; 6.2 km east of the junction with Highway 22.

The saddle showing between the two summits of Saddle Mountain. Photo Gillean Daffern.

137

44 The Mountains of the Crowsnest Pass

From Blairmore

Highway 3, 14.2 km west of the junction with Highway 507; 19.5 km east of the B.C. border.

Phillipps Peak (left) and Mount Tecumseh.

Although there are several interesting mountain views as one enters the Front Ranges on Highway 3, it is not until the highway reaches Blairmore that the peaks of the Continental Divide come into view. While passing the golf course to the north of the highway, a beautiful panorama of 10 mountains, including the dramatic Crowsnest Mountain itself, appears through low points in forested ridges.

The mountains that can be seen south of the Crowsnest Pass are part of a small range called the Flathead, which was named in 1904 after the Flathead Indians of Montana. The southernmost five peaks in this panorama honour individuals who played prominent roles in the early history of communities located in this the most southerly major pass through the Canadian Rockies.

The high forested ridge at the far left was named **Willoughby Ridge** (2057 m) in honour of a family of early settlers who ran a boarding house near Sulphur Springs at the base of Turtle Mountain. The ridge reaches an elevation of 1686 m and is part of the Crowsnest volcanics. This is one of the few areas in western Canada where volcanic rock has been forced through the limestone beds to the surface. The Ironstone forestry fire lookout is located on the top of the ridge.

Mount Coulthard (2642 m), the southernmost peak visible, was named for R. W. Coulthard. He was a prominent mining engineer and the general manager of West Canadian Coal Company in the early part of the century.

To the north of Mount Coulthard is **Andy Good Peak** (2621 m), named in 1960 to honour an early resident of the area who was involved in prospecting and many other interesting activities.

Sherman Parrish was the first settler in the Crowsnest Pass area. In 1898 he homesteaded at the foot of what is now known as **Mount Parrish** (2530 m) and began raising cattle. A big man with very large hands, Sherman Parrish was also an artist and inventor. One of his hobbies was making model steam engines that really worked.

138

Mount McLaren (2825 m) lies somewhat to the east of the main range, and unlike the other peaks has a rather gentle east slope. In 1881, Senator Peter McLaren, a lumberman from Perth, Ontario, purchased a small lumbering operation from John Kean on Mill Creek. His company's busiest time was during the construction of the Crowsnest Pass Railway in 1897 and 1898, when the Peter McLaren Lumber Company had the contract for ties. All along the right-of-way his loggers hand-hewed the numerous Douglas firs in advance of the rails.

Mounts McLaren, Parrish, Andy Good and Coulthard form a semicircle that contains the headwaters of North York Creek. In the upper reaches of this cirque are the entrances to a major cave system within Mount Coulthard. In addition, one can find the remains of a Royal Canadian Air Force DC-3 aircraft. It was on a flight from Comox, B.C. to Greenwood, Nova Scotia, on January 9, 1946, when it struck one of the peaks of the Flathead Range. Rescue crews took several days to locate the crash site and then another 10 more to remove the seven bodies on toboggans.

To the right of Mount McLaren on the skyline is **Chinook Peak** (2591 m). The mountain was named by Jim Kerr, a lifelong resident of the Crowsnest Pass who lived on Sherman Parrish's original homestead. Jim looked directly at the peak from his living room window and during a cold spell he would watch it and when the snow started to blow off the top from the west he knew a chinook was not far behind.

Sentry Mountain (2435 m) is the northernmost peak of the Flathead Range and is just visible to the right of a large, unnamed flat-topped ridge. Sentry was formerly named Sentinel Mountain, but was renamed in 1915 to avoid confusion with another peak named Sentinel that lies at the headwaters of Willow Creek west of Nanton. Presumably, Sentry Mountain keeps watch over the traffic through the Crowsnest Pass.

Mount Tecumseh (2549 m), which lies to the north of Crowsnest Pass, is the southernmost peak of the High Rock Range. It has had a complex history in terms of its name. It was originally called Mount Wilson, but members of the Boundary Survey had the name changed to avoid confusion with the Mount Wilson above the Icefields Parkway. The mountain was also known locally as "The Sleeping Giant," as its profile was thought to resemble one. For a period of time it was known by this name, Phillipps Peak and Mount Tecumseh.

In 1960 the name Tecumseh was confirmed and the slightly lower southwest shoulder was named **Phillipps Peak** (2500 m). Tecumseh, which means "Shooting Star," was a Shawnee

Indian brave who as a brigadier general led his warriors to fight alongside Sir Isaac Brock against the American invaders in the War of 1812. It is unusual for a mountain in western Canada to be named after events in eastern Canada that took place almost 100 years prior to settlement in the west. It is likely the mountain was named after another place or person that had previously been named after the Indian who fought with Brock.

Michael Phillipps was a Hudson's Bay Company clerk in charge of a post at the mouth of the Wild Horse River. While searching for gold in 1873 he became the first white man to visit the Crowsnest Pass area.

This is the southern end of the **High Rock Range**, which forms the Continental Divide for almost 100 km from Phillipps Peak to Mount Muir in the upper Highwood Valley. To the north of Mount Tecumseh there is a break in the range at Deadman Pass, which is only 200 m higher than Crowsnest Pass. To the right of Deadman Pass unnamed high points on the High Rock Range are the most distant features in this panorama.

Looming at the far right is the highest and most outstanding peak in this panorama, **Crowsnest Mountain** (2785 m). To its right is the southern end of the **Seven Sisters** (2591 m), a high narrow ridge with seven distinct high points. It was first named The Steeples by John Palliser's expedition. The first ascent of the "Main Tower" of the Seven Sisters was made in 1951 with considerable difficulty by the well-known guide, skier and photographer, Bruno Engler, who lived in the Crowsnest Pass for four years.

DC-3 crash site in the Flathead Range.

Seven Sisters. Photo Gillean Daffern.

Andy Good

Andy Good at his zoo. Courtesy Glenbow Archives, NA-1384-5.

Andy Good Peak was named after one of the most interesting of the early residents of the Crowsnest Pass. In 1897, when the railway was under construction through the pass, Andy and Kate Good decided that the hotel business offered great potential. At the point where the railway was to cross the border between British Columbia and what was then part of the North West Territories, they set up a hotel using tents. Before long they realized they did, indeed, have a good location and built a wooden structure to replace the tent hotel. It was an impressive structure, featuring twin stairways to a large front porch area supported by fine stonework. The upper floor of the hotel featured a large balcony. As it was on the Continental Divide, they called it the Summit Hotel.

Baptiste La More, a hunter of French origin, supplied wild meat for the hotel's dining room. The hotel must have had some excellent chefs because it became known across the continent for its fine food. Renowned as well was the collection of mounted trophy game heads in the bar and lobby.

In order to offer visitors even more in the way of memorable attractions, Andy had a zoo. He tamed birds and animals, including bears, and taught them to do numerous interesting and challenging tricks. As the years went by the Summit Hotel became a popular resort. In 1909, the Goods were able to advertise the largest dance pavilion under cover in British Columbia.

CPR crew at the Summit Hotel, early 1900s. Courtesy Glenbow Archives, NA-1384-3.

Portion of Mount Coulthard, Andy Good Peak, Mount Parrish, Mount McLaren and Chinook Peak.

Crowsnest Mountain

"Crowsnest Mountain, seen from the south, stands out as an isolated massif, rising in terraces and resembling a great fortress or keep."[210]

One of the Rockies' "Calendar Peaks," Crowsnest Mountain is a spectacular sight as one drives through the Crowsnest Pass. It stands aloof, in front of the main High Rock Range and this, together with its steep cliffs on all sides, is what makes it so eye-catching.

George M. Dawson, who was surveying in the area on behalf of the Geological Survey of Canada in 1883-84, noted that the mountain, as well as the pass and the river, were named by the Cree Indians after big black birds that nested in the area. The Cree were referring to ravens, but unfortunately the white men of the day translated the name as Crowsnest when it should have been Ravensnest.

The steep cliffs of Crowsnest Mountain attracted none other than Edward Whymper, the famed British mountaineer who had been the first to climb the Matterhorn in Switzerland. Whymper, owing to a combination of age and alcohol, was well past his prime at this point. However, in 1903 he made arrangements with Tom Wilson and two Swiss guides, and together they travelled to the unclimbed peak that Whymper had been told could not be climbed.

When the day came to climb the mountain, Tom Wilson and the two guides, one of whom was Hans Kaufmann, succeeded in reaching the summit but were forced to leave the famous Whymper in camp as he was suffering from having had too much to drink.

The cliffs forming the upper part of the mountain are limestones of Paleozoic age, while the more gentle slopes below the cliffs are much younger, being of Mesozoic age. Because of this, some people believe that Crowsnest Mountain is "upside down."

The rocks that make up the cliffs were once connected with the rocks forming the High Rock Range to the west. The rock sheet, moving along the Lewis Thrust Fault, was pushed upward and eastward to ride over the younger rocks. On Crowsnest Mountain the fault is horizontal and is located just below the cliffs.

Gradually the streams cut down all around the mountain and left the peak isolated, an island of old rocks sitting on younger rocks known as a klippe.

The ballad following explains the geology and was found in the register on the summit of Crowsnest Mountain in 1992. Al Bradley is a geologist and, together with his brother Fred, spearheads the "Crow Cavorters," a group that has been meeting each year since 1971 for a weekend of "mountain climbing, caving and cavorting" in the Crowsnest Pass area. Al's poem was written partly to commemorate the twentieth anniversary of the "Cavorters."

The Ballad of the Upside-down Mountain

There've been strange tales told, by cavorters bold,
round the campfire late at night.
When cavorting juice, makes the tongue go loose,
and all reason takes a flight.
The Crowsnest Pass, has heard many an ass,
spin tall tales about the town.
But the best of them all, is the one about how,
this mountain got turned upside-down.
Now I know it sounds strange,
to those who don't range,
the mountains high and low.
But I've been there, and by God I swear,
that indeed I believe it is so.
Now upside-down, is a relative noun,
the meaning not always the same.
Is not bottom over top, a reasonable spot,
to end debate on the upside-down claim.
For this is what's so, on the mountain called Crow,
where tectonic upheaval has reigned.
The Lewis Thrust, has ripped the Earth's crust,
to create the present terrain.
The rocks at the bottom, are the youngest in place,
while the oldest crowd the sky.
Now that's upside-down, so let's go to town,
and drink beer as long as you buy.
—A. R. Bradley, P. Geol.

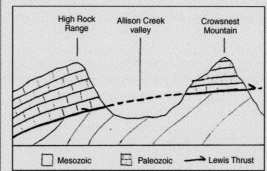

Left: Crowsnest Mountain from Allison Road. Photo Gillean Daffern.

Right: Geological cross-section through the High Rock Range and Crowsnest Mountain.

Whistler Mtn. Lys Ridge Barnaby Ridge Southfork Mtn. Mt. Haig Gravenstafel Ridge St. Eloi Mtn. Syncline Mtn.

45 Some Peaks of the Castle River Headwaters

From the confluence of the Castle and West Castle rivers
Highway 774, 16.5 km south of Beaver Mines.

As one drives south on Highway 774, this viewpoint provides the last broad panorama before the highway turns to the southwest toward the recreation area and the headwaters of the West Castle River. Beyond this point the valleys become narrower and the views much more limited.

Rising behind a low forested ridge in the foreground is **Whistler Mountain** (2210 m), named after the whistling or hoary marmot. A forestry lookout building is located on the slightly lower, western peak.

The headwaters of the Castle River lies near the boundary of Waterton Lakes National Park, some 25 km up the valley beyond Whistler Mountain. **Lys Ridge** (2522 m) lies to the east of the river and stretches for eight km. It is one of several features in this area named after locations in France where Canadian troops fought during the First World War. The Lys River flows through the city of Armentières. A high point on the ridge is named West Castle, probably because it is directly across the Castle River valley from Castle Peak.

The massive **Barnaby Ridge** (2471 m) lies between the Castle and West Castle rivers and dominates the centre portion of the panorama. There are four distinct high points on this nine km-long ridge, the lowest and closest being named **Southfork Mountain** (2330 m). The origin of both names is not known. Barnaby Ridge was named in 1916 and is probably related to World War One in some manner. It is difficult to imagine how the name Southfork Mountain came into use. The peak lies between the two rivers and they both flow from south to north.

Mount Haig (2610 m), which looms up above the western slopes of Southfork Mountain, lies on the interprovincial border and

is the most distant and highest peak in this view. Captain R. W. Haig was the chief astronomer and senior military officer for the British Boundary Commission of 1858-1862, which had the task of mapping the international boundary from the Continental Divide to the Pacific. The surgeon and naturalist on the commission, Dr. David Lyall, was also honoured in this way by having a prominent peak at the headwaters of the Oldman River named after him. What is interesting is that both these individuals were so well respected by members of the Interprovincial Boundary Survey who named the peaks some 55 years after Captain Haig and Dr. Lyall did their work.

Gravenstafel Ridge (2391 m) is the mountain where the Westcastle ski runs are located. The original Gravenstafel Ridge is located in the Flanders area of northern France. One of the highest points in the area, the ridge was the scene of several battles involving the Canadian Army including the Second Battle of Ypres in 1915. Their efforts and sacrifices were honoured by the naming of this attractive feature.

To the right of Syncline Brook rise the slopes of **St. Eloi Mountain** (2504 m). The summit is hidden behind the eastern peak of **Syncline Mountain** (2441 m). The Interprovincial Boundary Survey members generally named mountains after individuals, locations or warships that were playing a role in the war. Syncline Mountain is an exception, however, and the surveyors noted in their report, almost as if to excuse themselves, that the mountain was named after, "a very apparent physical feature."[211] The word syncline is a geologic term that refers to rock layers that have been folded in such a manner that the beds form a trough.

The headwaters of Suicide Creek lie between the two peaks of Syncline Mountain. It was named by Morris Bridgland in 1915, but the origin of this name is not known.

Canadians at the Battle of Ypres. Courtesy We Stand on Guard.

Hoary Marmot

"As I smoked away, silent as all about me, suddenly a sharp clear whistle that awoke the echoes far and near, thoroughly roused me, and sent all other thoughts to the rout."[212] This was John Keast Lord's introduction to the hoary or "whistling" marmot. Lord, a naturalist attached to the British Boundary Commission in 1861, was quietly smoking his pipe near the point where the provinces of Alberta and British Columbia, and the United States meet, above Cameron Lake in Waterton Lakes National Park.

Living in colonies, these badger-sized animals inhabit high alpine meadows and live in holes that they excavate under large rocks. They spend the summer eating as much grass, flowering plants, roots and berries as possible in order to acquire a thick layer of fat to sustain them through seven or more months of hibernation.

Marmots are wary creatures. A group generally has a sentinel posted on a prominent boulder to warn of predators such as grizzly bears and golden eagles. The warning sound is a resounding, shrill whistle of alarm at the sound of which the colony often dashes off to the safety of their burrows. The sound of a marmot whistle is very special to most hikers and climbers who visit their habitat, as it means one has reached the alpine level with all its special attractions.

The Castle River area is not the only one in the Alberta Rockies to have a feature named in honour of this animal. Farther to the northwest in the Egypt Lake area of Banff National Park there is a high valley known as Whistling Valley, which culminates in Whistling Pass. Farther northwest yet lie two different Marmot mountains, a Marmot Creek, a Marmot Pass, a Whistlers Creek, a Whistlers Pass and a mountain near Jasper known as The Whistlers.

The animal's name is attached to mountain features in both of Canada's official languages. The marmot was referred to by the early French Canadian fur traders as the siffleur after the French word siffleur, which means "to whistle." Siffleur Falls, Siffleur River and Siffleur Mountain all lie near the headwaters of the North Saskatchewan River in Banff National Park. Lastly, the marmot's scientific name, *genus arctomys columbianus*, was the basis for Arctomys Peak and Arctomys Creek northwest of Saskatchewan River Crossing.

The fact that so many natural features in Alberta are named in honour of the marmot indicates it was a favourite animal of the early explorers and travellers.

Marmot. Photo Gillean Daffern.

Mount Haig (left) and Gravenstafel Ridge.

Victoria Peak

Mt. Matkin

Windsor Mtn.

Castle Peak

Mt. Gladstone

Table Mtn.

46 An Island of Paleozoic

From the Gladstone Valley road

The Gladstone Valley road, 5.3 km south of the junction with Highway 507. The Gladstone Valley Road begins 4 km east of the junction with Highway 774 and 4 km west of Highway 775.

Table Mountain. Photo Gillean Daffern.

"Looking to the mountains ahead of us I picked out the most prominent, and took bearings on them. There were two near one another bearing thirty miles south, one of which, from the resemblance to a castle on its summit, I named Castle Mountain."[213] The peaks at the head of the Gladstone River clearly caught Thomas Blakiston's eye as he travelled along the eastern edge of the Rockies in 1858.

Attractive mountains with the well-known names of **Castle** and **Victoria** may be seen from this viewpoint on a "road less travelled" in the Mill Creek valley west of Pincher Creek. The Gladstone Valley road does not connect with any others. It simply follows the valley into the headwaters of Mill Creek, and serves as access to local ranches.

Where the Gladstone Valley road turns sharply to the right after cresting a ridge 5.3 km from the junction with Highway 507, it provides a striking view of the mountains at the head of the valley. One can even see the tip of a distant peak beyond the Castle River on the Continental Divide.

Rising from behind a forested hill on the left side of the panorama is **Victoria Peak** (2569 m). Named in honour of Queen Victoria, the peak and its east-facing slopes are also part of the Twin Butte panorama.

To the right of Victoria, a high, forested hill looms in the foreground between Whitney Creek to the left (east) and Mill Creek to the right (west). Rising above the hill's low point, the distant summit of **Mount Matkin** (2418 m) is just barely visible. This 2418 m-high peak lies 27 km away across the Castle River and on the Alberta-British Columbia border.

Windsor Mountain (2558 m) is the highest and most striking feature in the Gladstone Valley panorama. The two peaks that make up the mountain are 1.5 km apart. The eastern peak is not named but the western one is known as **Castle Peak** (2558 m).

Windsor Mountain shows up clearly on a surface geological map as an island of Paleozoic rock within a large area of Precambrian. This is apparent when one looks carefully at the facing cliffs and notes their colour and the strata, which is more similar to mountains farther north than it is to neighbouring peaks.

Although **Mount Gladstone** (2370 m) is 100 m lower than Castle Peak, it is 3.5 km closer and so seems to loom over more distant peaks. It was named in honour of "Old Glad," William S. Gladstone, and lies between Mill Creek to the east and Gladstone Creek to the west. The headwaters of both valleys are clearly visible from this angle.

The small peaks between Gladstone and Table Mountain are unnamed.

Table Mountain (2232 m) lies west of Gladstone Creek and east of Beaver Mines Lake. It is named for its striking likeness to a table. From this angle only a portion of the table can be seen and the nearer, highest point of the mountain is not table-like at all.

"Old Glad" (William Shanks Gladstone)

W. S. Gladstone was born in Montreal, Quebec, in 1832 and joined the Hudson's Bay Company at the age of 16 as a carpenter and apprentice boat builder. He was sent west shortly after joining the HBC and spent five years working at Rocky Mountain House in the winter and Fort Edmonton in the summer. During his years with the Hudson's Bay Company he acquired the nickname "Old Glad." In the spring of 1853 he was sent down to York Factory with a load of furs and instructions to bring back additional trade goods. On his return he also brought a passenger, Father Lacombe, who was to have a crucial influence on the history of Alberta, particularly in the area of new settlers and native people relationships.

In 1855, so the story goes, "Old Glad" wanted to marry a native girl at Fort Edmonton. The girl was Roman Catholic and Father Lacombe wanted Gladstone to change his religion but he refused. The priest finally agreed to marry them but told Gladstone that he would not be able to wear his vestments during the service. "Old Glad" is said to have replied, "I don't care if you're bare naked just as long as you marry us."[214]

For the next nine years Gladstone travelled widely over western Canada, meeting up with the members of the Palliser Expedition at one point and later joining a group of prospectors who were heading for Montana following the discovery of gold. However, upon arriving in the goldfields he set up a carpentry shop instead. In 1870 he was involved in the building of Fort Hamilton just west of Lethbridge. The previous fort at this site had burned down and because there was so much money to be made selling whiskey to the Canadian natives, its American owners hired "Old Glad" to put up a strong, well-fortified trading post. Business was so good at the new fort it soon became known as Fort Whoop-up. "Old Glad" worked at the fort during the winters until 1874 when the arrival of the North West Mounted Police brought an end to the whiskey trade by the Americans.

Taking advantage of new opportunities, Gladstone then operated a sawmill near the creek that bears his name and prepared lumber, windows and doors for the North West Mounted Police fort that was built at Macleod.

"Old Glad" continued to live in the Mill Creek valley until he passed away in 1911. The mountain and creek were named in his honour in 1916.

*William Gladstone with his granddaughter.
Courtesy Glenbow Archives, NA-184-23.*

Windsor Mountain

The natives had referred to this peak as "Queen Mountain" when Thomas Blakiston of the Palliser Expedition noticed the prominence in 1858 and named it Castle Mountain. Its fortress-like appearance is obvious from the Gladstone Valley viewpoint. His colleague with the expedition, James Hector, had also named a mountain "Castle" in the Bow Valley between Banff and Lake Louise. So in 1915 the peak was renamed Windsor Mountain as it was felt the mountain's profile resembled Windsor Castle in England. The name "Castle" was retained, however, when it was decided to name the higher of the two peaks Castle Peak.

An interesting parallel to this evolution of names is found in the naming history associated with the other Castle Mountain. After being named Castle Mountain by James Hector because of its fortress-like appearance, it was renamed Mount Eisenhower in 1946 in honour of American General Dwight D. Eisenhower, the supreme commander of the Allied Forces during the final year of World War Two. Bowing to public pressure, the naming authorities officially changed the name back to Castle Mountain in 1979. However, as a compromise, a prominent feature on the mountain was given the name "Eisenhower Peak."

Windsor Mountain.

The Matkin Brothers and their Mountain

F/O Merlin Matkin. Courtesy Garth and Violet Matkin.

Mount Matkin. Photo Murray Anderson. Courtesy Castle-Crown Wilderness Association Slide Library.

In Alberta alone, the names of some 120 peaks relate to the First World War, including 25 that were named after Royal Navy warships. Mount Matkin is one of only seven in the province named in honour of Albertans who gave their lives for their country during the Second World War. The place-naming policies of the day were, inadvertently, not followed properly but even if they had been, the peak would still be named Mount Matkin.

The mountain was unnamed and no one seemed concerned about this until 1962 when the Geological Survey of Canada, which must have been doing some work in the area, suggested to the federal Department of Mines and Technical Surveys that the name Citadel Peak be approved for the mountain. However, the department noted there was already a Citadel Peak on the B.C.-Alberta border and suggested to the Geographic Board of Alberta that, "an Alberta casualty name" be used. At this time there was a policy to name features after individuals who had been killed in action during World War Two and whose home was closest to the feature.

The provincial department, in error as it turned out, determined that Cardston was the nearest hometown of a casualty and recommended the name Mount Forsyth. Flying Officer Thomas R. Forsyth was a 21 year-old navigator who had served with the Royal Canadian Air Force. His Halifax bomber was part of 431 Squadron when it was lost on April 28, 1944.

But the federal department pointed out that there was already a Mount Forsyth in the East Kootenay district of British Columbia, only 140 km away, and asked the provincial department to suggest another name. The department then recommended Mount Matkin and the name was approved. Sergeant Philip Matkin, a bomb aimer with the RCAF, listed his home as Leavitt, just west of Cardston. At the time of his death at aged 24, he was still training with #12 Operational Training Unit and had not seen any action. He was tragically killed when he was struck by a car on Bayswater Road in London after getting out of a taxi. Although not an operational casualty, the accident was clearly war-related as it took place at night when London was blacked-out.

As it turned out there was another World War Two casualty whose home was closer to the mountain than Leavitt. Merlin Leigh Matkin, Philip's younger brother, listed his home as Waterton Lakes Park as his family had recently moved there. Flying Officer Matkin was a 21 year-old pilot assigned to 514 Squadron of the Royal Air Force when he was killed on January 17, 1945. Bomber Command crews were a closely knit unit and it was considered bad luck to fly with another crew. Despite this F/O Matkin volunteered to fly with a crew whose regular pilot was unavailable. One hundred and thirty-eight aircraft attacked the benzol plant at Wanne-Eickel, Germany, and F/O Matkin's Lancaster was the only one not to return to base. All seven crew members were killed.

So the mountain would have been named Matkin even if the oversight had not been made. It seems fitting that the memory of both brothers be honoured by this mountain's name. The Matkin brothers and F/O Forsyth were just three of 10,000 young Canadians killed while serving with Bomber Command during the war.

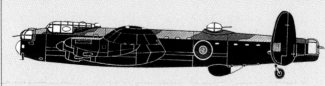

Lancaster bomber. Courtesy Lancaster in Action.

Mt. Galwey   Mt. Dungarvan   Cloudy Ridge   Mt. Glendowan   Spionkop Ridge   Loaf Mtn.   Drywood Mtn.   Pincher Ridge   Victoria Peak   Prairie Bluff

47 From Prairies to Peaks

The view to the west from the crest of a hill south of Twin Butte is unique in Alberta in that the mountains rise abruptly out of flat grasslands. As well, the mountains are more sculptured than those seen farther north. Here the Front Ranges have been dissected by various creeks into a number of clearly defined peaks.

The southernmost peak seen from the Twin Butte viewpoint is **Mount Galwey** (2377 m), which lies at the left side of the panorama. Mount Galwey is a low mountain (2348 m) at the southern end of an unnamed range that terminates about six km from Waterton Lakes. It was named after Lieutenant W. J. Galwey who was the assistant astronomer for the British Boundary Commission from 1872 to 1876.

There is a peak to the right of Mount Galwey that is actually some 60 m higher. However, this peak remains unnamed.

Mount Dungarvan (2575 m), which lies some four km north of Mount Galwey, is a much more massive peak. Dungarvan is an Irish term for a rough and broken mountain. It is also the name of a seaport in County Waterford, Ireland. The summit ridge consists of basalt pinnacles of the Purcell sill, a sill being a layer of igneous rock that was forced between layers of sedimentary rock and then cooled and solidified.

Cloudy Ridge (2606 m) is a 4.5 km-long sloping ridge that extends in a northeasterly direction from its highest point on the main range to the prairies. It is named, presumably, because the upper part of the ridge is often hidden by clouds.

Mount Glendowan at 2673 m is the highest peak visible from the Twin Butte viewpoint. Lying near the headwaters of Yarrow Creek, the mountain was named by Morris P. Bridgland in 1915 after a range of mountains in County Donegal in Ireland. Glendowan means deep glen, so Bridgland may have been influenced by the narrow, steep-walled valley to the northeast of the mountain.

All of the peaks in this panorama from Mount Glendowan south are in Waterton Lakes National Park.

From Twin Butte
Highway 6, 2.3 km south of Twin Butte; 9.5 km north of the Pine Ridge viewpoint.

Mount Galwey from the Blakiston Valley. Photo Doug Elias.

Mount Dungarvan (left) and Cloudy Ridge.

The Calgary memorial to those who served in South Africa. Photo Janet Scase.

Spionkop Ridge (2576 m) is seven km in length and trends WSW-ENE. Its high point lies at its western end. From the Twin Butte viewpoint one can only see the eastern summit (2444 m), which is sometimes referred to as Spread Eagle Mountain. Its profile is very similar to that of Mount Burke, a peak in the northern part of the Livingstone Range at the headwaters of Pekisko Creek, west of Nanton. The original Spion Kop is a mountain in southern Africa and was the site of a battle in the South African (Boer) War of 1899-1902. It is unusual to find a mountain in the Canadian Rockies with a name related to this war.

The viewpoint allows one to see up a very straight valley to the north of Spionkop Ridge to the headwaters of Spionkop Creek. **Loaf Mountain** (2639 m) lies at the western end of a ridge that lies to the north of the creek. The mountain that appears to rise to the right of Loaf Mountain is actually the western part of the ridge. Although there is no resemblance to a loaf of bread from this angle, the origin of the name is thought to be descriptive.

Drywood Mountain (2514 m) is a low peak that lies between South Drywood Creek and Drywood Creek. The origins of the names are not known but have been in use since 1904.

Beyond Drywood Creek lies the west end of **Pincher Ridge** (2423 m), which is located just south of Pincher Creek.

Victoria Peak (2569 m) was named by the well-known mountain surveyor J. J. McArthur in honour of Queen Victoria. This prominent peak lies between the Gladstone River valley and Pincher Creek.

The distant **Prairie Bluff** (2254 m) is an isolated point that frames the right side of this beautiful panorama from Twin Butte. Prairie Bluff lies 21 km to the northwest of the viewpoint.

Victoria Peak.

Spion Kop Mountain, January 24, 1900

Colonel Thorneycroft looked Winston Churchill in the eye and told him he was not going back to the top of Spion Kop. Churchill had just delivered an order from Thorneycroft's superior. The colonel was on his way down Spion Kop Mountain and met Churchill who was on his way up. The 26 year-old future prime minister of Great Britain—the man who was to lead the Free World in its great war against Nazi Germany four decades later—had just delivered General Warren's directive that the British position on top of the mountain was to be held. But the general's headquarters was in a valley two miles west of Spion Kop. He could observe nothing and had to rely on messengers to bring him reports. He was not aware that Colonel Thorneycroft and 4,500 British troops had just spent a very full day on the mountain.

The Boers were white residents of Dutch, German and Huguenot descent who had formed the South African Republic and the Orange Free State. They resented the fact that the British had gradually laid claim to south African lands and taken control of its mining operations and commerce. After declaring war on Britain and winning some initial victories, they were eventually overwhelmed by the reinforced British in what became known as the South African or Boer War (1899-1902).

Some 8,000 Canadians, almost all cavalrymen, sailed to South Africa to support the Mother Country. The troops distinguished themselves, and Canadians at home viewed their soldiers' success with pride and marked their victories by massive parades and demonstrations.

Spion Kop is a three-cornered, table-mountain near the headwaters of the Orange River in southeastern Africa. It dominated the area in which the Boers and the British were fighting. At 9:00 pm on January 23, 1900, Colonel Thorneycroft led his force of 1,700 men up the southern side of the peak, reaching the top seven hours later. The soldiers immediately tried to dig themselves in but their tools were almost useless against the solid rock. When the mists lifted at 8:00 am the British found the shallow trench they had so labouriously scraped out was in the centre of an exposed plateau. It became a lovely clear day and well-placed Boer marksmen began to fire upon the huddled British troops with rifles, heavy guns and two pom-poms, causing heavy casualties.

At about 1:00 pm the strain proved too much and some soldiers surrendered. A more complete collapse was only prevented by the personal intervention of Thorneycroft who rallied the fainthearted, and the bitter struggle was resumed. During the afternoon reinforcements arrived until almost 2,500 troops were packed on the summit while another 2,000 waited just below. As darkness arrived, a steady trickle of men began to descend and at 8:00 pm Thorneycroft ordered the abandonment of the mountain.

As the day wore on the Boers also became disheartened and many deserted. At nightfall they too retreated. When the Boers reoccupied the summit the next day they were horrified with what they saw on the top of Spion Kop Mountain. The British had suffered 350 killed and the Boers about 300.

Because no Canadian units were involved in this battle, one wonders who it was whose view of the mountain brought back to mind these horrors from the South African War.

The east end of Spionkop Ridge.

Geology of the Southwestern Corner of Alberta

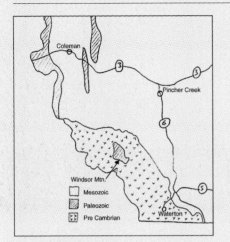

Geological surface map of southwestern Alberta.

South of the Bow Valley, the geology of the mountains remains quite consistent until about 40 km north of the international border. Until this point the trend of the Front Ranges and the Continental Divide has been slowly curving away from the general northwest-southeast trend to almost exactly north-south just north of Highway 3.

About 10 km south of Beaver Mines a significant change in the orientation of the mountain front occurs with very noticeable changes in the geology and the general look of the peaks. At this point the orientation of the Front Ranges abruptly changes to northwest-southeast, then for a distance of approximately 25 km, from Syncline Mountain on the international border to Prairie Bluff, the trend is essentially east-west.

North of this point the Precambrian rocks are not seen at the surface in the thrust faulting that created the Front Ranges. South of Beaver Mines the Lewis Thrust Fault that began at Mount Kidd in the Kananaskis Valley cuts more deeply and the Precambrian rocks are brought to the surface. Throughout this area they are virtually the only rocks to be found from the initial mountain slopes to the Continental Divide, some 20 km to the west.

Mountains composed of rocks of this age can also be found in the Rocky Mountains between where the Continental Divide enters Alberta from the north to just south of Lake Louise.

The Precambrian rock exposed in the mountains of southwestern Alberta is said to be among the best preserved sedimentary rock of that age in the world. Because rocks of Precambrian age are in excess of 570 million years old, the fossils found in them are of only the most primitive animals such as sponges and worms.

These Precambrian rocks that form the view from Twin Butte are made up of layers of sandstone, shale, limestone and dolomite of the Purcell Group. They are more easily eroded than the hard Paleozoic limestone that forms the steep cliffs of the Livingstone Range to the north. This is why the view from Twin Butte includes a number of individual peaks whereas the Livingstone Range, particularly south of the Oldman River, tends to have few isolated mountains.

Another change that is very obvious when viewing the Front Ranges south of Prairie Bluff is that the foothills have been largely eroded. The peaks rise abruptly out of flat grasslands.

Prairie Bluff.

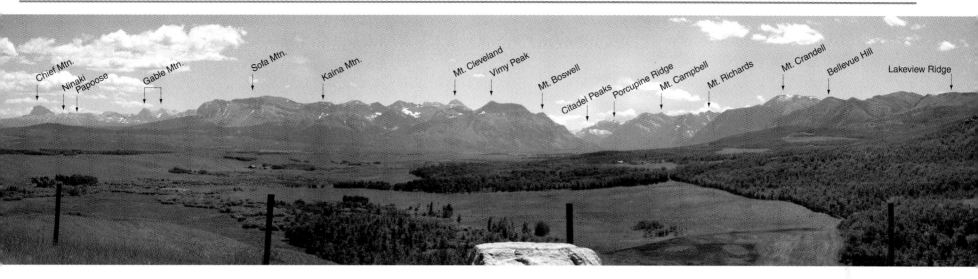

Chief Mtn. · Ninaki · Papoose · Gable Mtn. · Sofa Mtn. · Kaina Mtn. · Mt. Cleveland · Vimy Peak · Mt. Boswell · Citadel Peaks · Porcupine Ridge · Mt. Campbell · Mt. Richards · Mt. Crandell · Bellevue Hill · Lakeview Ridge

48 An International View

As one drives south from Pincher Creek through the Twin Butte area, the mountains to the south are hidden until the road crosses over Pine Ridge. From this location the gently rolling prairie provides foreground for a spectacular, international panorama.

It was in 1865 that Kootenai Brown first viewed this area after travelling over South Kootenay Pass. He later recalled: "…we climbed to the top of one of the lower mountains. The prairie as far as we could see east, north and west was one living mass of buffalo. Thousands of head there were, far thicker than ever range cattle grazed the bunch grass of the foothills."[215] The grasslands in the foreground of the Pine Ridge panorama are what Kootenai was looking at but one can only imagine the "living mass of buffalo."

The panorama from Pine Ridge is one that undoubtedly was welcomed by Brown in later years as he paused on the ridge during his many trips from the more developed areas of southern Alberta to his home beneath Goat Mountain near Waterton Lakes.

Chief Mountain (2768 m), the block-shaped peak on the left side of the panorama, lies 99 km away and nine km across the border in the United States. Located on the western boundary of Montana's Blackfoot Indian Reserve, its isolated location and imposing silhouette have made it one of the most recognizable mountains in southern Alberta. When the lighting is good, **Ninaki**

(Chief's wife) (2475 m) and **Papoose** (2275 m) may be seen to the right of the Chief.

The twin-peaked **Gable Mountain** (2823 m) lies six km southwest of Chief Mountain.

Sofa Mountain (2520 m) is in Canada and lies 16 km in front of Gable Mountain. It rises to the west of Chief Mountain Highway (Highway 6) and the Chief Mountain port of entry into the United States. Kootenai Brown recalled his first impression of the mountain: "Coming down from the mountain, where we got our first glimpse of the buffalo, we soon reached the prairie shore of a large lake at the further side of which a mountain rose to a sofa-like peak among the clouds. This mountain was afterwards called Sofa Mountain."[216] When viewed from the north on Highway 6 it is easy to see the large cirque that forms the seat of Brown's sofa.

Thirteen years later Kootenai Brown led a group of six Indians in the search for a hunter and two women who had climbed part way up Sofa Mountain to skin two sheep that the hunter had killed the day before. Leaving the women to skin the sheep, the hunter climbed still higher after another sheep. Suddenly, a storm blew in and trapped all three on the mountain. Brown and the rescue party found the two women wrapped in the sheep skins but frozen stiff. The hunter, too, had frozen to death after exhausting all his matches in trying to start a fire. He had also tried to kill himself with his

From Pine Ridge
Highway 6, 9.5 km south of Twin Butte; 10 km north of the turn-off to Waterton Lakes townsite.

Vimy Peak from across Middle Waterton Lake.

Oil derrick at Oil City, c. 1905. Courtesy Glenbow Archives, NA-670-65.

rifle. The Indians brought the body of the hunter down to where the women had perished and built a stone cairn around them.

Kaina Mountain (2892 m) rises in the distance behind the Front Ranges. The name Kaina (formerly Kainah) refers to the Blood tribe of the Blackfeet Confederation. It may derive from the word "Kai" for (dried) blood, or perhaps it is from the word "Akaina" meaning many chiefs.

The highest peak, suitably located at the centre of this panorama, is **Mount Cleveland** (3190 m). The mountain is named in honour of Grover Cleveland, the 22nd and 24th president of the United States.

Vimy Peak (2385 m), over 800 m lower than Mount Cleveland, is a Front Range mountain located west of the valley that contains Waterton Lakes. Upper Waterton Lake lies below its western slopes and Middle Waterton Lake below its northern slopes. Vimy Ridge stretches for three km to the southeast of the peak. The mountain was originally known as Goat Mountain until it was renamed in 1917.

On Easter Monday in that year, four divisions of the Canadian Army attacked and held the most heavily defended German position on the western front during this point in the First World War. The French and British had attempted to take Vimy Ridge and both had failed at tremendous cost, the French alone having lost 150,000 men. On this occasion, the Canadians went over the top at dawn and captured the ridge by noon, establishing new positions on the top of the ridge as well as, some say, a new image of Canada to the world and in the eyes of the Canadian people themselves. It remains one of the proudest days in Canadian military history and a mountain in such a prominent location is a fitting tribute.

Mount Boswell (2400 m), which lies just north of the international border, was named after Dr. W. G. Boswell, the veterinarian for the International Boundary Survey.

Citadel Peaks (2440 m) and **Porcupine Ridge** (2775 m) come into view behind the western slopes of Vimy Peak. Both are situated beyond the southern end of Upper Waterton Lake, Porcupine Ridge lying 10 km across the international border.

Mount Campbell (2513 m) lies across the border in the United States. **Mount Richards** (2416 m), 3.5 km closer in, lies on the west side of the upper lake, just north of the border. Archibald Campbell and Captain George Richards both played roles in mapping the international border.

Unlike the other survey members who are honoured in this area, Captain George H. Richards of the Royal Navy was involved in the 1856 to 1863 survey that mapped the boundary from the Pacific to the Continental Divide. Richards, the second commissioner of the British Boundary Commission, later participated in extensive hydrographic surveys of the B.C. coast as captain of the *HMS Plumper*. After completing a resurvey of Vancouver Island waters, he was recalled to England to become hydrographer to the Royal Navy.

Mount Richards was originally known as Sleeping Chief Mountain, a name still used by some people. The east ridge is said to resemble the profile of an Indian's face.

When the mountains that form this panorama were being considered for inclusion in a possible national park, a Department of the Interior report referred to the Wilson Range that stretches from the Belly River in the east to Waterton Lakes. It may have been biased when it stated, "The culminating point of this range, Mount Cleveland, 10,535 feet in height is in Montana, but its most significant peak is its Canadian summit, Sheep Mountain, which though only 7,580 feet high, makes up what it lacks in altitude by its situation at the angle of the Waterton Lakes."[217] In fact, Sheep Mountain is not even part of the Wilson Range. However, the significance of its location directly northwest of Waterton townsite and the northern end of Upper Waterton Lake is correct. Sheep Mountain was Kootenai Brown's favourite mountain. He enjoyed looking at it as well as hunting on it in the fall.

Sheep Mountain was renamed **Mount Crandell** (2381 m) in 1914 after Edward Henry Crandell, a pioneer Calgary businessman and city councillor who had an interest in the first producing oil well in western Canada, Discovery No. 1.

After Kootenai Brown and his companion William Aldridge noticed beads of oil floating on Cameron Creek, John Lineham of Okotoks, Alberta, formed the Rocky Mountain Development Company in 1902. Shares were sold, and a drilling rig shipped from Petrolia, Ontario. The following year the roar of heavy machinery reverberated through the Cameron Creek valley, just west of Mount Crandell, where oil was discovered at a depth of 311 m. In preparation for the expected boom, a townsite named Oil City was cleared, streets were surveyed and several buildings constructed. However, the flow of oil came to a halt, the boom didn't materialize, and after three years of work the well was abandoned.

Blakiston Brook flows east between Mount Crandell and **Bellevue Hill** (2125 m), Bellevue being French for "Beautiful View." **Lakeview Ridge** (1925 m) forms the right edge of this spectacular mountain panorama.

Chief Mountain

When Peter Fidler travelled as far south as the Oldman River in 1792, he made notes regarding this spectacular and well-known peak. According to Fidler it was known by the Indians as "Nin nase tok que" or "The King." Thomas Blakiston, as part of the Palliser Expedition in 1858, first saw the mountains that lie to the east from what is now Waterton Lakes National Park from just south of the Oldman River. He wrote in his journal that "From reports which I had previously heard, I took the most easterly one, standing by itself, to be the 'Chief's Mountain,' which the Indian on coming up confirmed."[218] He later noted that his calculations showed that the 49th parallel passed directly over this block-shaped landmark.

Unfortunately, his surveying was not quite correct and Chief Mountain is not on the border but south of it in the United States. As one drives south along Highway 6 toward the Chief Mountain border crossing, the views of the peak keep improving and it becomes easy to see "Ninaki" and "Papoose" to the right of the "Chief." At the U.S. border the mountain is only eight km away and appears to loom over the customs buildings.

The mountain presented a challenging puzzle to geologists who first visited the area in the late nineteenth century. Fossils in the rocks of the upper 600 m were found to be considerably older than those in the underlying rocks, but all the layers seemed to be essentially flat-lying and there was no obvious discontinuity between them. In 1902, however, it was determined that the Lewis Overthrust Fault that extends south from the Kananaskis area does indeed cut through the two layers but does so horizontally.

Chief Mountain is most impressive from the prairies and carries with it a powerful presence. It would certainly have been used by the natives as a focus for vision quests. During this ritual, a young man would be required to journey to an isolated location and spend a few days alone, fasting and seeking guidance on how to plan his future.

Chief Mountain, Ninaki and Papoose.

Kootenai Brown

Kootenai Brown, c. 1910. Courtesy Glenbow Archives, NA-678-1.

"I had settled long before that when the time for squatting came I would come back to this spot."[219] The time came in 1877, following his murder trial and subsequent acquittal in a Montana courtroom.

John George Brown was 26 years old when he travelled the old Indian trail over South Kootenay Pass, first saw the area around Waterton Lakes, and determined that this would eventually be his home. His association with the Kootenay Indians of southeastern British Columbia led to his nickname, Kootenai. Born in County Clare, Ireland, Brown had served with the British Army during the Indian Mutiny before sailing to North America in 1861. He was attracted to the goldfields of Barkerville, British Columbia, about which he later wrote, "I had no money when I went to the Cariboo and I had none when I came out in 1864, but I had a little fortune for a while in between."[220] He then went on to serve as a constable in the gold rush town of Wild Horse Creek. In the summer of 1865, while travelling with four companions, he quickly passed though the Waterton Lakes area. It made a lasting impression on him. He would return 12 years later to play a pivotal role in the development and history of this area that so impressed him.

Those 12 years would see Kootenai wounded in the back by a Blackfoot arrow (it is said he pulled the arrow out himself and treated the wound with turpentine), spend time as a Pony Express rider, endure capture by Sitting Bull and a band of Sioux, and then subsequently escape. By 1877, with the buffalo rapidly disappearing, he turned to hunting wolves. Brown was then accused of murder in Fort Benton, Montana, and after his acquittal crossed the border with his family to settle in his chosen area.

Kootenai ran a trading post at Waterton but later turned to hunting, ranching, commercial fishing and serving as a guide to travellers passing through the area. Constantly extolling the area as one of great beauty with excellent fishing and hunting nearby, Brown played a key role in promoting it. In an article written for the *Fort Macleod Gazette*, the reporter described the attractiveness of the area and then went on to promote Brown's guiding business. "There is a boat on the lake and horses can be procured from the guide, Mr. Brown. For trolling and fly-fishing there is abundant tackle and all the necessary requisites, and parties visiting his place are always sure of their fish as Mr. Brown can catch them where all others fail."[221]

In 1885 Brown spent three months serving with the Rocky Mountain Rangers, a cavalry unit raised to quell the Métis uprising led by Louis Reil.

The southwestern corner of Alberta, like all the prairies, was changing as ranches were established and grasslands ploughed. Kootenai Brown began to worry that the beauty and wildlife of his home would be unable to withstand the coming onslaught. He was able to convince others, in particular rancher F. W. Godsal, to lobby the government to take action. Godsal wrote a letter that according to the *Lethbridge Herald*, "crystallized into action the wishes of Kootenai Brown [that the] Waterton Lakes District should be erected into a national park for the preservation of its natural beauty and its wildlife for all time."[222]

After this experience as a political activist and nineteenth century conservationist, Kootenai went on to play yet another role. In a letter to his friend and member of parliament, he wrote, "A park overseer is required. There have been over 500 people, picnic and tourist, here this season; a great number are here now (August 16, 1909). Many of them wantonly or thoughtlessly destroy shade trees and leave campfires burning which are a menace to all of us, the mountains and all things. If I can obtain this office I am willing to put up an office close to the lake and look after things to the best of my ability."[223]

Kootenai got the job and when the area became Waterton Lakes National Park in 1911, he was appointed the park's first superintendent. Already a legend in southern Alberta, the small, 70 year-old man with the white handlebar moustache continued to look after "his" park and successfully recommended in 1914 that it be increased in size from its initial 35 sq. km to 1095 sq. km. At this point the management required a younger man but Kootenai Brown continued to "look after things to the best of (his) ability" as a park ranger until his death in 1916. He was buried along the shores of Lower Waterton Lake.

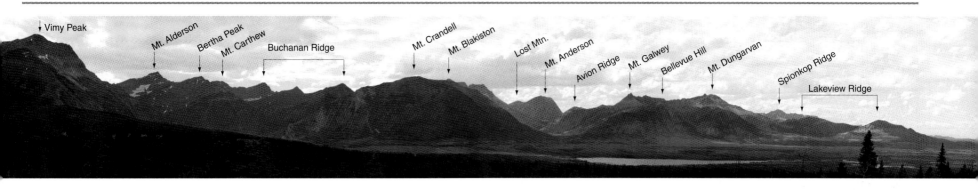

49 Waterton from the East

Located over 300 m higher than Waterton Lakes, this viewpoint provides an outstanding look at many of the mountains in Waterton Lakes National Park as well as Lower Waterton Lake.

The reddish slopes of **Vimy Peak** (2385 m), named for the World War I battle, frames the panorama on the left. The mountain beyond is **Mount Richards** (2416 m), its summit hidden behind Vimy Peak. It was named after a prominent Canadian participant in the defining of the international boundary in this area.

In the distance beyond Mount Richards is **Mount Alderson** (2692 m), which in midsummer has the largest accumulation of snow of all the mountains in this panorama. Named by Morris Bridgland, the peak honours Lieutenant General E. A. H. Alderson who commanded the Canadian Expeditionary Force in France during 1915 and 1916.

To its right is **Bertha Peak** (2454 m) whose gentle slopes rise above Waterton townsite. Its lower slopes feature several broad avalanche tracks that are a brilliant green colour during the early summer. Bertha Ekelund was an early resident of the area who gained notoriety by attempting to pass counterfeit money and ended up in jail as a result.

Just to the right of, and beyond Bertha Peak, one can see **Mount Carthew** (2636 m). Dominion Land Surveyor, William Morden Carthew D.L.S., spent time in the Waterton area as an assistant to R. W. Cautley who was working on the Interprovincial Border Survey in 1914. Carthew made what was probably the first ascent of the mountain to "set a signal" for Cautley. In June of 1916 Carthew was killed at the Battle of Ypres while serving with

the 49th Battalion of the Canadian Expeditionary Force. The mountain was named in his honour later that same year.

The three high points to the right of Mount Carthew are all part of **Buchanan Ridge** (2530 m), which stretches for about four km between Carthew Creek and Cameron Creek. Senator William A. Buchanan was the founder, editor and publisher of the *Lethbridge Herald* and went on to become the first provincial legislative librarian before serving in the first Alberta government as minister of municipal affairs.

Beyond the northern slopes of the smoothly-contoured **Mount Crandell** (2381 m) looms the highest mountain in Waterton Lakes National Park, **Mount Blakiston** (2910 m). Although 542 m higher than Mount Crandell, only the tip of the summit and some of its northern cliffs may be seen because it lies over eight km behind the nearer mountain. Clearly, it is the outstanding peak in the park, despite not lying on the Continental Divide like most other dominant mountains in southern Alberta. Thomas Blakiston was associated with the Palliser Expedition and named the mountain after himself in 1858. An ideal viewpoint for a closer look is from the Waterton Townsite Road, 1.2 km west of the junction with Highway 6. From here the valley of Blakiston Creek permits a good view of the entire mountain.

Beyond and to the right of the northern slopes of Mount Blakiston, the dome-shaped **Mount Anderson** (2652 m) appears in the distance, with **Lost Mountain** (2512 m) between the two. Lost Mountain's name is said to have been derived from its isolated location although it does not appear to be particularly isolated. There may be some other explanation for its name.

From Sofa Mountain Hill
Highway 6, 6.5 km south of the junction with Highway 5; 21.9 km north of the Belly River bridge at the entrance to Waterton Lakes National Park.

Mount Alderson. Photo Gillean Daffern.

Mount Blakiston from the Waterton Townsite Road.

Lieutenant Anderson, as the chief astronomer for the International Boundary Survey, would have played a crucial role in determining the location of the 49th parallel. The peak formerly known as Millionaire's Peak was renamed in his honour.

The most distant point in the panorama is **Avion Ridge** (2437 m), which was thought to resemble an airplane in shape. The name "avion" is French for airplane.

Mount Galwey (2377 m) features some small spires, uncommon in this area where the rocks are generally quite easily eroded. It rises beyond **Bellevue Hill** (2125 m). The name Bellevue is taken from the French, "Quelle une belle vue," which means "What a beautiful view." The lower and middle Waterton Lakes with Sofa Mountain and Vimy Ridge in the background certainly provides a beautiful view from the top of the hill.

The eastern end of **Spionkop Ridge** (2576 m) rises in the distance between **Mount Dungarvan** (2575 m) and the appropriately named **Lakeview Ridge** (1925 m) from where the prairies stretch off to the east.

Thomas Blakiston

Thomas Blakiston. Courtesy The Palliser Expedition.

Thomas Blakiston was a remarkable man who travelled the world pursuing adventure and his scientific interests. Born in England, he obtained a commission as a lieutenant in the Royal Artillery, serving in England, Ireland, Nova Scotia and the Crimea.

In 1858 he travelled west with the Palliser Expedition in the capacity of magnetic observer. His special assignment was to explore the southern passes of the Rockies to determine a feasible route for a transcontinental railway.

Lieutenant Blakiston was certainly gifted but he may have been difficult to work with and had his differences with John Palliser. After setting off to the mountains with Eugene Bourgeau and James Hector, he left a letter for Palliser, "wherein I threw off his command."[224] Setting out on his own, he travelled down the eastern edge of the Rockies, along the route of the present-day Highway 22 from Turner Valley to the Crowsnest Pass and into the southwest corner of what is now Alberta. Here he thoroughly explored the Kootenay passes, determining they were wholly in British territory and were unsuitable for a railway. Later he travelled over South Kootenay Pass into Blakiston Creek, which he followed past Mount Blakiston to a series of lakes that he named Waterton.

Although he followed his previously issued instructions regarding his exploration objectives and used expedition men, horses and supplies, Blakiston refused to hand over his observations and maps for the expedition's records. Returning to England in 1859, he submitted a separate report on his own personal findings.

The year 1861 found this adventurer up the Yangtze River in China, travelling 1500 km farther up the river than any Westerner had previously gone. After retiring from the army he visited Japan by way of Russia and Siberia where he pursued business interests. During the 1870s he compiled a catalogue on the birds of Japan, which was the authoritative document for years in that country.

In 1884 he retired from his Japanese business interests and settled in the United States where, pursuing his interest in ornithology, he completed publications for the United States National Museum.

Mt. Boswell

Mt. Cleveland

Stoney Indian Peaks

Cathedral Peak

Wahcheechee Mtn.

West Flattop Mtn.

Citadel Peaks

Mt. Campbell

Porcupine Ridge

Mt. Richards

50 The View from the Lobby

In most mountain panoramas one is looking at a group of peaks that are all roughly the same distance away from the viewer. A different situation occurs at this vantage point and makes for a very special view. Here, one is looking down the long, narrow valley that contains Upper Waterton Lake and, farther to the south, the Waterton River in the United States, the lake and distant river valley lying in an almost straight north-south line for a distance of 23 km. The panorama is framed by the slopes of Vimy Peak on the left and Mount Richards on the right, both of which are less than five km away. The most distant point, West Flattop Mountain, lies 23 km to the south and some 17 km beyond the American border.

Mount Boswell (2400 m) was formerly named Street Mountain after Jack Street who was an early avalanche victim in this area. It was renamed in 1917 by the International Boundary Commission after their veterinarian, Dr. W. G. Boswell.

Mount Cleveland (3190 m) is both the highest peak in this panorama and in the northern Rockies of the U.S. Lying nine km beyond the slopes of Mount Boswell, it rises 751 m higher. An attractive horizontal band of snow lingers into late July, forming a base for the peak's triangular-shaped summit. It honours a former president of the United States, Grover Cleveland.

One of the view's special features are the "towers" that frame the lake. On the left side are the **Stoney Indian Peaks** (2849 m), visible behind the western slopes of Mount Cleveland.

Matching the Stoney Indian Peaks on the right side of the lake are the **Citadel Peaks** (2440 m), a spectacular set of small spires that lie three km south of the southern end of Waterton Lake, just to the west of two small lakes known as Kootenai Lakes.

Cathedral Peak (2756 m) is the most distant high mountain that can be seen from the Prince of Wales Hotel. This beautiful peak is often snow-capped and although it is 434 m lower than Mount Cleveland, the way it rises behind a far-off ridge makes it one of the most appealing mountains in the panorama.

From the Prince of Wales Hotel
On the Waterton Townsite Road, 8.5 km southwest of Waterton Park gates.

Only the twin peaks at the very top of **Wahcheechee Mountain** (2584 m) are visible behind the upper west ridge of Stoney Indian Peaks. The origin of this very intriguing name is, unfortunately, not clear. Records indicate it is based on "ochichak," the Cree word for the sandhill crane, which was believed to carry smaller birds on its back and was also regarded by the natives as the "Spirit of the Mountains." It is important to remember that these native names were recorded, spelled and pronounced by people of European origin. The name Wahcheechee appears to be, at least to some extent, the result of an error.

Although the broad, flat-topped mountain that appears to the right of Wahcheechee appears to be a separate feature, it is actually the northwest end of Cathedral Peak. The steep cliffs of this western part of the mountain are most impressive as the mountain rises 1050 m above the upper Waterton River valley. Shaded from the sun for most of the day, snow lingers below these cliffs well into the summer.

At centre right one can see the valley down which the Waterton River flows from the south into Waterton Lakes. Rising above it on the skyline is, at 2082 m, a high point that is not really a mountain at all. It is known as **West Flattop Mountain** (2082 m) and is actually two km farther away than Cathedral Peak. It is most unusual that this most distant feature, which is the focal point for the view, has the lowest elevation in the panorama. It is actually 300 m lower than the next lowest point.

Mount Campbell (2513 m) and **Mount Richards** (2416 m), which frame the panorama on the right, are separated by West Boundary Creek. The creek is well named as it flows almost directly east for nine km, touching the 49th parallel at one point and never straying more than half a kilometre from the boundary.

Mount Campbell's location looking over the international boundary from the American side is most appropriate. Archibald Campbell was the United States commissioner of the International Boundary-Line Survey, which marked the 49th parallel across the prairies to the Continental Divide.

Porcupine Ridge (2775 m) is a long, high feature that begins at Citadel Peaks at its eastern end and reaches a high point some five km to the west. It can just be seen in the distance between Mount Campbell and Mount Richards.

Top: Waterton townsite from the Prince of Wales Hotel. Mount Campbell (left) and Mount Richards in the background. Photo Ray Djuff.

Bottom: Close-up of the Prince of Wales Hotel. Photo Ray Djuff.

Waterton Lakes and the Prince of Wales Hotel

Waterton Lakes were originally known as Kootenai Lakes after the Kootenai Indians of southeastern British Columbia (for some reason this Indian name is spelled "Kootenay" in B.C.). Although they were renamed by Thomas Blakiston of the Palliser Expedition in 1858, they continued to be referred to as the Kootenai Lakes for some time after that. In 1895 the federal government set aside a "reservation for park purposes" that included the lakes and adjacent area. Despite the fact that the lakes had been officially named Waterton Lakes for 37 years, the new area was named Kootenai Lakes Forest Reserve. It wasn't until the reserve's status was changed and it became Waterton Lakes National Park in 1911 that use of the original name dropped off.

Charles Waterton was an explorer and naturalist who Blakiston would certainly have known by reputation and may have known personally. In the early 1800s Waterton was involved in four journeys through the rain forests of South America following which his most famous book, *Wanderings in South America*, was written. He preferred to do his own study of the natural world rather than rely on the reports of others. During his research on the reported bloodsucking vampire bats of South America, he actually slept with his bare feet exposed to further his studies. Following his marriage in 1829, Waterton began to focus on birds. His estate, known as Walton Hall, became a large bird sanctuary—the first to be established in England.

Given his scientific interests, it is not surprising that Waterton was somewhat eccentric. It is said that he refused to sleep in beds, only wore shoes when he was indoors and loved to climb things. He once climbed to the top of St. Peter's Cathedral in Rome.

The view of the lakes and mountains from the low knoll at the northern end of Upper Waterton Lake provided the Great Northern Railway with an excellent location upon which to build its new hotel. Several luxury hotels had already been constructed in neighbouring Glacier Park and the railway had plans for bus tours that would extend from the American park all the way to Jasper. The Canadian government authorities quickly approved the project and a Swiss architect was retained to draw up plans. The design had to take under consideration the strong winds that often gust down the valley and over the knoll.

At one point during the construction in early 1927, a gale force wind pushed the 50 m-tall building framework 23 cm off the foundation. It was pulled back by horse-powered winches but still remains somewhat off of its original location. Another problem was how to deliver the huge boilers for the heating system from the railway north of Pincher Creek, some 57 km away. They were too heavy for any vehicle or wagon in the district, but following a late spring snowfall the contractors quickly built two large sleds, hooked up 30 horses, and spent two days dragging the boilers to the new hotel.

Whether you are outside on the lawn or inside the grand hotel lobby looking through the huge window, the view down the upper lake is one of the classic panoramas in the Canadian Rockies.

Prince of Wales Hotel. Photo Ray Djuff.

The International Boundary Survey (1872-76)

Canadian International Boundary Commission staff (l-r) (back) G. Burpee, W. F. King, G. Coster, L. Herchmer, S. Anderson, George M. Dawson, W. M. Ashe, L. Russell; (front) W. J. Galwey, A. C. Ward, D. R. Cameron, Capt. A. Featherstonhaugh, W. G. Boswell, G. Burgess. Courtesy Glenbow Archives, NA-249-1.

Much of the early exploration of Canada was undertaken by explorer-surveyors. Alexander Mackenzie, David Thompson, John Palliser and Simon Fraser were explorers and adventurers of heroic stature. But the surveying of the new lands through which they travelled was a critical part of their work and each produced maps that were of great importance to the country's development.

Others, such as Dr. W. G. Boswell and Donald Cameron, were explorer-surveyors in a more limited sense, their work involving the more mundane task of determining the location and marking of the precise boundary that separated what was to become Canada's prairie provinces from the United States. These explorer-surveyors, seldom far from their bulky surveying instruments, had their own challenges and rewards as new areas of Canada were made ready for orderly development. Undoubtedly they enjoyed the pleasure of exploring this corner of Alberta and were responsible for naming many of its features.

Differences of opinion between Canada and the United States concerning the placement of the international boundary through the islands in the Strait of Georgia between the mainland and Vancouver Island were settled cordially by an International Boundary Survey commission that existed from 1857 to 1862. This success led to the formation of a similar commission in 1870, which was given the task of marking the boundary from Lake of the Woods, Manitoba, to the Continental Divide. Archibald Campbell was chosen to be the

United States commissioner of the survey. Prime Minister John A. Macdonald recommended a Scottish-born officer of the Royal Artillery, Captain Donald Cameron, to be Campbell's Canadian counterpart.

The natural history of the areas surveyed was to be studied as well and this was put under the direction of 25 year-old George Mercer Dawson, the son of the principal of McGill University. During the course of the survey Dawson gathered information that was eventually published as a 387-page "Report on the Geology and Resources of the Region in the Vicinity of the 49th parallel from the Lake of the Woods to the Rocky Mountains." This document established the scientific reputation of George Dawson. He became known as "Dr. George" and went on to become one of the most outstanding scientists Canada has ever produced, building the basis for much of the geological and botanical knowledge of western Canada.

The year 1873 saw the beginning of the long trek westward. The contrast in policy toward the continent's native population was evident as the American surveyors were supported by 230 armed men, two companies of cavalry and a company of infantry as a precaution against possible Indian hostility. On the other hand, the British did not consider an armed escort necessary. In Cameron's opinion, the British flag was all the protection they required.

The surveyors and their supply trains made for an impressive sight as they travelled across the dusty, desolate plains. The Americans used mules to haul their wagons; the British employed oxen to pull the legendary two-wheeled Red River Carts. Prairie fires and snowstorms hindered progress as summer ended. The surveyors evolved into expert plainsmen, adapting to challenging frontier conditions while remaining devoted to the scientific methods of their day.

Through 1874 and 1875 the survey continued, extending the cairn-marked boundary line across the three prairie steppes to the mountains and finally to the Continental Divide. By the time the final meeting of Commissioners Campbell and Cameron was held in London in 1876, 388 survey monuments such as iron pillars, stone cairns, earth mounds, timber marks, and mounds of mixed earth and stone had been established

along the 49th parallel of latitude. The now visible evidence of an international border was quickly put to use by the North West Mounted Police. The bootlegging of liquor by Americans to the Canadian Indians could now be controlled. One of the first to make effective use of the newly marked border was Sitting Bull and his Sioux warriors who fled to safety in Canada after the massacre at Little Big Horn in Montana.

At the conclusion of their work the surveyors must have taken some satisfaction from the naming of some of the mountainous features after themselves. Cameron Falls in Waterton townsite and Cameron Lake, which straddles the international border, were named after the Canadian commissioner. Dr. W. G. Boswell, who was in charge of veterinary duties, was honoured by Mount Boswell across the 49th parallel on the east side of Upper Waterton Lake. Lieutenant Anderson, who was Cameron's chief astronomer, was honoured by having a mountain known locally as Millionaire's Peak renamed Mount Anderson, while the survey's geologist, Hilary Bauerman, was recognized by the naming of a neighbouring peak. Both these latter mountains lie near the headwaters of Blakiston Brook in the northwestern corner of Waterton Lakes National Park.

The Americans honoured their commissioner, naming a peak just south of the border on the west side of Upper Waterton Lake Mount Campbell.

Boundary mound. Courtesy Glenbow Archives, NA-249-25.

References

16th Report of the Geographic Board of Canada. Ottawa, March, 1919.

ACC editorial. An Act of Heroism. *Canadian Alpine Journal*. Calgary: Alpine Club of Canada, 1909.

Amery, Leopold. *In the Rain and Sun*. London & New York: Hutchinson, 1946.

Appleby, Edna. *Canmore, the Story of an Era*. Canmore: Privately published, 1975.

Barkhouse, Joyce. *George Dawson—The Little Giant*. Toronto: Clark Irwin, 1974.

Beaty, Chester B. *Landscapes of Southern Alberta*. Lethbridge: University of Lethbridge, 1975.

Bennett, Geoffrey. *Battle of Jutland*. Newton Abbott, Devon: David & Charles, 1964.

Birney, Earle. *Selected Poems 1940-1966*. Toronto: McClelland & Stewart, 1966.

Birrell, Dave. *Calgary's Mountain Panorama*. Calgary: Rocky Mountain Books, 1990.

Blakiston, Capt. Thomas J. *Report on the Exploration of the Kootenai and Boundary Passes of the Rocky Mountains in 1858*. The Palliser Papers. Toronto: The Champlain Society, 1968.

Bradley, Al. *The Ballad of the Upside-down Mountain*. Unpublished, 1991.

Bridgland, M. P. Report on Yoho Camp. *Canadian Alpine Journal*, Vol. I. Calgary: Alpine Club of Canada, 1907.

Burpee, Lawrence J. *Among the Canadian Alps*. Toronto: Bell & Cockburn, 1914.

Burpee, Lawrence J. *On the Old Athabasca Trail*. Toronto: Ryerson Press, 1926.

Buzzell, Nora. (ed.) *The Register of the Victoria Cross*. Gloucestershire: This England Books, 1988.

Campbell, Robert E. *I Would do it Again*. Toronto: Ryerson, 1959.

Carmichael, Lieut. E. K. Letter from E. K. Carmichael to Sid Unwin's mother. Quoted in Sid Unwin's obituary written by Mary Schaffer. *Canadian Alpine Journal*. Alpine Club of Canada, 1917.

Cautley, Richard. *Highlights of Memory*. Unpublished. Whyte Museum of the Canadian Rockies photocopy 02.5 C31. B.C. Archives.

Christensen, Lisa. *A Hiker's Guide to the Art of the Canadian Rockies*. Calgary: Glenbow Museum, 1996.

Cochrane and Area Historical Society. *A Neighbour of Quincy Coleman's*. Cochrane: Big Hill Country, 1977.

Coleman, Arthur P. *The Canadian Rockies, New and Old Trails*. Toronto: H. Frowde, 1912.

Collie, J. Norman, Hugh Stutfield. *Climbs and Explorations in the Canadian Rockies*. London: Longmans, Green, and Co., 1903.

Coues, Elliott. *New Light on the Early History of the Greater Northwest: The Manuscript Journals of Alexander Henry and David Thompson*. Minneapolis, 1897.

de Smet, Father Pierre. *Oregon Missions and Travels over the Rocky Mountains in 1845-46*. New York: Edward Dunigan, 1847.

Douglas, David. *Journal, 1823-1827*. London: William Wesley and Son, 1914.

Edwards, Ralph. *Trail to the Charmed Land*. Victoria: Herbert R. Larson Publishing Ltd., 1950.

Erasmus, Peter. *Buffalo Days and Nights*. Calgary: Glenbow-Alberta Institute, 1976.

Fairley, Bruce. (ed.) *Canadian Mountaineering Anthology*. Edmonton: Lone Pine Publishing, 1994.

Fidler, Peter. *Peter Fidler Fonds*. Calgary: Glenbow Archives, 1792, 1969.

Fraser, Esther. *The Canadian Rockies*. Edmonton: Hurtig, 1969.

Fraser, Esther. *Wheeler*. Banff: Summerthought, 1978.

Freeman, Lewis. *On the Roof of the Rockies*. Toronto: McClelland & Stewart, 1925.

Gadd, Ben. *Handbook of the Canadian Rockies*. Jasper: Corax Press, 2nd edition, 1995.

Grant, Rev. George. *Ocean to Ocean*. Toronto: James Campbell and Son, 1873.

Hallworth, Beryl, Monica Jackson. *Pioneer Naturalists of the Rocky Mountains and Selkirks*. Calgary: Calgary Field Naturalists, 1985.

Hart, E. J. *Diamond Hitch*. Banff: Summerthought, 1979.

Hart, E. J. (ed.) *A Hunter of Peace*. (A reprint of *Old Indian Trails*, including her unpublished account of the 1911 expedition to Maligne Lake.) Banff: Whyte Museum, 1980.

Hart, E. J. *Jimmy Simpson—Legend of the Rockies*. Vancouver: Altitude, 1993.

Hoehling, A. A. *A Whisper of Eternity*. New York: Thomas Yoseloff Inc., 1957.

Holterman, Jack. *Place Names of Glacier/Waterton National Parks*. Montana: Glacier Natural History Association and Falcon Press, 1985.

Ingersoll, Ernest. *Canadian Guide Book*. New York: D. Appleton and Co., 1892.

Ireland, Bernard, Eric Grove. *Jane's War at Sea 1897-1997*. London: Harper Collins, 1997.

Jeal, Tim. *Livingstone*. London: Heinemann, 1973.

Kain, Conrad. The First Ascent of Mount Robson (1913). *Canadian Alpine Journal*. Winnipeg: Alpine Club of Canada, 1915.

Kain, Conrad. *Where the Clouds Can Go*. New York: American Alpine Club, 1935.

Karamitsanis, Aphrodite. *Place Names of Alberta: Mountains, Mountain Parks and Foothills. Volume I*. Calgary: Alberta Culture and Multiculturalism, Friends of Geographical Names of Alberta Society and University of Calgary Press, 1991.

Kauffman, Andrew J., William L. Putnam. *The Guiding Spirit*. Revelstoke: Footprint Publishing, 1986.

King, Donald R. *Beyond the Hills*. Privately published, 1975.

Kinney, G. B., Donald Phillips. To the Top of Mount Robson. *Canadian Alpine Journal*. Winnipeg: Alpine Club of Canada, 1910.

Larocque, Baptiste. *Legends of French Canada*. Toronto: Paul Wallace, 1923.

MacCarthy, A. H. The First Ascent of Mt. Louis. *Canadian Alpine Journal*. Winnipeg: Alpine Club of Canada, 1917.

MacEwan, Grant. *Pat Burns—Cattle King*. Saskatoon: Western Producer Prairie Books, 1979.

MacGregor, J. G. *Peter Fidler*. Calgary: Fifth House Ltd., 1998.

Mackey, R. S. G. *Lancaster in Action*. Carrollton, Texas: Squadron/Signal Publications, 1982.

Macmillan, Ernest. (ed.) *A Canadian Song Book*. London/Toronto: J. M. Dent and Sons, 1929.

Marteinson, John. *We Stand on Guard*. Montreal: Ovale Publications, 1992.

Marty, Sid. *A Grand and Fabulous Notion*. Toronto: NC Press, 1984.

Masson, Madeleine. *Pictorial History of Nursing*. Twickenham, Middlesex: Hamlyn, 1985.

McGowan, Dan. *Hilltop Tales*. Toronto: Macmillan Company of Canada, 1950.

Merk, Frederick. (ed.) *Fur Trade and Empire—George Simpson's Journal*. Cambridge: Harvard University Press, 1931.

Milton, Viscount William Fitzwilliam, W. B. Cheadle. *The North-West Passage by Land*. London: Casell, Petter, and Galpin, 1865.

Mitchell, B. W. *Trail Life in the Canadian Rockies*. New York: Macmillan, 1924.

Mountains Named After War Veterans. Calgary: Calgary Herald, July 4, 1994.

Outram, James. *In the Heart of the Canadian Rockies*. London & New York: Macmillan, 1906.

Palliser, Capt. John et al. *The Journals, Detailed Reports, and Observations Relative to the Exploration by Captain John Palliser...During the Years 1857, 1858, 1859, and 1860*. London: H. M. Stationary Office, 1863.

Parker, Elizabeth. In Memoriam. Obituary of Edward Whymper. *Canadian Alpine Journal*. Winnipeg: Alpine Club of Canada, 1912.

Patterson, Raymond M. *Buffalo Head*. New York: William Sloane Associates, 1961.

Patterson, Raymond M. *Far Pastures*. Sidney, B.C.: Gray's Publishing, 1963.

Patton, Brian. *Tales from the Canadian Rockies*. Edmonton: Hurtig, 1984.

Phillips, Walter. *Colour in the Canadian Rockies*. Toronto: Thomas Nelson & Sons, 1937.

Pincher Creek and Area Historical Society. *Prairie Grass to Mountain Pass*. Pincher Creek, 1974.

Pocaterra, G. W. *Among the Nomadic Stoneys*. Alberta Historical Review, Vol. II, No. 3, summer, 1963.

Putnam, W. L., G. W. Boles and R. W. Laurilla. *Place Names of the Canadian Alps*. Revelstoke: Footprint Publishing, 1990.

Report of the commission appointed to delimit the boundary between the provinces of Alberta and British Columbia. Ottawa: Surveyor General, 1917-1955 (4 volumes).

Rodney, William. *Kootenai Brown*. Sidney, B.C.: Gray's, 1969.

Ross, W. J. *The Travels of George Dawson in Alberta and British Columbia in the Years 1883 and 1884*. Privately published.

Royal Flying Corps Combat Report. Combats in the Air. University of Western Ontario: Beatrice Hitchens Memorial Aviation Collection.

Sandford, R. W. *The Canadian Alps*. Banff: Altitude, 1990.

Simpson, George. *Narrative of a Journey Round the World during the Years 1841 and 1842*. London: Henry Colburn, 1847.

Sissons, C. B. In Memoriam. Morris P. Bridgland. *Canadian Alpine Journal*. Alpine Club of Canada, 1948.

Smythe, Frank. *Climbs in the Canadian Rockies*. New York: Norton & Co., 1950.

Spry, Irene M. *The Palliser Expedition*. Toronto: Macmillan Co. of Canada Ltd., 1963.

Swanson, James L. *George Kinney and the First Ascent of Mount Robson*. Banff: Digital Banff, 1999.

Swettenham, John. (ed.) *Valiant Men*. Toronto: Hakkert, 1973.

Taylor, William C. *The Snows of Yesteryear*. Toronto: Holt Rinehart Winston, 1973.

Taylor, William C. *Tracks Across My Trail*. Jasper: Jasper-Yellowhead Historical Society, 1984.

Temple Patterson, A. *Jellicoe*. London: MacMillan, 1969.

Tetarenko, Kim, Lorne Tetarenko. *Ken Jones Mountain Man*. Calgary: Rocky Mountain Books, 1996.

The Great War, Vol. 7. London: Amalgamated Press Ltd., 1916.

The Story of 25 Eventful Years in Pictures. London, 1936.

Thomson, Don W. *Men and Meridians*. Ottawa: Queen's Printer, 1966-69.

Thorington, J. M. Interpretation of some old map names in the vicinity of Kananaskis Pass. *Canadian Alpine Journal*. Winnipeg: Alpine Club of Canada, 1923.

Thorington, J. Monroe. *The Glittering Mountains of Canada*. Philadelphia: John W. Lea, 1925.

Thorington, J. M. Jean Habel in the Canadian Rockies. *Canadian Alpine Journal*. Alpine Club of Canada, 1947.

Tyrrell, J. B. (ed.) *David Thompson's Narrative of his Explorations in Western America 1784-1812*. Toronto: The Champlain Society, 1916.

Victory Readers. *The Boy Hero*. Toronto: Canadian Readers Book IV, Gage and Nelson, 1924.

Walcott, Charles D. *Cambrian Geology and Paleontology V*. Washington: Smithsonian Institution, 1928.

Warren, Mary S. In Memoriam. Sergeant Sidney J. Unwin. *Canadian Alpine Journal*. Winnipeg: Alpine Club of Canada, 1917.

Waterton, Charles. *Wanderings in South America*. London: Charles Knight, 1973.

Wheeler, Arthur O. ACC Expedition to Jasper Park, Yellowhead Pass, and Mt. Robson Region, 1911. *Canadian Alpine Journal*. Winnipeg: Alpine Club of Canada, 1912.

Wheeler, E. O. In Memoriam. Morris Bridgland. *Canadian Alpine Journal*. Alpine Club of Canada, 1948.

Wilcox, Walter D. *Camping in the Canadian Rockies*. New York: G. P. Putnam's Sons, 1897.

Willes, John A. *Out of the Clouds*. Privately published, 1981.

Wordsworth, Dr. J. S. Parliamentary proceedings. Ottawa: Hansard, 1938.

Notes

Introduction

1. Outram, James. *In the Heart of the Canadian Rockies*. London & New York: Macmillan, 1906, 1.
2. Ibid., 383.
3. Barkhouse, Joyce. *George Dawson—The Little Giant*. Toronto: Clark Irwin, 1974, Foreword.

Panorama 1

4. Grant, Rev. George. *Ocean to Ocean*. Toronto: James Campbell and Son, 1873, 226.
5. Palliser, Capt. John et al. *The Journals, Detailed Reports, and Observations Relative to the Exploration by Captain John Palliser…During the Years 1857, 1858, 1859, and 1860*. London: H. M. Stationary Office, 1863, Vol. 2, 124.
6. de Smet, Father Pierre. *Oregon Missions and Travels over the Rocky Mountains in 1845-46*. New York: Edward Dunigan, 1847, 197.
7. Grant, Rev. George. *Ocean to Ocean*. Toronto: James Campbell and Son, 1873, 227.
8. de Smet, *Oregon Missions and Travels*, 197.

Panorama 2

9. Palliser, *The Journals, Detailed Reports*, Vol. 2, 124.
10. Swettenham, John. (ed.) *Valiant Men*. Toronto: Hakkert, 1973, 114.
11. Fidler, Peter. *Peter Fidler Fonds*. Calgary: Glenbow Archives, 1792, 1969, 9.
12. de Smet, *Oregon Missions and Travels*, 146.

Panorama 3

13. Grant, *Ocean to Ocean*, 235.
14. Masson, Madeleine. *Pictorial History of Nursing*. Twickenham, Middlesex: Hamlyn, 1985, 10.
15. Hoehling, A. A. *A Whisper of Eternity*. New York: Thomas Yoseloff Inc., 1957, 171.

Panorama 4

16. Amery, Leopold. *In the Rain and Sun*. London & New York: Hutchinson, 1946, 178.
17. Hart, E. J. (ed.) *A Hunter of Peace*. Banff: Whyte Museum, 1980, 95.
18. Ibid., 97.
19. Ibid., 96.
20. Ibid., 150.
21. Ibid.
22. Ibid., 97.
23. Ibid., 8.
24. Grant, *Ocean to Ocean*, 235, 236.
25. Hart, *A Hunter of Peace*, 96.
26. Ibid., 19.
27. Ibid., 18.
28. Ibid., 80.
29. Mitchell, B. W. *Trail Life in the Canadian Rockies*. New York: Macmillan, 1924, 78.
30. Ibid., 109.
31. Hart, *A Hunter of Peace*, 93.
32. Warren, Mary S. In Memoriam. Sergeant Sidney J. Unwin. *Canadian Alpine Journal*. Winnipeg: Alpine Club of Canada, 1917, 132.
33. McGowan, Dan. *Hilltop Tales*. Toronto: Macmillan Company of Canada, 1950, 209.

Panorama 5

34. Milton, Viscount William Fitzwilliam, W. B. Cheadle. *The North-West Passage by Land*. London: Casell, Petter, and Galpin, 1865, 237.
35. Ibid., 233.
36. Wheeler, E. O. In Memoriam. Morris Bridgland. *Canadian Alpine Journal*. Alpine Club of Canada, 1948, 221.
37. Sissons, C. B. In Memoriam. Morris P. Bridgland. *Canadian Alpine Journal*. Alpine Club of Canada, 1948, 220.

Panorama 6

38. Smythe, Frank. *Climbs in the Canadian Rockies*. New York: Norton & Co., 1950, 121, 122.
39. Milton and Cheadle, *The North-West Passage by Land*, 257.
40. Kain, Conrad. *Where the Clouds Can Go*. New York: American Alpine Club, 1935, 321.
41. Wheeler, Arthur O. ACC Expedition to Jasper Park, Yellowhead Pass, and Mt. Robson Region, 1911. *Canadian Alpine Journal*. Winnipeg: Alpine Club of Canada, 1912, 53.
42. Ibid., 19.
43. Swanson, James L. *George Kinney and the First Ascent of Mount Robson*. Banff: Digital Banff, 1999, 2.
44. Kinney, G. B., Donald Phillips. To the Top of Mount Robson. *Canadian Alpine Journal*. Winnipeg: Alpine Club of Canada, 1910, 23.
45. Ibid.
46. Kain, *Where the Clouds Can Go*, 321.
47. Kinney and Phillips, To the Top of Mount Robson, 40.
48. Kain, *Where the Clouds Can Go*, 321.
49. Taylor, William C. *Tracks Across My Trail*. Jasper: Jasper-Yellowhead Historical Society, 1984, 133.
50. Ibid., xi (preface).

Panorama 7

51. Buzzell, Nora. (ed.) *The Register of the Victoria Cross*. Gloucestershire: This England Books, 1988, 146.
52. Ibid., 182.
53. Ibid., 6.

Panorama 8

54. Smythe, *Climbs in the Canadian Rockies*, 96.
55. Ibid.
56. Ibid., 99.
57. Fraser, Esther. *The Canadian Rockies*. Edmonton: Hurtig, 1969, 21.
58. Ibid.
59. Ibid.
60. Patton, Brian. *Tales from the Canadian Rockies*. Edmonton: Hurtig, 1984, 19.
61. Sandford, R. W. *The Canadian Alps*. Banff: Altitude, 1990, 46.
62. Ibid., 47.
63. Thorington, J. Monroe. *The Glittering Mountains of Canada*. Philadelphia: John W. Lea, 1925, 107.
64. Coleman, Arthur P. *The Canadian Rockies, New and Old Trails*. Toronto: H. Frowde, 1912, 79.
65. Ibid., 208.
66. Collie, J. Norman, Hugh Stutfield. *Climbs and Explorations in the Canadian Rockies*. London: Longmans, Green, and Co., 1903, 153, 154.

Panorama 9

67. Cochrane and Area Historical Society. *A Neighbour of Quincy Coleman's*. Cochrane: Big Hill Country, 1977, 107.
68. Taylor, William C. *The Snows of Yesteryear*. Toronto: Holt Rinehart Winston, 1973, 105.
69. Outram, *In the Heart of the Canadian Rockies*, 382.
70. Ibid.

Panorama 10

71. Collie and Stutfield, *Climbs and Explorations*, 102.
72. Ibid.
73. Wilcox, Walter D. *Camping in the Canadian Rockies*. New York: G. P. Putnam's Sons, 1897, 155.
74. Ibid.
75. Ibid., 156.

76. Collie and Stutfield, *Climbs and Exploration*, 121.
77. Ibid., 103.
78. Taylor, *The Snows of Yesteryear*, 105.

Panorama 11

79. Thorington, *The Glittering Mountains of Canada*, 85.
80. Kauffman, Andrew J., William L. Putnam. *The Guiding Spirit*. Revelstoke: Footprint Publishing, 1986, 181.
81. Amery, *In the Rain and Sun*, 165.
82. Ibid.
83. Ibid., 170.
84. Kauffman and Putnam, *The Guiding Spirit*, 106.
85. Ibid.
86. Ibid., 107.
87. Ibid.
88. Thorington, *The Glittering Mountains of Canada*, 85.
89. Ibid., 88.

Panorama 12

90. Coues, Elliott. *New Light on the Early History of the Greater Northwest: The Manuscript Journals of Alexander Henry and David Thompson*. Minneapolis, 1897, Vol. II, 689.
91. Collie and Stutfield, *Climbs and Explorations*, 88.
92. Ibid., 89.
93. Fraser, *The Canadian Rockies*, 16.
94. Ibid.
95. Taylor, *The Snows of Yesteryear*, 120.
96. Outram, *In the Heart of the Canadian Rockies*, 352.
97. Ibid., 3.
98. Taylor, *The Snows of Yesteryear*, 117.
99. Hart, E. J. *Diamond Hitch*. Banff: Summerthought, 1979, 63.
100. Hart, E. J. *Jimmy Simpson—Legend of the Rockies*. Vancouver: Altitude, 1993, 34.
101. Ibid.
102. Outram, *In the Heart of the Canadian Rockies*, 385.
103. Fraser, *The Canadian Rockies*, 178.
104. Palliser, *The Journals, Detailed Reports*, Vol. 2, 111.

Panorama 14

105. Collie and Stutfield, *Climbs and Explorations*, 113.
106. Hart, *A Hunter of Peace*, 27.
107. Outram, *In the Heart of the Canadian Rockies*, 332, 333.
108. ACC editorial. An Act of Heroism. *Canadian Alpine Journal*. Calgary: Alpine Club of Canada, 1909, 129.
109. Ibid.
110. Ibid.

Panorama 15

111. Collie and Stutfield, *Climbs and Explorations*, 42.
112. Ibid., 30.
113. Ibid., 31, 32.
114. Hart, *Jimmy Simpson*, 25.
115. Ibid., 26.
116. Ibid., 212.

Panorama 16

117. Thorington, *The Glittering Mountains of Canada*, 25.
118. Palliser, *The Journals, Detailed Reports*, Vol. 2, 105-6.
119. Erasmus, Peter. *Buffalo Days and Nights*. Calgary: Glenbow-Alberta Institute, 1976, 76.
120. Palliser, *The Journals, Detailed Reports*, Vol. 2, 107.
121. Erasmus, *Buffalo Days and Nights*, 75.

Panorama 17

122. Palliser, *The Journals, Detailed Reports*, Vol. 2, 101.
123. Walcott, Charles D. *Cambrian Geology and Paleontology V.*

Washington: Smithsonian Institution, 1928, 268.
124. Birney, Earle. *Selected Poems 1940-1966*. Toronto: McClelland & Stewart, 1966, 118.
125. Palliser, *The Journals, Detailed Reports*, Vol. 2, 101.

Panorama 18

126. Ibid., 103.
127. Ibid.
128. Parker, Elizabeth. In Memoriam. Obituary of Edward Whymper. *Canadian Alpine Journal*. Winnipeg: Alpine Club of Canada, 1912, 126.
129. Tetarenko, Kim, Lorne Tetarenko. *Ken Jones Mountain Man*. Calgary: Rocky Mountain Books, 1996, 46.
130. Ibid., 5.

Panorama 19

131. *Mountains Named After War Veterans*. Calgary: Calgary Herald, July 4, 1994.
132. Coleman, *The Canadian Rockies*, 134.

Panorama 21

133. Palliser, *The Journals, Detailed Reports*, Vol. 2, 100.
134. Appleby, Edna. *Canmore, the Story of an Era*. Canmore: Privately published, 1975, 9.
135. Ibid., 103.
136. Ibid., 104.

Panorama 22

137. MacCarthy, A. H. The First Ascent of Mt. Louis. *Canadian Alpine Journal*. Winnipeg: Alpine Club of Canada, 1917, 79.
138. Ibid.
139. Kain, *Where the Clouds Can Go*, 443.
140. Ibid., 441.

Panorama 23

141. Palliser, *The Journals, Detailed Reports*, Vol. 2, 100.
142. Ibid., 101.
143. Ibid.
144. Ibid.

Panorama 24

145. Christensen, Lisa. *A Hiker's Guide to the Art of the Canadian Rockies*. Calgary: Glenbow Museum, 1996, 14.
146. Palliser, *The Journals, Detailed Reports*, Vol. 2, 101.
147. Hallworth, Beryl, Monica Jackson. *Pioneer Naturalists of the Rocky Mountains and Selkirks*. Calgary: Calgary Field Naturalists, 1985, 19.
148. Spry, Irene M. *The Palliser Expedition*. Toronto: Macmillan Co. of Canada Ltd., 1963, 206.
149. Outram, *In the Heart of the Canadian Rockies*, 31.
150. Marty, Sid. *A Grand and Fabulous Notion*. Toronto: NC Press, 1984, 50.
151. Ibid., 51.

Panorama 25

152. Thorington, *The Glittering Mountains of Canada*, 4.
153. Sandford, *The Canadian Alps*, 109.
154. Ibid., 110.

Panorama 26

155. Collie and Stutfield, *Climbs and Explorations*, 312.
156. Wilcox, *Camping in the Canadian Rockies*, 93.

Panorama 27

157. Hart, *Diamond Hitch*, 4.
158. Taylor, *The Snows of Yesteryear*, preface.
159. Wilcox, *Camping in the Canadian Rockies*, 115.

Panorama 28

160. Edwards, Ralph. *Trail to the Charmed Land*. Victoria: Herbert R. Larson Publishing Ltd., 1950, 7.
161. McGowan, Dan. *Hilltop Tales*, 191.
162. Edwards, *Trail to the Charmed Land*, 9.
163. Thorington, J. M. Jean Habel in the Canadian Rockies. *Canadian Alpine Journal*. Alpine Club of Canada, 1947, 58.
164. Ibid.
165. 16th Report of the Geographic Board of Canada. Ottawa, March, 1919.

Panorama 30

166. Patton, *Tales from the Canadian Rockies*, 25.

Panorama 31

167. Bennett, Geoffrey. *Battle of Jutland*. Newton Abbott, Devon: David & Charles, 1964, 138.
168. Ibid., 141.

Panorama 32

169. Jones, Ken, 1989, personal communication, Nanton, AB.
170. Kauffman and Putnam, *The Guiding Spirit*, 130.

Panorama 33

171. Report of the commission appointed to delimit the boundary between the provinces of Alberta and British Columbia. Ottawa: Surveyor General, 1917-1955 (4 volumes), 128.

Panorama 34

172. Pocaterra, G. W. *Among the Nomadic Stoneys*. Alberta Historical Review, Vol. II, No. 3, summer, 1963, 13.

Panorama 35

173. Macmillan, Ernest. (ed.) *A Canadian Song Book*. London/Toronto: J. M. Dent and Sons, 1929, 6.
174. Bishop, Billy. Combat Report, June 2, 1917.
175. Ibid.
176. Patterson, Raymond M. *Buffalo Head*. New York: William Sloane Associates, 1961, 165, 165.
177. Ibid., 171, 172.
178. Ibid., 172.
179. Ibid., 173.
180. Ibid., 173.
181. Patterson, Marigold, July 1990, personal communication, Victoria, BC.
182. Swettenham, *Valiant Men*, 93.
183. Ibid.

Panorama 36

184. Bennett, *Battle of Jutland*, 80.
185. Ibid.

Panorama 37

186. Marteinson, John. *We Stand on Guard*. Montreal: Ovale Publications, 1992, 76.
187. Buzzell, *The Register of the Victoria Cross*, 317.
188. de Smet, *Oregon Missions and Travels*, 146.
189. Outram, *In the Heart of the Canadian Rockies*, 38.

Panorama 39

190. Blakiston, Capt. Thomas J. *Report on the Exploration of the Kootenai and Boundary Passes of the Rocky Mountains in 1858*. The Palliser Papers. Toronto: The Champlain Society, 1968, 564.
191. Ibid.
192. Report of the commission, 103.
193. Ibid.
194. Fraser, Esther. *Wheeler*. Banff: Summerthought, 1978, 110.

Panorama 40

195. MacEwan, Grant. *Pat Burns—Cattle King*. Saskatoon: Western Producer Prairie Books, 1979, 125.
196. King, Donald R. *Beyond the Hills*. Privately published, 1975, 29.

Panorama 41

197. Thorington, J. M. Interpretation of some old map names in the vicinity of Kananaskis Pass. *Canadian Alpine Journal*. Winnipeg: Alpine Club of Canada, 1923, 248.
198. Patterson, Raymond M. *Far Pastures*. Sidney, B.C.: Gray's Publishing, 1963, 117.
199. Ibid., 118.
200. Ibid.
201. Ibid.
202. Ibid., 119.
203. Ibid., 120.

Panorama 42

204. Victory Readers. *The Boy Hero*. Toronto: Canadian Readers Book IV, Gage and Nelson, 1924, 239.
205. Ibid.
206. Ibid., 239, 240.
207. Ibid., 244.
208. Marteinson, *We Stand on Guard*, 144.

Panorama 43

209. Ross, W. J. *The Travels of George Dawson in Alberta and British Columbia in the Years 1883 and 1884*. Privately published, 21.

Panorama 44

210. Report of the commission, Vol. III, 62.

Panorama 45

211. Ibid., Vol. I, 77.
212. Patton, *Tales from the Canadian Rockies*, 68.

Panorama 46

213. Blakiston, *Report on the Exploration*, 564.
214. Pincher Creek and Area Historical Society. *Prairie Grass to Mountain Pass*. Pincher Creek, 1974, 560.

Panorama 48

215. Rodney, William. *Kootenai Brown*. Sidney, B.C.: Gray's, 1969, 61.
216. Ibid., 62.
217. Ibid., 197.
218. Blakiston, *Report on the Exploration*, 564.
219. Rodney, *Kootenai Brown*, 123.
220. Ibid., 52.
221. Ibid., 129, 130.
222. Ibid., 173.
223. Ibid., 191.

Panorama 49

224. Spry, *The Palliser Expedition*, 162.

Mountain Names

Mountain Names

Mountain People